IN THE
SHADOW OF
GREATNESS

★ ★ ★

In the Shadow of Greatness

★ ★ ★

VOICES OF LEADERSHIP, SACRIFICE, AND SERVICE
FROM AMERICA'S LONGEST WAR

The U.S. Naval Academy Class of 2002
Joshua Welle, John Ennis,
Katherine Kranz, and Graham Plaster
Foreword by David Gergen

NAVAL INSTITUTE PRESS
ANNAPOLIS, MARYLAND

The statements in this book do not represent the official viewpoints or policies of the U.S. Naval Academy, U.S. Navy, Marine Corps, or the Department of Defense. The statements herein are exclusively the opinions and recollections of the individual authors.

Naval Institute Press
291 Wood Road
Annapolis, MD 21402

First Naval Institute Press paperback edition published in 2017.
ISBN: 978-1-68247-247-7 (paperback)

The Library of Congress has cataloged the hardcover edition as follows:
In the shadow of greatness : voices of leadership, sacrifice, and service from America's longest war : the U.S. Naval Academy Class of 2002 / edited by Joshua Welle ... [et al.].
    p. cm.
  ISBN 978-1-61251-138-2 (hbk. : alk. paper) — ISBN 978-1-61251-139-9 (e-book) 1. United States Naval Academy. Class of 2002—Biography. 2. United States. Navy—Biography. 3. United States—History, Naval—21st century—Anecdotes. I. Welle, Joshua W.
  V415.K42002 I52 2012
  359.0092'273—dc23
                    2012018295

♾ This paper meets the requirements of ANSI/NISO z39.48-1992 (Permanence of Paper).
Printed in the United States of America.

25 24 23 22 21 20 19 18 17   9 8 7 6 5 4 3 2 1
First printing

Dedication

To those who served in uniform after 9/11

and the thousands who never returned home

To our Naval Academy 2002 classmates who

left this earth much too early

And to our mothers, who allowed us to embark

on an adventure of service and never lost faith

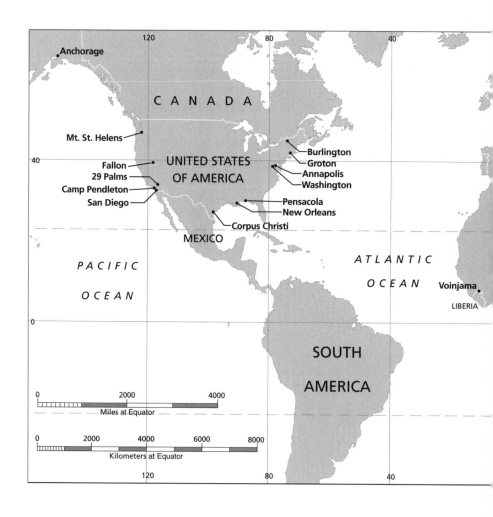

Anchorage

CANADA

Mt. St. Helens

UNITED STATES
OF AMERICA

Fallon
29 Palms
Camp Pendleton
San Diego

Burlington
Groton
Annapolis
Washington

Pensacola
New Orleans
Corpus Christi

MEXICO

Burlington

PACIFIC

OCEAN

ATLANTIC

OCEAN   Voinjama

LIBERIA

SOUTH

AMERICA

0   2000   4000
Miles at Equator

0   2000   4000   6000   8000
Kilometers at Equator

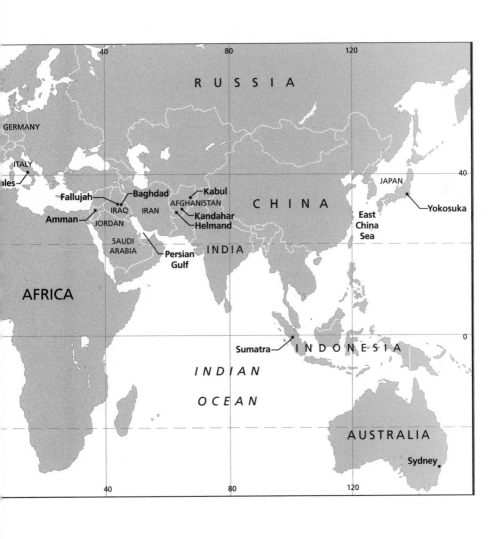

Contents

PHOTOGRAPHS

Foreword

David Gergen

In the spring of 1994, preparing for the fiftieth anniversary of D-day, President Bill Clinton invited a group of veterans and scholars to the White House for a private session so that he might better understand that special moment from the past. Each visitor was stirring, but none more so than Steven Ambrose, a marvelous historian and storyteller.

As U.S. troops began to storm the beaches, German machine guns up on bluffs cut them to pieces. A senior officer would fall, and a junior officer would quickly fill in; he, too, would go down, and a noncommissioned officer would take command, pushing men forward. Had positions been reversed, so that Germans were pouring out of the landing craft, argued Ambrose, they would have stopped in the water and called Berlin for instructions—and they would have lost the most crucial battle of the war. But the men hitting those beaches, he said, were "sons of democracy"—young warriors who had learned to think and act for themselves, who had grown up in freedom and would instinctively step up in a time of crisis.

As Ambrose finished, all of us in the room wondered whether our young men and women of today could match the "greatest generation," whether they had the right stuff. Ambrose insisted that if another moment came, despite the apparent softness of so many, the new generation would rise to the occasion because they, too, were "sons and daughters of democracy." They, too, knew the blessings of liberty and would volunteer their lives.

Anyone who has the pleasure of reading the essays in this book would surely agree: Ambrose was right. The young men and women here were members of the first class to graduate from the U.S. Naval Academy after al-Qaeda struck the United States. They rose to the challenge and soon became known as the "9/11 generation." One day they could be called the "next greatest generation."

Among the silver linings to be found in these past ten years of continuous war, there is one that shines brightest: the courage, character, and leadership of the young men and women who have answered the country's call to duty. I see some of them every day passing through the hallways of Harvard and on other campuses. They are part warrior, part scholar, all leader.

The Naval Academy, for more than a century and a half, has produced some of America's finest warriors, scholars, and leaders, from Alfred Thayer Mahan and Albert Michelson to President Jimmy Carter and Senator John McCain. Years ago, I had the privilege of working with some of them during a stint as a naval line officer, a chapter distinctly unheroic but full of lessons about leadership. (Serving as a damage control officer was also great preparation for working in Washington.)

Speaking at the Naval Academy's commencement in 1916, ten months away from America's entry into World War I, President Woodrow Wilson told the graduates, "You do not improve your muscle by doing the easy thing; you improve it by doing the hard thing, and you get your zest by doing a thing that is difficult, not a thing that is easy." The young men and women who have written this book have voluntarily chosen the hard thing, and they richly deserve our honor and our appreciation. Just as much, they deserve our attention, because they have provided in this volume first-person accounts of courage and integrity under the most trying of circumstances. They tell us of crucible moments—coming to the aid of soldiers pinned down in Iraq, landing a Tomcat on a carrier in pitching seas, rescuing men from drowning, watching a buddy die. Women are right there on the front lines, again proving their worth. These stories are gripping; some are heart wrenching. All of them show what their generation has accomplished, can accomplish, and God willing, will yet accomplish.

Let's be clear: This book is military in subject matter, but national in scope and relevance. It is penned by those in uniform but is written for citizens and others of all stripes. These accounts will inspire, they will impress, but most important, they will fill you with hope that this rising generation, forged in tragedy and war and called to difficult, often thankless duty, will help all Americans, both in and out of uniform, unite to rise to the occasion once more.

Introduction
Non Sibi Sed Patriae

The current generation of young Americans has its share of stereotypes. Many assume this group lacks vision and ambition or the ability to lead in a time of great peril. At Annapolis, we knew differently. We were the midshipmen of the United States Naval Academy, Class of 2002. We longed to be tested, to prove others wrong about their impressions. We wanted a destiny of purpose, a higher calling.

The Naval Academy, with its glossy catalog depicting college seniors saluting crisply and brandishing swords, promised to make us heroes. Perhaps only the enlisted service members of our class truly knew what uniformed service entailed, but for those fresh out of high school, the ideal of the Naval Academy was like an invitation to join King Arthur's Round Table. A magnificent chapel stands on the campus grounds. At the entrance, a magnificent door, twenty feet high, is inscribed *Non sibi sed patriae*—"Not for self, but for country."

On Tuesday, September 11, 2001, the purpose and test of seniors at the academy became clear. Al-Qaeda attacked the United States, and our commander-in-chief assumed the lead in protecting our allies and our coasts from threats to American interests. Our abilities as tacticians and deckplate leaders would be tested. Our moral compasses would be rattled and recalibrated amid the realities of war. We would suffer losses—of blood, friends, family, and innocence.

These times are of almost limitless access to free media, overwhelming consumption, and layers of instant gratification. We seek greater connectedness online, yet we must also acknowledge that the virtual public sphere fosters an unhealthy state of individualism. We have seen a growing cultural gap between the military and civilian sectors of American society that must be bridged. Integrity, the bedrock of leadership, is today a rare virtue, not a common character trait.

In the Shadow of Greatness presents first-person accounts of junior officers during two wars, on the front lines and at home, in times of valor, humor, and tragedy. It explains how their experiences at Annapolis prepared them for what would be a decade at war. It also explores the nuances of a generation struggling to achieve something big—to earn the distinction of the next greatest generation.

This literary endeavor began in late 2009 after reflection on countless deployments, great victories, and much sorrow among various members of the Class of 2002. Their stories of bravery and service needed to be told. This book provides a podium for voices normally hesitant to write publicly about their experiences. The stories allow readers to meet an array of personalities; each writes in a way that every parent can enjoy and most people could be inspired. The body of work represents the effort of hundreds of people, among them advisers, classmates, friends, and professional writers; they all helped make this book a reality. The stories were selected from a pool of submissions to highlight the most important themes from this age of conflict.

The "war on terror" remains an ambiguous concept. We ask ourselves, time and again, Was it worth it? More than 6,000 American servicemen were killed and more than 46,000 wounded during Operation Iraqi Freedom and Operation Enduring Freedom. Thousands of Iraqi civilians were displaced, or worse, died from the armed conflict in their homeland. Now, with the United States suffering under the weight of crushing financial debt and a wide array of other domestic problems, the sacrifices of those who served run the risk of being eclipsed by the crises of the moment.

The writers in this volume are true believers. They have done a great deal of soul searching and invite you to join them on a journey of remembrance of their generation's Long War. We all believe that the futures of Iraq and Afghanistan look promising, if not assured. We are bearing witness to a global community that has renewed its commitments to combating diffuse extremist groups.

More to the point, those who have served in a decade of conflict and are now returning from war are prepared and ready to lead our country through tumultuous times at home. More than a million men and women served in Iraq and Afghanistan from 2001 through 2011. This great reservoir of leadership is being tapped and called to duty at home, making America great again.

We, the members of USNA 2002, are humbled and proud to be among the many who have served, and we will continue to answer the call. We believe the nation is ready for a new generation of leaders, made up of men and women who have served after 9/11. These are our stories.

PART I

★ ★ ★

FOUR YEARS BY THE BAY

Inside the Gates of Annapolis

During my time as commandant, a question often posed to me was, Why should our nation invest so much in service academies and the young men and women who are chosen to attend them? My reply was simple: The support and defense of the Constitution of the greatest nation in the world demands a cadre of handpicked men and women who, without distraction, are rigorously prepared morally, mentally, and physically for this challenging but sacred duty. Our country deserves nothing less.

There are always those who doubt. They opine that America's youths are increasingly incapable of shouldering the challenges we face as a nation. They believe that the next class will somehow be less capable, less honorable, and less willing to make the sacrifices necessary to defend the nation and fulfill the call to duty. Nothing could be further from the truth. In the history of the United States, our Navy and our Naval Academy have always, without hesitation, answered the call of duty. No graduating class has failed to inspire us with its honor, courage, commitment, and sacrifice. Graduates willingly leave the comforts of home to patrol the world's oceans and defend our nation and our way of life. It is a dangerous undertaking. Many give their last full measure.

On September 11, 2001, as I sat at my desk in the "Dant's" office, I recall vividly watching the al-Qaeda attacks on the World Trade Center and the Pentagon and the plane crash in Pennsylvania. When the images reached the Brigade, and the uncertainty of the events rapidly became reality, I asked myself, Are these men and women, these young patriots, ready for the challenges that most certainly lay ahead? A decade of war has proven that they were more than ready. Fortunately for us all, they remain ready today. We are extremely proud of all they have accomplished and thankful that we chose the right men and women to lead the next great generation.

ADM. SAMUEL J. LOCKLEAR
Commandant of Midshipmen, 2000–2002

T here are many reasons to seek an Annapolis diploma. Some dream of glory, to be the next astronaut to explore the final frontier, or perhaps to be a senator, representative, or even president of the United States. Others want to further a legacy because their fathers or mothers served with distinction. As the price of a college education continues to skyrocket, many are driven by a desire for a free education. Though all are conscious of the fact that the Annapolis experience imbues characteristics that support success, each midshipman's intent is unique.

The United States Naval Academy was established under Secretary of the Navy George Bancroft in 1845. Bancroft envisioned and ultimately succeeded in creating a center of excellence charged with providing future naval officers a scientific education centered on mathematics, navigation, gunnery, steam power, and chemistry, complemented by humanities courses in English, French, and philosophy. The Naval School, the Academy's first incarnation, was established at Fort Severn, a ten-acre Army post. Its first class consisted of a mere fifty midshipmen taught by seven professors. The curriculum's scope evolved as the United States grew in strategic importance and as technology progressed from tall sailing ships and coal-powered ironclad vessels to nuclear-powered submarines and sophisticated marine amphibious forces. The Naval Academy has consistently produced graduates prepared to become experts in the latest technology.

By providing a true liberal arts education in the classical tradition, the Naval Academy has been heralded among the top schools in the country by *U.S. News & World Report*. Although academically impressive, a USNA education extends beyond books. As set out in the Academy's mission statement, its goal is also "To develop midshipmen morally, mentally and physically, and to imbue them with the highest ideals of duty, honor, and loyalty in order to graduate leaders dedicated to a career of naval service."

Induction Day, 1998

The humidity and simmering heat felt like someone breathing down the necks of the thousand-plus plebes converging on Alumni Hall. The transition from civilian to military life had, for most of us, finally come to fruition. We were a hodgepodge group of seventeen- to twenty-three-year-olds representing every state in the Union as well as Bahrain, Cameroon, Croatia, and Turkey. Among us were high school standouts in debate and music, scholastics and student government, volunteer work, and athletics. While a few dozen were exceptional enlisted men and women, the morning of July 1, 1998, leveled the playing field and made each of us a member of one team.

Induction Day, commonly known as I-Day, transformed this rag-tag group of young men and women into crisply dressed and shorn midshipmen equipped with everything they needed to begin their journey. I-Day is a mix of excitement and foreboding, the first of many such days to come during the next four strenuous and tumultuous years. While high school friends basked in the freedom of their summer vacation and prepared to attend civilian colleges, this small cross-section of American teenagers opted for a more rigid lifestyle, defined by regulations and abject obedience to orders.

One by one, we entered Alumni Hall armed only with our unique talents, ready to join the team that would become the Naval Academy Class of 2002. Each of us carried a manila folder with identification forms and a single, authorized duffle bag containing a toothbrush (but not toothpaste), seven pairs of "tighty-whitey" underwear, one pair of running shoes, and five white t-shirts. None of the accoutrements of a normal dormitory were permitted, and family members were told to wait outside. A barrage of unique accents was heard; distinctive ethnic backgrounds were apparent in the winding corridors of Alumni Hall. In short, a look out upon the class reflected America's demographic tapestry.

Blue-chip varsity athletes, who chose to attend the Academy after being recruited to play one of the NCAA Division I sports, were sprinkled among the group. The male athletes, standing 6 feet 3 inches or taller and with massive muscles, were easy to spot. They were basketball or football athletes assuredly, all trying to be the next David Robinson or Joe Bellino, Navy's first Heisman Trophy winner. With slight embarrassment or unabashed honesty, some came because they could not afford college and judged four years of relative pain to be a small price for a free education and five guaranteed years of employment following graduation. Many others were still discerning their intent, but nonetheless answering the same call of duty as those who from an early age knew it was their destination.

Whether a person's reasons were self-centered or selfless, no one was judged on their past; all were accepted on the precept that they were now in this together. All held in common a humble appreciation for the prestige of the institution and the challenging journey on which they were about to embark. The only thing that truly mattered was how well the class performed and whether its members could work as a team.

Bancroft Hall is the world's largest dormitory and home to the Brigade of Midshipmen—all 4,400 of its members. It boasts 1,700 rooms, 33 acres of floor space, and 4.8 miles of hallway, and is warmly referred to as "Mother B" or the Hall. Bancroft is large enough to have its own zip code, 21412. The building, designed in the eighteenth-century beaux-arts architectural style, is completely self-contained and functions like a small city. The Hall houses a cobbler shop, uniform store, tailor shop, laundromat, travel office, barbershop, bank, general store, medical and dental facilities, gymnasium, post office, and a dining facility that can feed every midshipman in one seating.

From Bancroft Hall, we were ushered in groups to Tecumseh Court, the main entrance to and gathering area outside the dormitory. We stood nervously at attention in our newly fitted white sailor uniforms or "whiteworks." All 1,231 of us had made it as one unit through the overwhelming process of I-Day and stood ready to tackle the rigors of plebe summer and the challenges that lay beyond.

We were directed to raise our right hands to swear an oath to the Constitution of the United States and to discharge the duties of a midshipman. Some followed the direction uneasily, some with timidity, most of us fearfully, but all voluntarily. Perspiration collected on our foreheads and streamed down our young, taut faces as we stood rank and file among the strangers who would become our shipmates and most committed lifelong friends.

Within hours of arriving on Induction Day, Midshipman 4/C Richard Ferrari and other members of USNA 2002 learn how to render a salute. (Courtesy U.S. Naval Academy)

Plebe Summer

Anyone who fails to pass plebe summer is expelled from the Academy. The program is the ultimate equalizer, spanning seven gut-wrenching, tearful, and draining weeks of military instruction and training. During this time, midshipmen become ingrained with valuable skills and enduring habits and characteristics that will help them persevere for the next four years.

The boot camp experience of plebe summer has two objectives. The first is to break individuals to a point where they are no longer encumbered by self-doubt, fear, and poor habits. They are taught a new way to stand, walk, talk, and think and are pushed to their limits. For some, the breaking point is physical, for others mental, and for some even spiritual. Most of them discover a reservoir of inner strength that keeps them of sound mind and body and allows them to soldier on through the trials of the summer. Inevitably, some do not, however, find it and are compelled to reconsider their oath. Some simply quit.

The second objective of plebe summer is to prepare young men and women to join the Brigade of Midshipmen—the military reference to the four thousand men and women who attend the Naval Academy at any given time. Rather than put plebes into the hands of active-duty personnel with extensive Fleet experience, upperclass midshipmen serve as the gatekeepers of the Brigade, the largest fraternity in the world. In other words, the more experienced midshipmen discipline, teach, and mold those who follow in their footsteps. In this way, the Academy uses plebe summer as a leadership forum for honing the command skills of upperclassmen on the path to graduation.

At the start of plebe summer 1998, everyone was assigned to a numbered platoon, two of which formed a company, which was assigned a letter. Each platoon was divided into four squads of nine to twelve individuals. These layers of companies, platoons, and squads provided support as well as motivation. We were reminded of our responsibility to each other by recitation of the Fifth Law of the Navy.

> On the strength of one link in the cable dependeth the might of the chain.
> Who knows when thou may'st be tested, so live that thou bearest the strain.

Our days began long before sunrise. The detailers, upperclass midshipmen pretending to be Parris Island drill instructors, yelled down hallways, abruptly kicked in doors, or banged metal rods against the tile walls to wake us at the hour of 0500. Within five minutes of reveille, we were standing outside our rooms in squad ranks, dressed in gym gear, holding canteen bottles in one hand and bed sheets crammed inside a pillowcase in the other.

Following a brief look of distaste from our detailers, we would be dismissed to our rooms to make our racks so precisely that the hospital corners could be measured with a protractor and so tightly that a quarter could be bounced off the top sheet. Mere minutes later, we would form up again and march out to Farragut Field for ninety minutes of physical training that increased in intensity and became more challenging as the summer progressed.

After daily physical training, there was a morning's worth of work to accomplish in only minutes. In Bancroft Hall, the three individuals (on average) assigned to each room would sequentially shower and choreograph the morning rituals of shaving, preparing a uniform, polishing shoes, applying edge dress to soles, "brasso" (shine) name tags, read three newspaper articles on sports and current events, memorize the menus for the next three meals and the plan of the day, learn the names of the on-duty leadership, and prepare the room to be inspection ready. All of this had to be done in a mere twelve minutes. Meanwhile, the detailers—who were somehow faster, smarter, and more capable—would pound on the door and yell at us, reminding us that they were ready and wondering why we were not. It was frustrating, confusing, and demoralizing. Perfectionists bristled with agitation, and those who were unaccustomed to having their failings made public lamented silently. Over time, as intended, we came to appreciate just how much one can accomplish in a little more than ten minutes.

No matter how hard we worked individually or tried to help each other, it was impossible to satisfy the detailers' ever-increasing requirements of fastidiousness and their demanding nature. It seemed that even with their backs turned, they could spot an errant thread or nearly unnoticeable blemish on a uniform, a scuff on a shoe, or a quirk in a facial expression. Something always caught their attention.

One might think that mealtime would be the one activity offering a shred of physical satisfaction or comfort, but even this most basic ritual of consuming food was transformed into a tormenting and dissatisfying ordeal. We ate while perched on the front three inches of wooden chairs, sitting ramrod straight, with our "eyes in the boat"—focused straight ahead—and our hands on our knees, only removing them to eat one bite at a time. Variations to the ritual included a defined number of chews and putting one's fork down between bites.

We soon became a team, first as squads and then as platoons, companies, battalions, and as a regiment. We also learned to march in these units to display team unity. We spent hours in the hot sun learning marching techniques and practicing formations. Those of us already motivated to join the Marine Corps perhaps relished these evolutions more than others because we needed to perfect the skill to someday march as a Marine. Even for future sailors destined for ships, submarines, and aircraft, marching developed rhythm, reinforced discipline, emphasized meticulous attention to detail, teamwork, and leadership as well as followership. We marched not only on the parade and athletic fields, but also to the sailing center and even to religious gatherings. We often ran in formation, barking motivating cadences.

Strangely, the days felt longer than the weeks. Each day brimmed with physically challenging and mind-expanding activities. The detailers ran us ragged, leading us to every corner of the 338-acre campus and across the Severn River to the Naval Weapons Station. We participated in weapons qualifications, obstacle courses, swimming, sailing, wrestling, and parade practice. No day was easy, and rare was a second that passed unnoticed. Our detailers kept us engaged from 0500 to 2200. They scolded us, yelled at us, and noticed every minor deficiency. No matter how hard we tried, we were never perfect. Despite feeling as though we were giving 100 percent, it never seemed to be enough.

PROFESSIONAL TRANSFORMATION

The end of each plebe summer is marked by the return of the Brigade of Midshipmen, tipping the plebe to upperclassman ratio from 10:1 to a threatening 1:3. With every second of the day planned for us under the watchful eyes of our detailers, we wondered how we would juggle all of the tasks required if left to our own devices. After plebe summer, however, we would be forced to balance the military requirements of being a plebe with the rigors of the academic classroom.

Despite the military uniforms, countless formations, and relentless physical training, the Academy is actually a four-year college, though at the time none of us would have called it that in comparison to friends we knew at other civilian universities. Attendance at academic class was mandatory and closely monitored not only by the academic faculty but also by the officers and senior enlisted leaders charged with our supervision in Bancroft Hall.

The Naval Academy faculty is a talented and eclectic mix of civilian professors and military instructors. Unlike at civilian institutions, there are few publication requirements for obtaining tenure, therefore instructors can focus the entirety of their intellectual energy on imparting knowledge to midshipmen and are encouraged toward tenure almost exclusively through in-classroom performance.

The Academy was the only home we knew as plebes. We were not allowed to go outside its walls at any point during the week; on Saturdays, we could exit the grounds for about twelve hours, but we had to be dressed in an authorized uniform and remain within a twenty-two-mile radius of the chapel dome. Thanksgiving leave was the first time that we were allowed to remain away from the campus for any extended period of time, drive cars, wear civilian clothes, and feel like regular college students. These short-lived five days of relative freedom came to a halt as we experienced our first taste of December at the Naval Academy.

Between the bustle of the holiday season around us, the end of classes, the antics and pranks of Army Week—culminating in the boisterous excitement of the Army-Navy football game in Philadelphia—and final exams, we found ourselves exhausted and definitely ready for an extended holiday break from the Academy. During the winter and spring semesters, we endured the Dark Ages, a period of bleak, cold weather and long nights in the Nimitz Library studying for hellacious chemistry and calculus exams. When flowers began to bloom in spring, hope appeared on the horizon. Plebe year would soon be over.

Before we could celebrate the graduation and commissioning of the Class of 1999 and the completion of our plebe year, we had two more tasks to complete as a team. The first was to get through the newly established Sea Trials, a challenge modeled after the Crucible in Marine Corps basic training. It is a day-long test of teamwork and stamina, consisting of obstacle, endurance, and confidence courses and other physical activities designed to challenge personal strength and unit cohesion. Next we had to participate in the time-honored tradition of climbing Herndon, an obelisk-shaped monument in the middle of the Yard, to retrieve the blue-rimmed white "dixie cup" cover (cap) worn during plebe summer and replace it with a midshipman cover, symbolizing our passage from plebes to full members of the Brigade. The monument is covered in lard, and the dixie cup is affixed with superglue and duct tape to make achieving success more challenging.

The Class of 2002 worked as a team to climb the 21-foot gray monument in two hours and twenty-six minutes. (Courtesy U.S. Naval Academy)

Youngster Year

After summer cruises, during which we were exposed to Fleet-style military training, we returned to the Yard in August 1999 to begin the challenge of our sophomore or "youngster" year. Although each of us had already selected a major course
of study, the core curriculum still dominated most of our credit hours; thus, we
collectively took two more semesters of calculus and differential equations or
statistics, two semesters of physics, and American history. Aside from academics, we also played a unique role in the training of the new plebes, the Class of
2003. Although the Class of 2001 took on the more ruthless role of "trainers," we,
as youngsters, formally third class (or second-year) midshipmen, could assume
the role of guide or mentor. Each morning, the plebes could come to us for a final
check of their required rates and tasks before being inspected by the 2/C (a second
class, or third-year) midshipman. In addition, we had the responsibility of setting
an example for the plebes. Though there was no longer anyone constantly looking
over our shoulder to ensure that our uniforms were perfect and our shoes shined,
we still had to make sure these things were done while also guiding the plebes in
the right direction.

The end of youngster year was marked by important training for us as midshipmen, in large part because we knew that after the summer, we would be committed to serving as officers in the Navy or Marine Corps. Our summer training
to become 2/Cs, therefore, carried a significant amount of weight when it came
to our decision-making process. The most ambitious midshipmen looked to
break from the relative ease of youngster year and compete to be a plebe summer
detailer. Although challenging and exhaustive, the task of being a detailer that
year would define the way the entering Class of 2004 would evolve; our detailers made lasting impressions on us, and there was a great deal of pressure for us
to live up to the example set by those who had trained us. During summer training, we would also be exposed again to the Fleet, learning a particular warfare
community within the military and ultimately determining if that was in fact our
desired career path.

2/C Year: Eyes on Commissioning

Prior to the first day of classes of a 2/C year, a midshipman can choose to leave
the Naval Academy at no cost. After that day, a midshipman who decides to separate from the Academy must reimburse the government for his or her education
to that point, dollar for dollar. Military service requires a commitment entered
into with a clear head and open eyes. A two-year "free" exposure period to the
Navy and Marine Corps ensures that only the most committed and motivated
junior officers will be commissioned. Second class year allows midshipmen to

transition from followers to leaders. During 2000–2001, no longer responsible only for ourselves, we became accountable in the training of the Class of 2004. The academic program is tailored toward fulfilling requirements for majors, but courses in electrical engineering and thermodynamics are mandatory.

Senior year is not an electives cakewalk. While most colleges require 120 credits to graduate, the Naval Academy piles on professional development classes so that 150 credits are needed, and with very few exceptions, one must complete them within four years. On top of ongoing physical requirements, military obligations, mandatory extracurricular activities, and classes, every semester has a course devoted to professional development. The courses include seamanship and navigation, naval heritage, naval leadership, military ethics, naval law, weapons systems, and strategy. The results factor heavily into a midshipman's military order of merit and academic grade point average. Of importance, these courses provide, bit by bit, comprehension of future responsibilities as junior officers.

Professional education is not, however, limited to the classroom. In fact, midshipmen are required to attend monthly Forrestal Lectures, where the speakers typically are Medal of Honor recipients, Supreme Court justices, retired four-star generals, Nobel Prize winners, influential diplomats, renowned authors, or captains of industry. They offer, firsthand, a glimpse into their rise to prominence, their setbacks, and personal values. The professional and academic educations provided by the Academy overlap each other. Although the ubiquitous demands of both compete for a limited time and can result in many caffeine-induced, sleepless nights, the densely packed educational program elevates thought processes and compels one to learn more in less time.

First Class Year: Completing the Transformation

The Naval Academy has been described as a leadership laboratory where midshipmen can experiment with different styles leading peers and subordinates. Another popularized description refers to the Academy as "a quarter of a million dollars in education shoved up your ass one nickel at a time." First class midshipmen, having survived three years at the Academy, ultimately assume the role as the leaders of the Brigade, and all the sacrifices are worth it to take charge as the senior midshipmen on deck. Each semester, an individual is tasked as the Brigade commander, the highest-ranking midshipman, who sets policy for all 4,400-plus midshipmen. Other opportunities for hands-on management exist at the company commander level, leading 140 midshipmen, or as a squad leader, overseeing 12. Others are selected as varsity team captains or presidents of various extracurricular activities.

First class midshipmen are responsible for leading and upholding the Honor Concept of the Brigade. As the leaders of a Brigade-owned concept, first class midshipmen are ultimately responsible for its integrity, effectiveness, and longevity. Supporting the Navy core value of honor with constant reinforcement, the Honor Concept, in the simplest terms, states that "Midshipmen are persons of integrity: They stand for that which is right." This statement provides the framework and backbone for midshipmen's four years of training, from the moment they take their oath and don the cloth of the nation.

If a midshipman is reported to have engaged in plagiarizing, cheating, using a fake ID, or even giving a false answer to a harmless question—all honor violations—the honor staff, led by first class midshipmen, conduct a thorough investigation and convene an Honor Board of his or her peers before which the accused must appear. Honor was, and remains, an essential quality that permeates every facet of midshipman life. Because of it, midshipmen strove to be responsible, accountable, and trustworthy.

SEPTEMBER 11, 2001

The morning of September 11, 2001, began like any other during the academic year. Most midshipmen woke up around 0600, maybe some slightly earlier to exercise or finish a last-minute homework assignment. The reveille bell rang at 0630 as it always does, accompanied by the same morning announcement from Main Office. Plebes began their chow calls at 0650, a cycle we were growing tired of after four years. Thirty commanders called their companies to attention at precisely 0700, and the Brigade filed down to King Hall for breakfast and then shuffled off to first period classes. We had no idea that this day would be our coming of age, the day our lives and careers would be irrevocably changed. One of our classmates recalled that morning:

> I had first period off and was headed through the bottom floor of Bancroft Hall towards second period in Luce Hall. It was probably 0830 or so. I wanted to stop and say hi to my friend who had just graduated and was working in Bancroft Hall. I saw the news footage of the plane hitting the first tower on the TV in his office . . . when they were still reporting that it might be an accident. Another friend I passed on the way to class stopped me to ask if I had heard that a plane crashed into the Pentagon. . . . I corrected him, saying I had just seen it on TV and it was the World Trade Center. When I got to class, everyone had heard about it, and we realized it was both the Pentagon and the World Trade Center. We turned a TV on in the classroom and watched the second plane hit. Surely this wasn't an accident . . . but our teacher said that we needed to focus and he conducted class as usual. Needless to say, I can't remember anything I learned that day, or even what class it was.

We furiously tried to call friends and family members, even if they were nowhere near New York City or the Pentagon. We needed to know that our loved ones were safe. Busy signals and "could not connect" messages flowed from cell phones. It wasn't until around 1400 that Jeff Schwab, from 16th Company, learned that his father, who worked in the Pentagon, had survived and had ridden his bike the twenty-five miles to their home in Northern Virginia because traffic in the D.C. metropolitan area was completely gridlocked.

The Academy suspended classes after third period. Instead of eating lunch as usual as the Brigade, we went by battalions, one by one. We were told this was to ensure that the entire Brigade could not be targeted. The rumor mill was working overtime. Tarek Elmasry, from 29th Company, recalls, "I was the company duty officer on deck 8-3. Two things stand out from my CDO experience this day. First, the rumor of the day happened to be that the Naval Academy was on a 'top 10' list of Osama Bin Laden's targets. Second, the plebes and youngsters assigned as company mates of the deck were ordered to carry the dull bayonets in order to protect the rest of us."

September 11 was as personal for the Class of 2002 as December 7, 1941, had been for the USNA Class of 1942. Some of our friends and family members perished; all of us would eventually go forward in retaliation. If any doubt remained as to the purpose of our service and our education, those reservations disappeared that day. Life at the Naval Academy changed after 9/11. The training continued, but our individual anxieties and the pulse of the Brigade increased. Obviously, as a military installation, there were modifications in gate security for pedestrian and vehicle traffic. Grades in the professional courses, seamanship, tactics, and weapons systems became more important than other courses. We felt closer to combat and would graduate in wartime.

GRADUATION DAY

Of the 1,231 civilians who started the journey with the Class of 2002 on I-Day, 965 sat in ranks on the field at Navy-Marine Corps Memorial Stadium on May 24, 2002. We were ready to take the oath of office and begin our next chapter as commissioned officers. There is ultimately no difference between the person graduating first in the class and the one who holds the prestigious honor of being the "anchor man," a title of the individual who graduates with the lowest scores in military conduct, academics, and physical aptitude. After commissioning, both first- and last-ranked graduates warrant military salute, share the same title, and are addressed as "Sir" or "Ma'am."

Our Commandant of Midshipmen, then-colonel John R. Allen, USMC, recently turned over from Sam Locklear, recounts the following:

In 2002, I was nearing the end of my third decade of service in the Marine Corps and the start of my third tour at our beloved Academy. My first tour was as a midshipman, my second tour was as a political science instructor, and my third tour was as the Commandant of Midshipmen. Throughout those tours, totaling nearly a decade, I literally spent thousands of days on the Academy's grounds, met thousands of midshipmen, and amassed countless memories that sustain me and make me proud to be associated with an institution that is a shining beacon of honor and pride for our nation.

However, despite the many noteworthy memories I have of my time at Annapolis, three specific days stand out as truly memorable. The most memorable day, as it is for almost every graduate, is the day I arrived as a midshipman to join the Class of '76. The next most memorable day was the day when, after Four Years by the Bay, I graduated and was commissioned a second lieutenant. My third day . . . well, my third day was that beautiful, warm day when the Class of 2002 was commissioned.

Why that day? Simply put that day marked the convergence of several firsts, both for me and for the Academy. For me, the day was my first Graduation Day as the commandant of midshipmen, and since I was the first, and so far only, Marine officer to hold this position, I was particularly concerned that everything go smoothly. For the Academy, it was graduating its first class since the horrific attacks of 9/11—attacks that thrust our nation into a war that still continues over a decade later. Indeed, little did I know on that day at Annapolis . . . 11 September 2001 . . . that ten years later, on the anniversary of 9/11, I'd be in Afghanistan commanding the entire war effort.

On that Graduation Day, I remember looking across the stage at the hundreds of midshipmen about to be commissioned and who would soon complete their initial training and report to their respective Fleet and Marine Corps units. I distinctly recall thinking of the "sea change" that had occurred in the expectation of our graduates. The Academy has long been known as a bastion of leadership dedicated to producing leaders ready to lead our nation's forces in combat. It is an institution famous for grooming men and women of integrity and service.

Yet, on that day, looking out upon those bright faces, I knew that there were members of the class who would soon lead troops into battle and who would offer what President Lincoln referred to as their "last full measure of devotion" in defense of our nation. I knew that there were members of the class who would stand the watch with distinction in the face of challenges normally handled by those more senior. And, I knew, there was a core, not yet identified, who would, in uncertain times and in unknown places, perform decisive actions whose impact would have as much strategic importance as they would have impact on the tactical situation at hand.

In hindsight, it seems certain that the wars we have undertaken have not evolved the way we might have expected them to unfold. Instead of large ground wars through Europe's Fulda Gap, we found ourselves involved in counterinsurgency campaigns reminiscent of the brutal, communist-inspired wars of national liberation following World War II. Instead of conventional force-on-force battles at sea, we find ourselves conducting antipiracy operations that hearken back to the eighteenth century. Yet, we also find that those fundamentals . . . those immutable principles . . . that were true 237 years ago are still true today: that a nation, served by patriotic volunteers, dedicated to the principles enshrined in our Constitution, will stand as a beacon of freedom and liberty to the world.

I recall standing on the stage, in the bright morning sun, when I turned to the Chief of Naval Operations, Adm. Mike Mullen, and presented him 797 midshipmen ready to assume duty as ensigns in our great Navy, and then turned to the assistant commandant of the Marine Corps, and presented 162 hardened midshipmen ready to assume duty as lieutenants in our great Marine Corps. Each of them raised their right hand, listened to the oath of office, and in conclusion roared forth with a heartfelt, "I do!"

We did it. As individuals and as a class, we committed ourselves to service as commissioned officers. We sang "Navy Blue and Gold" for the last time together, hands over hearts. We threw our midshipman covers into the air. As a sea of white rained down on our heads, we laughed, cried, and celebrated, barely believing that we had made it through.

The Marine Corps required 16.5 percent of our graduating class. These new Devil Dogs would spend six months at the Marine Corps Basic School to prepare to become infantrymen, logistics specialists, intelligence officers, or aviators. Surface warfare officers would spend six months in Newport, Rhode Island, for professional seamanship training before meeting up with ships around the globe. Submariners had a two-year academic and practical nuclear educational timeline before attending their boats. SEALs and explosive ordnance disposal officers departed to begin the famed mental and physical training of their intense community, BUDS. Two hundred twenty-seven naval aviators entered the "cradle of naval aviation," Naval Air Station Pensacola in Florida, to begin a regime of more than eighteen months of written tests, training flights, simulated drownings, and POW training prior to entering the fight.

The global war on terrorism, catalyzed by the 9/11 attacks, created a ripple that took America into an extended conflict, a tidal wave of military activity not likely to be seen by it for many years. In March 2003, with military operations still under way in Afghanistan, the United States invaded Iraq. There was no turning back. The Class of 2002's time in service would be defined by war.

The Blue Angels fly over the graduation ceremony of the Class of 2002. (Courtesy U.S. Naval Academy)

PART II

───── ★ ★ ★ ─────

THE LEADERSHIP LABORATORY, FLEET TESTED

Leaders are made, they are not born. They are made of hard effort, which is the price which all of us must pay to achieve any goal that is worthwhile.

VINCE LOMBARDI

It is by no means enough that an officer of the Navy should be a capable mariner. He must be that, of course, but also a great deal more. He should be as well a gentleman of liberal educa-tion, refined manners, punctilious courtesy, and the nicest sense of personal honor. He should be the soul of tact, patience, jus-tice, firmness, kindness, and charity. . . . In one word, every commander should keep constantly before him the great truth, that to be well obeyed, he must be perfectly esteemed.

AUGUSTUS C. BUELL, reflecting on John Paul Jones in 1900,
Reef Points, 2003–2004

S ome call the United States Naval Academy a "leadership laboratory." The Academy exists to make naval officers, forming them "morally, mentally and physically" to exemplify "duty, honor and loyalty." While most of the midshipmen accepted to the Academy have received a fair dose of moral fiber from parents, teachers, and mentors along the way, the institution promises to take these lessons a step further. It accomplishes this by increasing the burden of leadership and raising the bar for personal and professional integrity.

At the epicenter of this leadership laboratory stands a building dedicated to Stephen Bleeker Luce, an American hero. Luce was a midshipman in 1848. He graduated and went to sea, later returning to the Academy to become commandant in 1865. He focused his efforts on educating men in the art of gunnery, seamanship, strategy, and most important, leadership. Today, Luce Hall overlooks the Navy's sailing marina, with its sailboats named for various midshipman virtues, such as courageous, fearless, dauntless, and so on. In front of this building stands a statue of Admiral James Stockdale in a fighter pilot uniform, honoring his service as senior officer while a POW during the Vietnam War. He later received the Medal of Honor for his leadership.

Classes in Luce Hall include ethics, navigation, strategy and weapons, and naval law. The curriculum incorporates case studies from real-world scenarios, discussion forums with junior officers, lectures by respected world leaders, ethics roundtables, and hours of homework. As with any laboratory, some of the experiments at Luce produced unintended results. Heightened idealism about one's ability to affect change as a junior officer may be a consequence of time spent in Luce Hall and the cause of some disenchantment. There are some things, however, especially pertaining to leadership, that can only be learned in the school of hard knocks. The Naval Academy was certainly that at times, but then again, it was called a leadership laboratory for a reason. As the first class graduating post-9/11, we stepped into a military requiring more advanced ethical leadership skills than the Naval Academy had had time to teach us.

Honor at Sea

Will Carr

O ur Honor Board hearings were held in a stately conference room next to Smoke Hall. Inside the room, there were three long mahogany tables, where I sat alongside twelve other midshipmen. Directly ahead of us was a smaller, detached table behind which sat a distraught second class midshipman who had been accused of plagiarizing a term paper crucial to his final grade. Presumably he had been struggling with his grades for months, and when faced with the prospect of failure, he had copied entire passages verbatim from other sources to get a passing grade. "Guilty" or "not guilty" were the only conclusions the board was allowed. If guilty, the Commandant of Midshipmen, Adm. Sam Locklear, would decide the punishment. No one held any illusions; a second class midshipman found guilty of an honor violation had an excellent chance of being expelled from the Academy.

I was the honor chairman, and it was my duty to make sure this man's peers asked the tough questions and ultimately made their decision according to the words of our Honor Concept. I felt the knot in my stomach tighten as I imagined myself in the accused's shoes: What would I have done if faced with that potent mix of pride and fear of failure? Integrity is a virtue that is talked about in most leadership seminars as a critical trait. It is an attribute that defines a person's character and behavior. It goes beyond not lying, not cheating, not stealing to serve as a guide to doing the right thing wholeheartedly. In short, it is an individual's ideology. At the Academy, we tried our best to nurture integrity within ourselves; the honor education focused on the "me," the individual, and my development as a person of integrity. Two sea tours in the Fleet, involving hundreds of watches for thousands of miles of ocean steaming, gives one time to think and to make a few big mistakes. What I learned from this experience is that successful leaders bring out integrity in others. Such leaders create a culture where the truth can readily be told.

★ ★ ★

On a moonless night in the Pacific, I struggled to stay awake through one of my first officer of the deck watches on USS *John S. McCain* (DDG 56). It had been a full day of drills, an hour or two of broken sleep, and then back to the bridge for the "reveille watch," from 0200 to 0700. We were under way as part of our destroyer squadron's group sail, during which all the ships in the force are put to sea for a series of exercises, to prepare for upcoming operations in the East China Sea. Each day featured an exchange of several officers and crew members to observe the operation from other ships in the squadron.

On this particular morning, the ships converged to close quarters before first light, put their small boats in the water, and conducted the personnel transfer. The radio crackled with the signal for each ship to close one another, and I ordered the conning officer to turn starboard to our appointed position in the darkness. The bridge was pitch-black, I could only see the outlines of those on watch, quietly focusing on their duties in order to make it through the long hours of the watch.

My quartermaster was diligently plotting our course and speed and entering them into a log. My junior officer of the deck walked over and examined the chart and radar every few minutes in the dim glow of red light. I knew they were all tired. The minutes before the first rays of sun reach above the horizon can last for what seems to be forever. This is the time when the human body reaches its nadir of energy. I had certainly reached mine, I thought, as I sipped the last, cold drops of the coffee I had poured myself hours before. Then the silence was broken by the radio chatter with new signal orders. I snapped at the other officers to write down the message quickly: "All ships ordered to close each other and take tight formation for personnel transfer." I strained through my binoculars to see the red and green running lights of the ships converging in the dark Pacific night ahead of us.

It was 0455. The captain had asked the officer of the deck, me, to wake him up at 0500, prior to the personnel transfer. It was a tradition to give the boss a wake-up call, not because he needed to be reminded to wake up, but because he worked eighteen-hour days and rarely slept for more than four hours at a time. No matter the time of day, the captain is on call and responsible for the welfare of the ship, its crew, and our mission. I was being trusted as the officer of the deck to keep us safe while on watch.

I rehearsed and revised the report that I would give the captain when I called him. I wanted to sound confident instead of exhausted. I had been on board for a little more than a year. I was ahead in my qualification exams, already having qualified as an officer of the deck on the best *Aegis* destroyer in the Pacific Fleet. We had returned from Operation Iraqi Freedom to our homeport in Japan only months before and were already preparing to sail again, which was the tough but proud life of a sailor in the forward-deployed naval forces. I had picked up tons of valuable experience in driving my ship halfway around the world and back. The last thing I wanted was to fail my first real test when in charge on the bridge.

I woke the captain and reported: "Sir, the time is now 0500; the ship is on course 050 at 13 knots; we are 5,000 yards away from the guide, USS *Curtis Wilbur,* and are closing to our assigned station of 500 yards astern for the personnel transfer; there are three other ships moving to their assigned station in the screen formation." The captain grunted his approval and asked if everything was okay up there. "Yes, Sir," I answered as confidently as I could.

The radio crackled again. The junior officer of the deck recorded a message that the ship ahead of us was turning to port, but clearly the ship was turning to starboard, its running light plainly visible and now only several thousand yards away. The ship directly off our port beam had started to turn as well. In an instant, I knew I had confused the identities of the ships around us as the formation grew tighter. It should have taken my watch team only moments to regroup, but we were now only focused on staying clear of collision. I looked at my conning officer, Ensign Cordray, still green and inexperienced after only three weeks on board. I felt the knot in my stomach and knew I was in over my head.

My first option was to muddle through the next few minutes and hope to recover situational awareness. My second option—the more humiliating of the two—was to call the captain to the bridge, admit I had lost "the bubble," and face reprimand or worse. My mind protested. Hadn't I just woken him with his wake-up call and told him everything was fine? It was decision time. I took a deep breath and picked up the phone. "Captain, I need you to come to the bridge now."

Seconds later, the captain was standing by my side. From the bridge, we could see that we were now only hundreds of yards away from several other warships, but we couldn't identify each ship because it was too dark to see their profiles and hull numbers. I expected a sharp reprimand right then and there for poor watch standing. Instead, something different transpired that helped shape my view of leadership, integrity, and what a command culture should be.

The captain listened to my explanation of what I knew and made a quick assessment. He then started quietly feeding me rudder orders to give to the conning officer. "Right 15 degrees rudder," he said. I echoed. "All engines ahead one-third for seven knots," he added. Again, I repeated. "Shift your rudder." I called the last order and suddenly felt the ship moving out of danger and into a clear path. The captain could have easily given these orders himself in a show of frustration but instead chose to work through me. In doing so, he helped me regain control of the situation as well as the trust of my team. It was the confidence boost I needed. Like many commanding officers under the stress and anxiety of having ultimate responsibility, he could have berated me and sent me off the bridge. By not making an example of me that morning, he allowed me to learn from my failure. An experience such as that was all the junior officers needed to know that the captain was someone they could trust and rely on in a dangerous situation.

★ ★ ★

One of my responsibilities as strike officer on an *Aegis* destroyer was to maintain custody of classified documents. There was strict accountability for top-secret paperwork and a requirement that two people handle the information. After the documents were reviewed and understood, they were required to be destroyed. One night, after a weeklong exercise in which my team had been called upon at intervals around the clock, I sat in the ship's radio shack next to the classified document shredder mulling a serious dilemma. The log showed that there should have been five documents in my possession, but the destruction record showed that only four had gone through the shredder. I asked my partner if he had seen the missing one, but he didn't remember. I traced my steps, walking from shredder to safe, shredder to the desk, shredder to anywhere that I might have conceivably gone and everywhere in between. Had I written my notes in the log incorrectly? Could I have been that careless in my fatigue? I played it cool and walked out of the radio shack trying to keep an impassive face while I pondered what would happen if I could not find this paper: court-martial? Fort Leavenworth? Discharge? The voice of my chief petty officer played nonstop in my head, warning me about how careful I had to be with classified material at all times. The knot in my stomach grew tighter and tighter.

Lying awake in my officer rack at 0300, I knew I could go back into radio easily enough and alter the destruction log and end the whole sorry episode. I wanted to talk to someone, but once I disclosed this violation, I would lose control of the situation. I would also lose the opportunity to cover my tracks. If I decided to falsify the destruction log, no one would ever know. At 0600 that morning, I found myself standing in front of my department head telling the story of how I had mishandled a document. I had looked everywhere and had retraced my steps, but without success. Losing the piece of paper was like falling on my own sword. I could lose my job. Yet, I would lose my integrity, and all the trust that had been given to me, if I turned my carelessness into a lie and my actions later came to light.

The sum of my experiences at the Naval Academy helped in always guiding me toward the right action, no matter the consequences. The hours of training we received as nervous plebes that first summer, the countless case studies, the skits and scenarios we enacted for plebes when it was our turn to lead them, and the numerous honor boards that I witnessed had all deeply imprinted in my mind that violating my integrity would have irrevocable consequences. This, however, didn't make swallowing my pride and admitting my mistakes and shortcomings any easier. Yet, my revelation was that the environment on USS *John S. McCain* encouraged integrity because I knew the commanding officer would deal with me fairly. Confidence and trust in the chain of command made doing the "right thing" not quite so hard.

Creating a command culture that encourages integrity in others does not mean ignoring mistakes and wrongdoing. John Paul Jones reminds us that a naval officer should "not be blind to a single fault in any subordinate, though at the same time, he should be quick and unfailing to distinguish error from malice, thoughtfulness from incompetency, and well meant shortcomings from heedless or stupid blunder." In each of my cases, no one overlooked my failure. After that morning watch, the captain made it clear that he expected more from me as an officer of the deck. Following an investigation into the missing document that concluded that I had most likely shredded the document inadvertently, I received formal counseling to help ensure that I never again repeated that mistake. Each incident reaffirmed my belief that it is better to go forward with bad news than to bury it.

What my captain showed me in his actions was that the officer who was forthcoming with problems and forthright about his or her failures could still maintain others' trust and continue to improve and excel. My captain viewed admitting one's faults as a sign of maturity and of officer development. What's more, that attitude was the bedrock of a solid, winning, and combat-proven destroyer crew. Our entire ship believed in integrity above all else. It was acceptable to strive for great things, and if something went wrong and one missed the mark, to grow from it.

Fleet experiences provided perspective on leadership that my four years as a midshipman had not. Annapolis espoused selflessness but rewarded individualism. If you made a mistake, you were responsible for the consequences. Even as midshipmen honor chairman, my development of integrity had been all about me—my personal choices and the negative consequences if I failed to live up to the Honor Concept. One's grades and push-ups score dictated one's own success, not the performance of subordinates. At sea, and in life, the performance of the team is the metric for excellence. After a year on a destroyer, and earning my salt at sea, I learned to use my own integrity as an example to foster the integrity of others.

Selflessness from the ICU

Anita Susan Brenner and Rachel Torres

GySgt. Curtis Sullivan, 11th Company senior enlisted adviser, paused in the doorway to Room 7345, clipboard in hand. The room's occupants, plebes Kurt "Nick" Fredland, Daniel "Gunny" Floyd, and Andrew Jacob Torres, stood at parade rest.

Gunny Sullivan's official assignment was to counsel and advise the plebes of 11th Company and to prepare them morally, mentally, and physically to become professional officers, preferably in the United States Marine Corps. He was well-acquainted with Fredland, Floyd, and Torres. The three roommates were bright, physically fit, and a constant challenge to their higher-ranking upperclassman detailers. Torres, in particular, was viewed as a bit of a troublemaker. Barely 5 feet 7 inches, Torres had been the smallest player on his high school football team, didn't mind getting yelled at, and wrote home that he was having "an outstanding time at plebe summer."

On this hot August day, Gunny Sullivan began the room inspection with a visual assessment to ascertain the material and sanitary condition of the room, which was poor. The inspection took a sudden turn for the worse when he saw a silver-framed photograph. The gunny glared at Torres and pulled out a contraband identification form. When he picked up the offending object for closer inspection, he noticed the genetically familiar swagger of another Marine from thirty-two years ago. It was Andrew's father, a young captain, standing a security detachment on the deck of USS *Galveston*, wearing Dress Blue "C"—blue trousers with a red "blood" stripe down the leg and a khaki long-sleeve button-up shirt. Gunny Sullivan squinted at the photo. The three rows of war ribbons were barely visible, but he noted a Bronze Star, jump wings, and a Vietnamese Cross of Gallantry. Sullivan sighed, put down the photo and tore up his paperwork. The photo would not be removed.

For the next four years, Fredland, Floyd, and Torres never failed a room inspection, though rumor has it that they never truly passed one either. Their decor and amenities expanded to eventually include a working air conditioner, a toaster oven, and a refrigerator, which was never confiscated despite sitting in plain view under Andrew's desk, barely covered by the original cardboard box. Torres thoroughly believed in honesty and was committed to the Naval Academy's Honor Concept, but minor rules were meant to be broken. When a plebe detailer asked, "What is in that box under your desk?" he answered respectfully and truthfully. "Sir, that is a refrigerator, Sir."

Floyd explains, "It wasn't just that Andrew had charmed Gunny Sullivan. A few years later, when the gunny left, CPO Sanders stepped right in line with the program, although he did make us get rid of the toaster oven. He said that it was a fire hazard."

Under Torres's dubious leadership, the room became a safe haven for other midshipmen. "Living with Andrew was like living in a commune," recalls Fredland. During plebe summer, the roommates began to share their clothes. All the clean clothing was stuffed into two laundry bags; all the dirty laundry was placed in a third. Problem solved—no more folding t-shirts. Nothing fit, but so what?

There was a "quarter jar" in the room. "If you need money for a soda, take some quarters. If you have change, put it in the jar," directed Torres. There were video games (from Floyd), a string of Christmas lights in the shape of red chili peppers (courtesy Torres), and a poster of John Belushi (Fredland's contribution but worshipped by all).

With his communal "share and share alike" outlook, Torres didn't realize that others might feel differently. Floyd remembers that anyone could come into the room, upset with one of the other three roommates, but after a short conversation with Andrew would leave on good terms. Since Torres was so giving with his friends, and everyone was his friend, what he had was theirs, and to some of their annoyance, sometimes what they had was his. Andrew wrote to his parents, "People from outside California are weird." Survival required a philosophy of "one day at a time," or as Torres put it, "some days you gotta live chili dog to chili dog."

As luck would have it, Torres found the perfect sponsor family. Capt. Rick Stevens, a JAG officer, and Connie, his wife, decided, sight unseen, to become Andrew's sponsor family after noting an interest in "cooking" on his sponsorship application. The Stevenses were accomplished home chefs. Whenever they offered to let Andrew cook, he would decline. Perplexed, Captain Stevens said, "But your application said that you like cooking." Andrew replied, typically, "I said that I liked cooking because I like to eat." Soon, the Stevenses were cooking for Andrew's classmates and friends.

Classmates describe an event during the 1999 Army-Navy game in Philadelphia during Andrew's "youngster" (sophomore) year. The story is told and retold, even by those who were not present. According to legend, Fredland, Floyd, and Torres had arrived separately at the Wyndham Franklin Plaza Hotel the day before the game. When he unpacked, Andrew realized he had forgotten an important component of his parade uniform—the shoes. All he had were Nikes.

"Didn't you bring my shoes?" he asked Fredland.

"No," said Fredland. "Why didn't you pack them?"

"I thought you would bring them," exclaimed Torres. "Did you bring any shoes?"

Nick Fredland handed over his one extra pair of civilian shoes—size ten, brown Timberland dress loafers. Andrew wore a size nine. "Apparently Andrew thought my brown loafers were more uniform-like than whatever pair of sneakers he had brought with him," recalls Fredland.

The next morning, exhausted after a raucous evening in Philadelphia, Torres and Jay Consalvi boarded the subway from downtown Philadelphia to Veteran's Stadium. They were dressed in Service Dress Blues, complete with overcoats, scarves, and covers, with one difference: Consalvi strode purposefully in the regulation black Corfams, while Torres slid along in Fredland's oversized, brown loafers. "It'll work out," Andrew told Consalvi.

Inside the subway car, Andrew spied a white-haired alumni. A true fan, the gentleman was dressed in a USNA jacket, a "Bill the Goat" scarf, dark slacks, and government-issued black Corfams, a relic from his days in service. Problem solved! Torres approached the gentleman. "Sir, I forgot my shoes. May I please borrow yours for the march on?" Of course, the gentleman agreed to the swap. Torres exchanged Fredland's loafers for the gentleman's size eight Corfams, wrote down the man's seat number, and arranged to switch shoes again during halftime. Trusting and trustworthy, likeable and charming, Andrew's defining characteristics avoided bringing the dishonor to the Academy's good name (and demerits to his record) that a march on without Corfams would have caused.

In the summer of 2001, just before his senior year, Torres signed up for a four-week training course called Leatherneck, held at Marine Corps Base Quantico. The course is required of all midshipmen who wish to be commissioned into the Marine Corps. Andrew made a point of calling home every night at midnight. He would ask for his father so that he could complain: It was hot. Why did he have to iron his uniform? There was nothing to do at night. After several weeks of such calls, his mother told him, "Well, at least you gave it a try. You don't have to be a Marine." Andrew immediately shot back, "What do you mean, not be a Marine!? Of course I want to be a Marine!" Later that summer, instead of returning home, he volunteered as a research intern at the USMC Historical Museum, then housed near the Navy Yard in Washington, D.C. In his spare time, Torres located his father's declassified Force Recon patrol reports.

From early childhood, Andrew Torres had wanted to be a Marine, like his father. "If I don't get into the Naval Academy," he said, "I want to enlist." In addition to his father, his great uncle had fought on Iwo Jima. Andrew grew up surrounded by heroes, including a little league coach who battled rheumatoid arthritis, who faced adversity but never complained.

Even after September 11, 2001, with war looming and uncertainty on the horizon, Andrew didn't falter in his desire to be a Marine officer. A high school friend asked, "Why do you want to be a Marine in wartime?" Andrew replied, "I think I can do some good, take care of my Marines, keep them safe." In January 2002, Torres got one step closer to his dream when he received a service selection from the Marine Corps.

A few weeks later, Torres confronted a danger different from war. Up to that point, his medical record at Hospital Point, where the midshipmen received medical care, had just two entries: a sore shoulder from a field ball game and a sore throat. He appeared to be strong, athletic, and healthy as a horse. On January 30, 2002, however, Torres was diagnosed with cancer. There were no symptoms other than some recent weight loss. He had no known risk factors. The cancer, a form of liver cancer called hepatocellular carcinoma, is generally fatal. The odds of developing this type of cancer are one in three million.

On February 14, Torres underwent extensive surgery at the National Naval Medical Center, in Bethesda, Maryland. The operation, which lasted five hours, included a liver resection. Before the surgery, the doctors told Andrew that there was a one in three chance that he would die on the operating table and a one in four chance of dying during the first week of recovery. The day after the surgery, Col. John Allen, USMC, the Naval Academy commandant (later promoted to four-star general), made a hospital call. Torres, lying in a bed in the ICU, was in great pain, attached to dozens of tubes and monitors. When Colonel Allen entered the room, Andrew seemed to stretch out, as if standing at attention.

Their visit was private. When the commandant came out of the room, he approached Anita and Len Torres and said, "I asked your son if he needed anything. He asked for only one thing. He said that the two of you have been staying here around the clock. He asked me to make sure that you leave the hospital and go to dinner." Colonel Allen then turned to Len Torres and said, "Captain Torres, your son is very brave. I look forward to welcoming him into the Marine Corps."

A few weeks later, Andrew returned to the Naval Academy. The Stevenses opened their home to Andrew and his family and loaned them a car. The first night, a bed had been made up for Andrew in a nook on the ground floor, but he gritted his teeth and walked up the stairs to one of the guest rooms. As the weeks went by, Andrew grew listless and unable to walk long distances. There were complications from the surgery. Captain Stevens sat him down and asked,

"Do you want to graduate with your class?" Andrew thought a while, and then said that he did. "You have to study," advised Stevens. "You need to call your professors." Stevens had a heart-to-heart with Andrew's parents, who reluctantly returned to California.

Andrew called his professors, who gladly agreed to help. Four days a week, different professors would come to the Stevens's house to tutor Andrew. On some days, Andrew read and wrote papers, and on others, he went to Bethesda for tests and treatment. "I'm not sure he can do it," said one of the professors. "He can do it," insisted Captain Stevens. At the end of the semester, Andrew passed every one of his final exams.

Andrew Torres, whose courage and smile will remain with us forever. Once a Marine, always a Marine. (Courtesy Torres family)

Dan Floyd remembers, "One thing that was remarkable about Andrew was how he was able to graduate alongside of us. He was really tired and he couldn't eat much food. He lost a lot of weight. Throughout this, he kept his studies on track and ended up graduating from the Naval Academy. I don't know how many people would have been able to do that."

The night before commissioning and graduation, Torres returned with Fredland and Floyd to sleep in Bancroft Hall for the first time since his diagnosis in January and for their last night as midshipmen.

As a young second lieutenant, Torres's first assignment was at the Senior Marine's Office at the Academy. By July 2002, the cancer had returned. During the next twenty-one months, Andrew participated in three separate clinical trials for the cancer, at MD Anderson, in Houston; Stanford Medical Center, in Palo Alto; and USC Norris, in Los Angeles. Regardless, Torres developed a routine. "Stashed" at the Naval Academy, he threw himself into his work. In his spare time he coached a soccer team of four-year-olds, all children of service members stationed at the USNA.

Classmate Ryan O'Connell remembers, "Andrew never said anything about the battle he was fighting. Our conversations were always about his life that he was living (seemingly to spite cancer) and never centered on his cancer or pain." The tumors would disappear for a while, but then return. There were more surgeries, more treatments, and new side effects. In December 2003, a gunnery sergeant told him, "Sir, you need to get your house in order." As things got worse, a high school friend asked Andrew, "If you knew it would turn out this way, would you still have gone to the Academy?"

"Yes," Andrew said, "for the friendships."

In his final hours, Torres said his goodbyes. He told the people he loved that he indeed loved them. Nothing was left unsaid. Andrew's courageous battle with cancer ended on April 3, 2004, at USC Norris. His parents, Leonard and Anita, his sister, Rachel, and his girlfriend, Ana Ortiz (USNA '03), then a Navy ensign, were at his bedside. Dozens of his friends were outside, sitting vigil. At Torres's funeral, Rabbi Gilbert Kollin, a retired Air Force chaplain, offered these words:

> Andrew was a remarkable person, blessed early on with a clear sense of self and a clear sense of purpose. In a world in which so many people transit youth and even middle age while still searching for their calling and purpose, Andrew focused clearly on what he wanted. He wanted to be an Annapolis graduate and a proud Marine, and that is what he became. And when he was knocked down and fearfully wounded by his illness, he fought back valiantly, and like the leader that he was, he marched toward his goal as long as his strength remained.

And when his illness ambushed him a second time, he accepted the fact that this was not a battle he could win. And it was here that he showed us a special form of leadership rooted in courage and compassion. He had the courage to face reality and—even as he hung on with all of his dwindling strength—to say fearlessly, "I am dying!" while at the same time reaching out to say farewell and try to comfort everyone he could reach.

The enemies we confront are not always other people or even the demons in our own souls. Illness can be a relentless foe as well and can test the qualities of our leadership and our love. Andrew fought with courage until he could fight no more, and then he faced his destiny with dignity. Cancer took his body, but not his soul; it sapped his strength, but never crushed his spirit. He was eminently worthy of the uniform he so proudly wore.

Ship, Shipmate, Self

Mike Johnson

In the Navy, selflessness is upheld as one of a sailor's finest qualities. We are taught to think of the ship first, shipmates next, and ourselves last. Many would be surprised to know what this means in practice, day in and day out on deployment. It's not always pretty, it doesn't come with great praise, and it takes a stubborn commitment, but it's the mantra that got me through my service and stays firmly lodged in my memory to this day.

I remember giving up my strong sense of self as early as my first few days at the Naval Academy, during plebe summer. My squad mates and I were forbidden from using personal pronouns to refer to ourselves and other plebes. The words "I," "he," "she," and "we" were off limits. Instead, we said "This plebe" or "These plebes," as in, "Sir! This plebe requests to have a drink of water, Sir!" To help us remember, my squad had frequent drills in which we would repeat after our squad leader and yell, "This plebe! *This plebe!* These plebes! *These plebes!*" The self was definitely last, because it no longer existed.

Later at the Academy, when I was a squad leader, I remember quizzing my plebes on the weekly professional knowledge they'd gained, including little-known Navy trivia and other military minutiae. I took my role as their leader seriously, and I did my best to infuse their brains with as much information as possible while still treating them as human beings. During our weekly Friday morning reviews, called "comearounds," I would tell them to stand at ease, rather than in their typical ramrod stance, along the wall, or bulkhead as we called it. I would have preferred a few extra minutes of sleep every Friday morning, but the Naval Academy was my ship, and my plebes were my shipmates. The mission of the Naval Academy to develop midshipmen into future officers came first, and the development of my plebes, who were my shipmates, came next. Although my position had changed since plebe summer, the lesson of selflessness continued to influence my leadership.

As a first-tour division officer in the Fleet, I found the virtue of selflessness to be invaluable to the mission of my ship, USS *Cowpens*, which was stationed in

Japan at the time. Whatever the order, we were called to be "ready for tasking," twenty-four hours a day, seven days a week. "Ship, shipmate, self" was a mindset for answering that call, but it was often a difficult standard to uphold. I tried to put my shipmates before myself, but I quickly learned from my chief, my mentor and the senior enlisted leader in the division, that I was not welcome to join in certain activities. "That's not your job, Sir," was something I heard frequently.

Another frequent occurrence on board *Cowpens* was blockage of the sewage system in the rear berthing compartment's bathroom. When this happened, my most junior sailor was responsible for cleaning up the mess. Once when I walked into the compartment and found him cleaning up sewage, I picked up a squeegee to assist him. I couldn't blame the others for not wanting to help; it was raw sewage, after all. It bothered me, however, that none of his shipmates helped him out anyway. The one mantra that had really stuck with me from the Naval Academy didn't seem to stick with everyone, but I didn't let that stop me from lending a hand to a shipmate.

Later, I had a chance to serve as a liaison officer on board the Japanese ship *Kirishima*. I was the watch officer for the Combat Information Center (CIC). *Kirishima* was also surface warfare commander, controlling the positions and tactical maneuvers of the combined U.S.-Japanese battle group operation. I had been in charge of welders in *Cowpens*, but in *Kirishima*, I was suddenly directing ship captains to steam at full speed as part of their naval exercises.

My experience in the Japanese ship deepened my appreciation for the word "shipmate" even more. The Japanese crew knew that I was an engineering officer on board *Cowpens*, and yet without a second thought, they put me in charge of their entire CIC watch team. They wanted me to talk to the U.S. ship captains and pilots, even though it was their ship and their chance to direct the Americans. Through their hospitality, they continually showed me that I was a respected shipmate.

I felt like their guest of honor, and even though I spoke very little Japanese, they made every effort to communicate with me. I ate meals in the admiral's mess with his full staff. I loved eating with them in part because the food was so good, but mostly because of how warmly they treated me. For starters, even as a lowly ensign, at the admiral's dining table I sat next to the captains, commanders, and other officers, all of whom outranked me. My appreciation for their customs and food only seemed to make our meals more enjoyable. They seemed amazed when I picked up my chopsticks and used them without a hint of hesitation, embracing the steaming rice, fresh fish, and tasty vegetables. At one meal, however, my appetite and demeanor led to more than I had bargained for. The meal included a dish called *natto*, which is made of fermented soybeans and looks like a blob of, well, very sticky beans. Even in Japan, it is known to be an acquired taste.

When I raised my chopsticks to my mouth, the pungent odor was overwhelming. I chewed and swallowed and managed to finish it all, much to the shock of the admiral and his officers. When they asked me if I liked it, I said yes, but I don't know if they believed me. Either way, I felt like a good shipmate, and they thought the same.

It was on board *Kirishima* that I also gained a new perspective on the term "ship." *Kirishima* was spotless, and not for lack of wear. Yes, *Cowpens* may have deployed more often than *Kirishima*, but the Japanese sailors could smoke inside their ship, and it was still ten times cleaner than *Cowpens*. I saw *Kirishima*'s smoke pits, and even they were immaculate. Everything was clean, and I soon realized why. The Japanese sailors were meticulous and kept the highest standards as a matter of routine. For example, the sailors would take off their shoes before walking into their berthing compartments, just like at home.

When it came time for new orders, I volunteered to deploy to U.S. Central Command forward headquarters in Qatar to conduct harbor security operations. The requirements were for a lieutenant with a top-secret security clearance. I was junior and lacked the appropriate level of clearance, but was encouraged to pursue the position anyway by my commanding officer from *Cowpens*. Within a week of volunteering, I was on a plane from Japan to attend training with the Army at Fort Bliss in El Paso. My lessons in the meaning of "ship, shipmate, self" were far from over.

While the Army may not use the word "shipmate," Army and Navy share a common core value of selflessness. Through training and deploying, I again saw how it was essential to making every mission a success. I soon found myself in Qatar in a joint command doing nothing related to harbor security operations. Instead, I worked on an antiterrorism vulnerability assessment team, traveling throughout the Central Command area of responsibility assessing military installations, embassies, and civilian facilities for antiterrorism weaknesses. During the course of six months, I deployed to Afghanistan, Kuwait, Kenya, Egypt, Iraq, Bahrain, and Kyrgyzstan.

I followed up that tour with a deployment with the Military Sealift Command, first in Bahrain for three months and then in Kuwait for nine months. In Kuwait, I worked at the Kuwait Naval Base and the port of al-Shuaybah, the latter being the single point of entry and exit for the vast majority of Army cargo to and from Iraq at the time. My ten-person command was all Navy, but the larger command structure at the port and base was mostly Army. I was in awe at how many Army bases were located throughout Kuwait, which I had caught a glimpse of during my previous Central Command tour. I saw how the services worked together as a team, an army of one, a "ship" with many "shipmates."

Mike Johnson with his "shipmates" at the Military Sealift Command in Kuwait. (Courtesy Mike Johnson)

The tour in Kuwait was challenging, working with Kuwaiti harbormasters, Indian subcontractors, and Filipino tugboat crews, as well as Americans in the Army, Coast Guard, and Seabees. Our motley crew worked together to move a massive amount of Army cargo in and out of Kuwait in nine months; it was definitely my most challenging assignment. By the time I left Kuwait, I was approaching four years in the Navy, and I had almost as much operational time with the Army in the Middle East as I had sea time on board *Cowpens*. It was an atypical career path, but the values were the same every place I went, and I always tried to be a shipmate. After Kuwait, I reported to Naval Station Great Lakes, not far from Chicago, for what I thought would be two years of restful shore duty. After little more than a year ashore, however, I deployed to Iraq, my third trip to the desert in three years.

This time, I worked on Gen. Raymond Odierno's staff at Camp Victory in Baghdad, in the Office of the Secretary of the Combined Joint Staff. My staff sought answers to a wide range of questions from the government of Iraq: Why did you arrest this person? Why did you demolish that building? Can you provide Minister X with medical assistance? Life in Baghdad was always about the mission of the ship, a joint allied effort. It was a fascinating tour, and the six months went by in a blur.

When I returned to the United States from Iraq, I had learned much about valuing the mission of the ship and working alongside shipmates of every branch and nationality. After six years as a naval officer, though, I decided to find a new ship and transitioned into the civilian world. Even though I am no longer in the military, "ship, shipmates, self" are words that I still live by. As I reflect on my formative years at the Naval Academy, I can clearly see that my identity and values were irreversibly shaped by my time as a plebe, when I began to lose my sense of self.

Fulfilling a Top Gun Dream

Meagan Varley Flannigan

My dream of graduating from the Naval Academy and serving the best Navy in the world began the first time I watched *Top Gun* as a little girl. Right then, I decided that someday I too would be a Navy F-14 Tomcat fighter pilot. Long before most Americans could fathom the horror and fear that the 9/11 attacks would bring, I had begun working tirelessly to fulfill my destiny. I didn't anticipate what a long, tough journey it would be.

While classmates were hurrying off after graduation to ships, submarines, or to the Marine Corps, and some were being deployed immediately, I had to wait. We had just finished four years of school, preparing to be naval officers, and now I had to complete at least two more years of flight school before I could strap into the cockpit of a Tomcat. I worried that I wouldn't get there in time to contribute to the fight, or worse, that I might miss my chance to fly Tomcats, since they were systematically being replaced with F/A-18 Super Hornets. To fly the Tomcat was the heart and soul of my dream. I remained focused through those days of flash cards, landing patterns, and emergency procedure drills because I knew I had the potential to actually see, hear, and feel the fight someday. I knew that I would be able to detect troops on the ground and fire weapons with my own hands to protect them. I would definitely be more "in" the fight than some of my counterparts, and to my twenty-two-year-old self that made it worth the wait.

Rather than dwell on worry, I took the bull by the horns and selected the earliest possible date for flight school following graduation. I finished in almost record time. I became a winged jet pilot in eighteen months! Not only did I join the Fleet almost a full year ahead of some of my aviator classmates, but I was also one of the lucky new aviators on January 30, 2004, selected to one of the last four F-14 Tomcat spots in the Navy. I almost couldn't believe it. I didn't realize at the time, but being selected to fly Tomcats also gave me another unique distinction: I would be the last female pilot to ever fly the F-14.

Initially, I didn't want this distinction to be part of the experience. I didn't want to be known as the "last female F-14 pilot." I just wanted to be "one of the last F-14 pilots." Then I began to think back to recent history, when women were not even allowed in combat, on the ground or in the air. During the 1991 Gulf War, women had not been part of the fight. Ten years later, I was being given the same opportunities as my male counterparts. Looking back, I came to accept the full honor because I realized that it was an important step for women in the armed forces, and it deserved recognition.

I was more than ready to work hard to show I was proud of my role in history. In February 2004, I found myself at Naval Air Station Oceana, in Virginia Beach, ready to take part in the Fleet Replacement Squadron (FRS), VF-101, where I would learn how to fly and fight with the F-14D Tomcat. From the moment I walked through the door, I knew this was a whole different ballgame. I was shocked to learn that people actually cared that I was a female. In flight school, I had been treated like everyone else more or less. Now my presence met with mixed responses. Although most of the instructors treated me the same as they did the guys, a handful made me aware that they didn't approve of me.

On my first day of FRS training, a lieutenant asked me, "Women have been blacklisted from piloting Tomcats, so how did you get here?" My heart sank, but I just smiled and respectfully told him that I was selected like everyone else. Other comments were more difficult to handle. One Navy captain said, "I don't think women should be allowed to be pilots, and I'll tell you why." I remember standing there, my feet rooted to the spot, stunned but curious to hear his justification for such a statement. Overall, I was more shocked than upset by these experiences. Not everyone in the squadron, however, was disapproving. I made wonderful friends along the way, both men and women. I also tried my hardest to focus on my training and the flying I had ahead of me. It helped that I did well in my carrier qualifications. I felt prepared for the Fleet and for deployment in a plane that was notoriously difficult to land on an aircraft carrier. When the time came, I headed to my Fleet squadron with confidence, albeit a confidence that was about to be shaken.

It was the middle of winter when we arrived at VF-213, a squadron known as the Black Lions, and almost immediately started an underway period on board USS *Theodore Roosevelt* to practice landings, or "traps" as we call them. The plan was for the "nuggets"—pilots like me, who were new to the squadron—to take most of the traps since we were the ones who needed the experience. We were in the middle of the Atlantic off the coast of North Carolina, and the weather was awful. As I sat in one of the Tomcats and watched the horizon disappear and reappear with each movement of the pitching deck, I knew this was going to be harder than my previous landings, but I was still sure of myself.

As I came down on one of my first passes, I realized that the plane was a bit too high to catch the wires on the ship, so I took off a small amount of power, similar to what I had done on passes in the past. With the high winds, however, it was too much of a correction. Luckily, the landing signals officer on the ship started giving me instructions on what to do. I added power each time he requested it, but I was coming down way too fast.

The officer's commands became louder and more forceful: "Wave off! WAVE OFF!" In response, I immediately went to full power to gain altitude and go around for another try, but still the jet descended too rapidly. There was nothing more I could do to change trajectory. I was like a passenger along for the ride. The plane slammed onto the flight deck and caught an arresting wire with its tail hook, which brought the jet to a quick stop. I had never been so scared in an airplane or in my entire life. My first bad pass at a ship had resulted in potential danger and shook me to the core. The rest of my passes that night were uneventful, as were the rest of my pre-deployment workups for that matter, but I was rattled, and I could feel cracks in my confidence beginning to show.

Ten months after joining the Black Lions, we departed on deployment and headed to the Persian Gulf. Finally, four years after the 9/11 attacks, I was given the chance to fight back. Although I was thrilled to be living my dream and contributing to the war against terror, I had no idea how much the next four months would test my courage and self-confidence.

As we transited the Atlantic and arrived in the Arabian Sea, I was consistently inconsistent with my landings. I would have five or six good passes and then one not-so-good pass. I was disappointed and frustrated with myself, and it turned out I was not the only one. Just as we arrived in theater, ready to contribute to the fight, my commanding officer pulled me into his office to tell me that he would not let me fly into Iraq until I got my landing grades up. I couldn't believe this was happening. I had worked so hard at the Naval Academy and flight school and the FRS. I knew I was a capable pilot and a confident person. I had always known throughout my life that I could accomplish anything I set my mind to. I could do anything! Now, however, I overanalyzed every landing and would focus on the bad landings for days, telling myself, "I can't have another landing like that." I would be so afraid of flying a low approach that I would fly too high and miss all the wires on the ship. Then the reverse would happen. I went back and forth in this downward spiral for months. For the first time in my life, I felt like I wouldn't be able to do better, to overcome a hurdle. It was unfamiliar territory. I knew that my landing grades were totally mental, just like many things in life, but I couldn't figure out how to get out of my rut.

I felt like I was letting everyone down, including my commanding officer, my squadronmates, as well as my family and friends back home who were so proud of me and what I had accomplished. Worst of all, I was letting down other women. I represented the few that were doing this job, and I needed to represent them well. I also wanted to set a good example and pave the way for the women behind me who dreamed of being fighter pilots. Not only were my insecurities affecting my flying and standing in the way of my dreams, they were also leading me toward being depressed. I couldn't seem to get back to being the outgoing person I normally was. I spent a lot of time talking to the more senior officers in my squadron and to my radar intercept officer (RIO), who was my "back-seater" in the cockpit.

One day, three months into our deployment, after another challenging landing, I took my RIO's advice and decided to call home and talk to my older sister. I confided in her about all of the troubles I was having and, most important, about how I felt like I was letting down so many people. She told me that as long as I was trying as hard as I could, that was all that mattered and that everyone back home was still proud of me. It was such a simple statement, which I had heard thousands of times during my youth, but it made all the difference to me now, when I felt so isolated and alone. I was able to slowly start to balance my mental state, my landing grades went up, and I became more consistent behind the boat. My commanding officer recognized my progress and finally began allowing me to do what I knew I had been put on this earth to do—fly in combat.

The combat situation on the ground during that period did not require the air wing to drop much ordnance. It seems odd at times to discuss combat support without dropping actual ordnance, because that is what we spend months training to do before deploying. Thankfully, the presence of a fighter jet in the air is often enough of a deterrent to the enemy for our troops on the ground to be safe. For the most part, our missions were relatively quiet. We simply provided an eye in the sky, telling troops what we saw around them that might be of interest or importance.

Every once in a while on a regular route, we were called into a "troops in contact" (TIC) situation to assist troops on the ground taking fire from the enemy or an unknown source. One mission in particular will always stand out. My RIO and I were on a routine flight when we were given directions by a ground controller to a TIC. We arrived on the scene and checked in with a unit that was taking fire and was unable to move from its position. One of the men on the ground said, "We're taking fire, but we don't know where it is coming from! What can you see? Can you do anything to help?"

We told our troops what weapons we had on board and that, yes, we could help. We had located the enemy forces and quickly relayed their location. Our directions enabled them to find the enemy and effectively fire back. We were anxious to do more to help them, but their proximity to the enemy troops did not allow us to drop weapons, for fear of hurting everyone in the vicinity. Instead, they requested that we do a "show of force"—a low-altitude, high-speed pass—to alert the enemy of our presence so as to act as a deterrent. There aren't any explosions or cinematic fireballs with a show of force, but it is a very effective tactic. We descended, sped up, did our pass, and sure enough, the enemy troops stopped firing and scattered. They knew what we were capable of doing. We watched the friendly forces regroup and safely begin their trek back to base.

Later during that same deployment, I would release live ordnance on a target, but this is the mission that I always remember with pride. We had made a difference without having to deploy deadly weaponry. It is almost more powerful to show yourself, show the flag of the United States, and have that make enough of a difference to those who would harm us.

I made a difference that day. It didn't matter to those on the ground whether it was a man's or woman's voice on the radio; they needed the help of a teammate, and I was that person. I still am. Sarcastic comments, difficult passes behind the boat, and confidence issues did not keep me from doing my job—providing support for the real heroes in the fight. Though the mighty F-14 Tomcat is no longer a part of the U.S. naval aviation arsenal, it will always be a part of me, and I am proud to have been a part of its history.

Meagan Varley Flannigan, recognized as one of the last pilots to fly the F-14D Tomcat operationally, flies her last flight to the "boneyard." (Courtesy Meagan Varley)

Find a Way, or Make One

Meghan Elger Courtney

T here are nine workout facilities, three running tracks, eighty-eight pull-up bars, and more than five acres dedicated solely to supporting the fitness of the Brigade at the Naval Academy. I'm well acquainted with these particulars from my years on the crew team. As my oar blade pushed against the waters of the Severn River, a glance toward the shoreline would catch someone running faster, jumping higher, or pushing themselves harder to stay physically fit. Upon reporting for duty on USS *John Paul Jones* (DDG 53), however, I was surprised to discover little more than two treadmills and a pile of mismatched free weights for nearly three hundred sailors. This was unacceptable. Being an avid marathoner, I knew the likelihood of staying fit (and sane) during the ship's underway periods was minimal without the right equipment. When I began soliciting feedback from sailors on their concerns and suggestions for improving the facilities, it became apparent that the lack of adequate fitness equipment was slowly deteriorating their stamina and, in turn, affecting our overall manpower readiness.

Now I'm not trying to make the case that fitness was my top priority as a naval officer. In my five years of active duty, I earned my gas turbine engineering certification and helped plan complex amphibious operations in several forward-deployed arenas as a tactical action officer. Interestingly, however, looking back from my current vantage point in corporate America, my gym initiative on *John Paul Jones* is my proudest accomplishment because in the end, it all really boils down to two things: having initiative and taking care of your people.

It is well known that the military regulates physical standards for its service members. Such standards are implemented to ensure the proper conditioning of the best-trained armed forces to defend the nation. The military's members are valued human capital, and exercising promotes their general health and well-being during deployments, which in the case of the Navy means long periods under way at sea. Whereas soldiers on the ground benefit from land-based training and exercise, those stationed on smaller naval vessels are at a significant disadvantage due to a lack of funding for equipment and the limited space on board ship. *John Paul Jones* was no exception. Albeit a marvel of modern-day engineering, this *Arleigh Burke*–class guided missile destroyer simply lacked adequate fitness facilities to accommodate the personnel that occupied it.

The onboard equipment at the time consisted of two treadmills, one elliptical, a Smith machine, and a hodgepodge of free weights, all relics of an earlier time and hardly capable of adequately serving the warrior elite. The prospect of standing in line for one of the two treadmills was sufficient incentive to blow off exercise and walk around the corner to the candy machine. These conditions—coupled with the ship's poor ventilation and average external temperatures in the Persian Gulf that reached 110 degrees Fahrenheit—gave our "gym" the same general appeal of the arid, uninhabitable deserts that would soon surround us.

By coincidence, the ship's scheduled six-month Western Pacific deployment coincided with the release of several Navy policy directives reinforcing the personal weight requirements of each sailor, including harsh punishment for those who did not meet the weight and body fat standards. This was a significant policy change at the time. Effective July 2005, the policy stated, "Sailors who do not attempt to maintain standards will be processed for administrative separation." The logic of the new policy made sense: A paradigm shift had taken place whereby sailors were now being sent to the front lines of Operation Enduring Freedom in ground combat units. It was, therefore, clear that having an agile, well-conditioned naval force was extremely important. Although not yet fully understanding the impact this measure would ultimately have on the Fleet, I did know that otherwise hardworking, patriotic sailors would be forced to terminate their service, and this prospect deeply saddened me.

As a junior officer, I struggled to reconcile our exercise equipment dilemma with a policy that stated that "mission readiness and operational effectiveness are built on the physical fitness of an individual; therefore, all Navy personnel shall maintain personal physical fitness by regular exercise and nutrition." Surely, physical fitness is an individual's responsibility, but commanders must also bear responsibility by providing sailors the means to stay fit on board ship. A provision to the policy stated, "Commanding Officers shall aggressively integrate physical readiness activities into the work week in the same manner as applied to meeting other mission and operational requirements." My thoughts flashed back immediately to Robert E. Peary's famous quote that hangs on a motivational placard in Halsey Field House on the campus of the Naval Academy: "I will find a way, or make one."

Fortunately, as the ship's morale, welfare, and recreation (MWR) officer, I was in a position to make a difference. Whereas my typical MWR duties involved menial tasks, like inventorying softball equipment, organizing raffle drawings, and running the holiday "Jingle Jog" on base, this endeavor was more crucial because sailors' careers were on the line. In addition to fulfilling my primary duties as the main propulsion division officer, I began searching for funding to outfit the ship with a gym. The stars soon aligned, when, during an off-chance discussion with the regional MWR director, I became aware that a surplus of cardiovascular and weight-training equipment was being warehoused nearby. There was one stipulation: We could have this $30,000 cache if, and only if, we could allocate space for it.

While this may seem like a simple problem with an easy resolution, it was actually quite complex given the organizational and architectural dynamics of the ship. Earlier, during the winter of 2004, I had found an underutilized supply storeroom in the belly of the ship that seemed ideal. It was roughly twenty by twelve feet in dimension and lined with shelving and haphazardly stored supplies. I instantly conceptualized what it *could* be: a bustling, state-of-the-art gym. There were two problems. First, I had to convince the supply officer and my entire chain of command of the merits of converting it into a fitness center. Second, and probably more important, I had to ensure that by reapportioning the existing supplies to another location, the weight of the resulting fitness equipment would not alter the ship's positive buoyancy and thus its stability on the water.

Initial meetings with department heads, my first leadership echelon, were fruitless. They were either too busy to hear me out or altogether disinterested. Frustrated but still determined, I scheduled a meeting with the command master chief (CMC). A CMC is almost equivalent in importance to a commanding officer, and sometimes more so in the eyes of sailors and junior officers seeking mentorship. This senior enlisted leader climbed the ranks from blue-shirt boot camp to be leader of the Chief's Mess. It is within the master chief "code" to put the sailors' welfare first, so I had reason to hope that he would listen to me.

After discussing my plans with him and showing him the initial design schematics, he too was convinced that we needed to do something. The following day, he privately corralled the Chief's Mess, laid out the plans, and directed that they fully support my initiative. Together, we scheduled naval architects familiar with the *Arleigh Burke* class to assess the likelihood of shifting weight without reducing the ship's stability at sea. With a few minor sacrifices by our supply officer, who gave up the ship's storage closet, it was determined that the project would not impact the integrity of the ship.

With the commanding officer's blessing, I went to work. During the planning phase, I developed a graphic model using computer-aided software to optimize the positioning of the equipment. Next, I recruited a team of ten sailors, with personnel representatives from every department on the ship, to collaborate on the project so that everyone would have equal ownership in it. Assigning tasks based on capabilities, I requested that the engineering department cut away the shelving to make room for the new equipment. The operations department, whose expertise lies in decking and bulkhead preservation, primed and painted the walls and installed rubber floor mats while the more strategically inclined combat systems and weapons departments masterminded the equipment disassembly on the flight deck and reassembly in the new gym. During the final phase, we collectively oversaw the crane operations lifting the remaining gear from the pier to the ship. Standing on the pier with my white safety helmet wedged against my Navy regulation hair bun, I felt like a powerful symphony conductor.

When the new fitness center was finally unveiled, I felt proud and validated by the overwhelming response from the crewmembers and my superiors. Those who had initially doubted its success had witnessed an organizational change for the better. Almost immediately, I saw a positive renewal in people's attitude toward fitness, healthy eating, and incorporating workouts into their daily routine as a way to relieve stress and stay in shape.

What some may have viewed as my silly pet project, the command master chief took seriously, and he became my closest ally in seeing it through. I never really knew how much the experience had impacted him until I saw him become visibly choked up recollecting it during his closing remarks when he transferred off the ship. I don't think he thought that a young officer like me could have cared about his crew so much, but I did, and I still do. Where there wasn't a way, I made one, and because of that, a community of sailors can better serve and protect our country.

Part III

★ ★ ★

Courage under Fire

The credit belongs to the man who is actually in the arena, whose face is marred by dust and sweat and blood; who strives valiantly; who errs, who comes short again and again, because there is no effort without error and shortcoming; but who does actually strive to do the deeds; who knows great enthusiasms, the great devotions; who spends himself in a worthy cause; who at the best knows in the end the triumph of high achievement, and who at the worst, if he fails, at least fails while daring greatly, so that his place shall never be with those cold and timid souls who neither know victory nor defeat.

THEODORE ROOSEVELT

M any candidates applied to the Naval Academy with aspirations of glory, inspired by military movies and the sea stories of veteran relatives. Sometimes truth is stranger than fiction, and the least dramatic moments, in hindsight, hold great importance in an epic story. This has been our experience, and to take a humble view, we are only beginning to see the pieces come together now. The reality of warfare does not always end with a ticker-tape parade.

The Naval Academy graduates officers into the Navy and the Marine Corps (and a select few to the Army and the Air Force). The Academy also trains each officer in a specialty, such as submarines, planes, and ships. Our visions of each of these "communities" led us early on to make serious career decisions. Some chose submarines because it was the "high IQ" community, aviation because it was cool, surface warfare because it offered leadership from day one, Marines for the esprit de corps and brotherhood.

We went from the homogenous nest of Annapolis and were "shotgunned" to all four corners of the globe. In every warfare community and in every case, there was a leadership challenge. Sometimes the challenge pertained directly to prosecuting the "war on terror," but often the challenge was something internal, created by the natural tensions of working under stress as a team. Both kinds of challenges helped to mature us as leaders. We learned that courage under fire doesn't always mean bullets overhead. Courage is a reservoir that should be tapped in peacetime as well as war.

A Lovely Afternoon over Baghdad

Jay Consalvi

I t was December 29, 2004, and I was twenty-four years old. It was my first combat deployment to the northern Persian Gulf, flying Tomcats with the Swordsmen of VF-32, onboard USS *Harry S. Truman*. By the end of December, I had flown a handful of missions over Iraq in support of Operation Iraqi Freedom. They had all been uneventful; any increase in heart rate was usually self-imposed. On this particular evening, I was scheduled to fly a standard mission "in-country." I was paired with an experienced radar intercept officer, call sign "Demo," and we had a Marine Hornet, flown by "Spaz," as our lead.

During our pre-mission planning and brief, our intelligence officers didn't provide any information out of the ordinary. We were on the hook to fly some pipeline routes in central Iraq, near Baghdad. One of many insurgent tactics was to plant explosives on the oil pipelines that crisscross the country. Our job was to either catch them in the act or deter them from acting at all. We expected to be staring at our sensors while trolling the pipelines for these bad guys. After about three and a half hours in Iraq, we'd cruise back to the boat for a greasy slider (cheeseburger) before bedtime. No big deal. As the old saying goes, "Ignorance is bliss."

★ ★ ★

As far back as I can remember, I had always wanted to be a Navy fighter pilot. Maybe it was the movies I watched, maybe it was the books I read or the stories I heard. Maybe it became a part of me on my third day of life when my father took a detour to the airport on the way home from the hospital and took me airborne for the first time. However it started, I have known from a young age that being a fighter pilot was my destiny. Dad died of a heart attack when I was two years old, but he remained a driving force in my life, motivating me to dream looking skyward.

My journey toward naval aviation was fairly typical. I studied hard and took flying lessons in high school. Thanks to the enthusiastic support and encouragement of my mother, I soloed an airplane when I was sixteen. That same year I was accidentally shot in the face, and I thought that my fighter pilot dreams were over. My seventeenth birthday, July 4, 1997, was spent in the hospital. As I watched the fireworks over Boston Harbor through my window, wiping drool from my chin and craving the next hit of painkiller, I wondered if I would ever fly again, never mind become a Navy fighter pilot.

I recovered and through my mother's unwavering support got my pilot's license when I was seventeen. I was inducted into the Naval Academy Class of 2002 two weeks later. I didn't stop flying while at the Naval Academy, nor did I stop facing adversity. Near the end of my junior year, the Navy Bureau of Medicine rejected my request for flight status. I was crushed. I appealed and appealed, fought and kept fighting. Finally, a year later, I was granted a waiver and flight status with no limitations on what I could fly. I service selected naval aviation and started flight school seven days after graduation. After a year and a half of flight training, I moved to Virginia Beach, Virginia, to begin the F-14 Tomcat training curriculum. My dream had come true. At that moment, I could never have imagined that a lifetime of dreaming and striving and working to become a naval aviator would eventually be summed up in one very poignant evening flying over northern Iraq.

★ ★ ★

It was a lovely afternoon over downtown Baghdad. I was a brand-new Fleet aviator on my first cruise. Everything was new to me, and in part because of that, I hadn't really explored the consequences of failure, or success for that matter. I was just happy to be there. Happy to serve, happy to fly.

We spent the first forty-five minutes of our mission searching for suspicious activity; eventually it just felt as though we were on a leisurely cruise through the countryside. I even commented to Demo, with a big yawn, that I was quite enjoying our sightseeing trip over the Tigris. Right about that time, our radios crackled to life.

"Viscous 45, 46, this is Warhawk. Be advised, there is a TIC in progress in Mosul. Your signal is buster. Meet your tanker fifty miles north of your position!"

Viscous 45 and Viscous 46 were our mission call signs, so I perked up quickly. Obedient to the anonymous voice on the radio, we turned our aircraft and "bustered" north as quickly as possible to get gas and help out the TIC (troops in contact). As briefed, "Exxon in the sky" was on our nose at fifty miles, heading toward Mosul. I was lucky to plug in first to fuel up, but it turned out the tanker's pumps weren't working. "Just stay in the basket," said the tanker pilot, "there is another tanker near Mosul. Take whatever gas we can give you in the twenty-minute transit. We'll drag you right to him." As we rendezvoused with our second tanker, Spaz elected to take gas first. While he was in the basket, we attempted to get an update on the situation on the ground. Just then, our primary radio gave up the ghost.

In general, operating on one radio is no big deal, but on this particular evening, it certainly would have been nice to have both radios working. Wartime operations require lots of coordination and lots of communication. The amount of communication over one radio was almost too much to handle, and it caused more than a little discomfort and misunderstanding throughout the remainder of our flight. We elected to stay up on the tanker frequency for safety, and therefore we were not able to get any more information about our troops and their fight in the city below us.

After fifteen minutes in the basket, Spaz had a full bag of gas and pitched off the tanker to provide support in Mosul. "Get your gas, report overhead," said Spaz over the static of our crackling radio. "See you in twenty minutes." With that, we were all alone. We got into the basket, again, and this time started to take on fuel. Five minutes later, a single Hornet from our Marine squadron showed up on the wing of the tanker. He had just come from the fight we were about to dive into. He was out of bullets and out of gas. When he checked in with the tanker I realized that it was a good friend of mine.

"What's going on Cleetus!" I yelled, hoping he could hear my broken transmissions over the din of static and radio noise.

"Is that you MJ!"

"You know it buddy! What's the story down there?"

Communications are normally kept succinct and professional in the air. Quiet time on the radio is golden, and filling that time with a running dialogue is not the norm. This evening, however, chatting casually with Cleetus provided us with some invaluable situational awareness that we had lost working with just one radio. Without him, we would have never learned what we were getting ourselves into. Despite the fact that our radio was scratchy and broken, I could still clearly hear the stress in his voice. As he described the battle that had unfolded in Mosul, I started shaking in my seat.

Cleetus spent some time describing the layout of the streets, the location of the friendlies, the buildings housing the enemy, and lots of other important details that helped us get our heads around the environment where we were about to immerse ourselves. He had done a good job of utilizing his Hornet's ordnance in support of the troops on the ground, but the battle was still raging. An Army Stryker unit had gone on patrol through the streets of Mosul, a common occurrence in the region. Ops were normal. What was not normal was that insurgent forces had planned an ingenious and deadly ambush. The convoy of vehicles, mostly heavily armed utility vehicles, had been rolling down the main drag on the west side of town. They were at the end of their mission when all hell broke loose. Multiple roadside bombs exploded simultaneously at intervals throughout the convoy, and the men and vehicles were stopped in their own bloody tracks. As soon as the men dismounted, gunfire rained down on them from all sides. They were trapped.

Full of fuel, we said goodbye to Cleetus, pointed the aircraft to the center of Mosul, and attempted to contact Spaz. I was scared, but I was ready to put my aircraft, and training, into service to help out my buddies in the street. Demo switched our only, shitty radio up to the frequency that we had been given, and the noise on that channel was startling. With the sun setting behind us, I peered down into the maze of streets, bridges, intersections, and smoking buildings. All I could think of was how our target resembled the Super Bowl—a grandstand full of flashing cameras above the heads of Army soldiers on the ground—but instead of thousands of flash bulbs, I was seeing the bright flashes of bullets, tracers, and grenades, all pointed at U.S. soldiers. I was now even more scared, but those were my brothers down there and I had to help them.

Gazing down at the maelstrom, I picked up the blur of a Hornet diving at the ground. Seconds later, a truck exploded, and more smoke poured over the battlefield. Though I knew I was safe in my cockpit, I was physically shaking. I had no idea what was next, and I had no idea how our boys were faring. The diving Hornet had been Spaz, on his last strafing run. Like Cleetus, he was out of bullets. The congestion of the city made collateral damage concerns too great for him to drop bombs, and he had to pitch out of the fight. We had bullets; it was our turn.

Demo began to get a talk-on to friendly and enemy positions, and an updated situation report from our joint terminal air controller (JTAC). The JTAC is like an offensive coordinator in football. He is with the guys on the ground, can see where the threat is coming from, and utilizes the aviation assets at his disposal to attack the threat. It's a tough job, but one that is absolutely crucial in a fight of this magnitude. This JTAC sounded young, and stressed, and he frequently took pauses to engage the enemy himself. The noises in the background were like something out of a movie. I was wet behind the ears, but I knew enough to realize that our team was in extremis.

The JTAC was begging for strafing attacks on the enemy, just eighty meters from their position. It took Demo and me a few minutes to get our bearings, but faster than I expected we were diving toward the ground, cleared hot—with permission to employ our 20 mm Vulcan cannon. I managed to get the gun sight squarely over the balcony from which the enemy was firing, but as I got lower and lower, the symbols in my gun sight weren't what I was expecting to see. I had to be sure that the bullets from my gun were not going to end up hitting the good guys or any nearby civilians. I pulled off without a shot.

"What happened?" came the voices from all sides as we recovered off target. "Why didn't you fire?!"

"I didn't fire because it didn't look right," I yelled into the radio.

Demo shouted back from the rear cockpit, "MJ, we gotta get bullets down there. These guys need us."

"Fuck. Okay, okay, I'll do it."

I knew that I needed to put bullets down on the second run, but I also knew that I still couldn't risk the lives of friendlies, so I pressed our Tomcat absolutely as low as I could before I pulled the trigger. It's amazing to me that I can still remember those few seconds so vividly. The gun spooled up, bullets came out, the earth started getting REALLY big in my windshield, and I pulled up, hard, and continued climbing back to our holding altitude. Through it all . . . silence. No static on the radios. No calls from the JTAC, or from Spaz. Oh my God, I thought, I just killed the friendlies. Seconds felt like hours as my stomach twisted itself into a pretzel.

"Good hits, those were good hits!" came Demo from the backseat. Then the radio crackled to life again, "Those were good hits, good hits! You are authorized for an immediate reattack!" I thought, "Holy shit! Thank you God! Here we go again!"

We rolled in again with the same results. Cleared for a third attack, we made our way around the circle and dove toward the target. Flashes whizzed past the canopy and our wings. It didn't even occur to me that those little guys were firing up at me. I only knew that I had to fire down at them. Ignorance was, indeed, bliss.

Coming off target, Demo yelled from the back seat, "Holy shit, break left!" I rolled and pulled about as hard as I possibly could, dumping flares out of the bottom of the aircraft. As I strained to see behind us, the spiraling smoke trail of a heat-seeking surface-to-air missile passed really close behind our tail and through the flares I had expended. Thank God for Demo. I probably wouldn't be recounting this story if he hadn't been watching our tail. Thanks, buddy.

The fight continued into the night, and the surface-to-air threat became more distinct. There were no more missile shots, but every time we rolled into our dive, tracer fire, and in some instances strings of antiaircraft artillery, followed our aircraft down the chute. It was terrifying, but our JTAC kept asking for support. We had gas and bullets, so we kept rolling in until we had spent all of our nearly seven hundred bullets.

After about an hour, we began to run out of gas. We had time for one last attack before we had to go back to the tanker. We coordinated the two aircraft, with Spaz pointing his Hornet at the target and shooting an air-to-surface missile. Demo used our targeting pod and laser to guide the missile into the very

Jay Consalvi and his wingman, "Spaz," receiving fuel over Iraq in support of combat troops on the ground. (Courtesy Jay Consalvi)

same building we had been attacking all night. The missile let itself in the front door and greeted the occupants of the building with a fiery blast. No more gunfire came from the building.

When we finally plugged into the tanker, very low on gas, we heard our JTAC report that the convoy was mounting up and heading for home. They made it out. Spaz, Demo, and I began the hour-and-a-half transit from Mosul back to the "boat," as pilots like to call home, in this case a floating city in the northern Persian Gulf. We spent the entire trip in almost complete silence. It was emotional detox time, coming down off an indescribable adrenaline rush. It was spiritual. I went over the fight in my head, said my prayers for those we tried to help and the souls we hurt. I then prepared myself for the nighttime carrier landing I was about to execute.

Every night when I come down the chute to land on the boat, I say a couple of Hail Marys. This short prayer always seems to calm me down. That night, to make matters even more worthy of divine intervention, my aggressive defensive maneuvering had severely damaged our Tomcat's wing-flap system. We had to land on the carrier without wing flaps or slats, which help the aircraft fly slower for a more manageable landing approach. It was a less than optimal configuration, controllable but certainly not comfortable. Our approach was much faster than normal, resulting in perhaps the scariest moments of the evening, including nearly being hit by a missile. That night I may have said a complete rosary on my way down the chute.

Once we were safe on deck, Spaz, Demo, and I debriefed with our intelligence officers, my skipper, and our air wing commander. As soon as we finished, we sat down and emailed the guys we had been supporting on the ground. Our message was simple: "Hope we helped you guys out. Let us know what we can do better next time." Less than two hours later, we received a reply: "Sir, helped out is a f-ing understatement. . . . You saved a lot of good guys' lives out there tonight. If you hadn't been there, we wouldn't be here. Thank you."

I sat back in my chair. Cold chills ran up the back of my neck, and then I breathed a long sigh of relief. Satisfaction, pain, pride, validation, and countless other emotions washed over me. Twelve years as a boy dreaming, four years at the Naval Academy preparing, and two years of flight school training to become a U.S. Navy fighter pilot had culminated in this one moment. My brothers made it home. It was all worth it.

Bad Karma

Wes Pass

As a student at the Naval Academy I realized that my perception of a task was not always right-on; some things that I thought would be hard weren't at all, and other tasks that I thought would be easy were anything but. This lesson carried over into combat as well. Often the "simplest" parts of our plan presented the biggest challenges, and the parts we meticulously prepared for would pass without a hiccup. This experience made me realize that it's just best to be prepared for anything.

I was selected by the Marine Corps to be a tank officer, and being an officer means assuming other combat responsibilities as well. I spent my first tour in Iraq with the 3rd Battalion, 4th Marines, which famously pulled down the statue of Saddam Hussein during the march to Baghdad in 2003. I had been at a mandatory Army school at the time, but was one of the first officers to check into 2D Tank Battalion after its return to the States that summer. At that time, the Army's mission in Iraq was focused on nation building, and no one expected the Marines to have to return.

A platoon of Marines is a unique thing. Their discipline and confidence can give one a false sense of comfort, but they are inherently untrusting of anyone outside their circle who has not proven his or her competence and, more important, courage. An effective platoon commander must demonstrate both traits to be successful in combat and must do so in the complex world of helping manage the Marines' day-to-day lives, giving advice on everything from financial decisions to family matters. Once attached to 2D Tanks, I had to prove myself to these tough critics while never having served with them in combat and knowing very little about the tanks, or "Hogs" as we affectionately refer to them. (My wife called my tank "the other woman.")

During a training exercise in Twentynine Palms, California, an area colorfully labeled "Satan's Asshole" because it looks like the worst place on earth, I received a radio call to come see the operation's officer. He didn't mince words: "You're leaving for Iraq in four days. I suggest you get back to North Carolina and pack your shit." The battalion needed more combat arms officers for its assigned push back into Iraq. Sure enough, within a few days, I was on a plane to Kuwait to meet my battalion.

★ ★ ★

My first thought upon landing in the desert in Kuwait was that I'd been sent to the dark side of the moon. It was four in the morning when I arrived at my tent. I didn't have any Marines, didn't know anyone, and didn't have any idea what I would be doing. When morning came, I learned that the battalion had not been expecting me, didn't really need me, and quite frankly didn't seem to want me there.

I was put into the operations shop, where I worked as an assistant for an arrogant helicopter pilot nicknamed "Fab," short for "feet, ass, and balls." We didn't stay long in Kuwait. The battalion was ordered to move, and we soon found ourselves at our new home in Haditha, Iraq. I spent the following week trying to avoid support duties and instead would slip off on patrol with the infantry platoons, acting as a rifleman where needed. Avoiding staff work could have gone badly for me, but I was fortunate enough to have an outstanding commander and executive officer who understood my passion to not be in garrison and who gave me a chance to prove myself with my own platoon. The sun shined on this dog's ass from that point on.

My Marines and I were running missions every day and night. Time flew by, and we grew very tight. This way of life continued for a few months, until one night when I entered the command center for a briefing on that night's mission. I was told without reason that everything had been scrapped for that night, so I headed back to our barracks at the bottom of the Haditha dam to get what I hoped would be a rare full night's sleep.

What I didn't know was that contractors from Blackwater USA, a private security company, had just been ambushed in Fallujah, dragged through the streets, and burned on a bridge. I was called back to the command center and given marching orders. We were given the order to press down to the city in direct support of an offensive operation. Within twenty-four hours, I was standing in a room at forward-operating base Fallujah looking at a two-story map on a wall. The map showed my battalion as the main effort, responsible for advancing through the city in what would take an estimated four days. It was at this particular point that our situation became sobering; my stomach sank and I completely forgot about the full night of sleep I'd been looking forward to.

★ ★ ★

The following morning, the song "Let the Bodies Hit the Floor" blared over the loudspeaker as we rolled into the city from the east. Due to successful operations from adjacent Marine Corps units, the enemy had assumed an attack was coming from another direction and had oriented their defenses westward. After gaining ground in the city, calls to halt our position started coming in over the radio from Division. It seemed to be a mistake, and these suspicions were confirmed when I heard our commanding officer, Lt. Col. B. P. McCoy, responding negatively and demanding that we be given an opportunity to establish a stronger foothold in the city if we were to be going to ground. The calls continued, and we were forced to halt. Much later I would learn that this had been a political decision, not a tactical one.

My Marines took a defensible position in a former insurgent's improvised fighting position as part of the Marines' defensive line in the city. At one point, it had been a family's home, and it was clear that the insurgents had chosen it based on its view and clear fields of fire. Before long, my platoon was pulled to support a battalion operation to reinforce a rifle company along with a CAAT (heavy mounted assault platoon organic to the battalion) and a light armored reconnaissance platoon.

The base in Fallujah had been taking sporadic mortar fire from a small town to the north called Karma (or al-Karmah), which at that time was thought to be relatively peaceful. With our additional firepower temporarily in the region, we were given the responsibility of conducting a night raid to break up the cell. The attached light armored vehicle (LAV) platoon, led by Lt. Knox Nunnally, a good friend and USNA 2001 graduate, knew there was more to this town than the intelligence reports had indicated. His platoon had encountered multiple exchanges of gunfire on the route to the town with an increasing level of ferocity.

We departed on our mission at 0200. Not even halfway through the route, at about five kilometers, we encountered an obstacle of tires, rebar, and concrete in the middle of the road that forced us to stop advancing. How such an enormous impediment was constructed without any aerial intelligence assets observing it is beyond me. During the halt, the AC-130 special operations aircraft attached to our mission checked in to help assess our situation.

We increased our security posture while halted and dismounted around the vehicles. I looked into a small building less than a hundred feet away and saw what I thought to be a couple of sandbags that could be used to set a machine gun. The thermal optics didn't indicate that there was anything alive in the building, but I wanted a bit more comfort, so I grabbed my security team leader, Cpl. Neal Regonini, and pushed forward to take a quick look. This was not one of my better decisions. As with many combat decisions, you can complete an action and then ask yourself, "What was I thinking," just before thanking God that that mistake won't be your last.

Regonini and I finished searching the inside of the house, and I let the Marines at our vehicles know we were coming back. I stepped out of the house only to be illuminated from the sky like I was being beamed up to outer space. I quickly adjusted our posture and position and came back out the door to the same light. I lifted my night vision goggles and could only see the darkness. I then realized where the light was coming from. I looked up and saw the AC-130 shining its infrared (IR) light while the gunners on board were trying to figure out what we were doing in the house. Our IR tape—used to identify us as friendlies—must have been dirty or worn down, so I flashed the IR light attached to my goggles to steer them away from our position. I looked back at Regonini and apologized for making such an unwise decision. The mission continued with the gunship directing us through alleyways in the dark from 10,000 feet overhead. I can still remember the radio transmissions: "Turn right, turn left, watch out for the right side of the road; there is an IED. . . . Oh man, these guys are coming out of the woodwork for you now. . . . Standing by." Our FAC responded, "Cleared hot." The AC-130 acknowledged us, "Cleared hot, roger," and I then became privy to the most glorious display of combat power I have ever seen.

For an unknowing al-Qaeda fighter, it must have looked like the heavens had opened up and Allah had unleashed fire. The 20 mm and 105 mm guns began to work what would soon be our battlefield as we began to free ourselves from the confines of the tight trail the gunship had steered us through. Still moving north, the company regained its dispersion, and platoon commanders began to reposition their Marines to engage the enemy. All the while, the AC-130 cleared every few meters with 105 mm howitzer rounds, far enough in front of the lead vehicle to prevent fragmentation, but close enough to catch the hajjis running from the side streets toward the Marines.

One round impacted too close to an adjacent platoon, and the flash washed out the vehicle driver's goggles, causing him to roll the seven-ton truck carrying Marines into a canal. These trucks were usually used for moving equipment, but they proved to be formidable at moving combat troops because of their IED-resistant design, often replacing Humvees when possible. This spot was where my Marines would make their home for the next eleven hours. I dismounted and moved up the road to the company commander's position, where I could see that he was making significant adjustments to the initial plan based on his radio conversation and hand signals to unit leaders. From the tree line in the distance, I could see the slow movement of tracer rounds from what had to be an RPK machine gun. I wish I had known that if you can see tracer rounds and they aren't moving much, it means they are coming directly at you.

The first burst passed between the sergeant major and me, causing me to look at Sgt. Maj. Dave Howell and say, "Holy shit, sergeant major, that one was close." I said it with a lack of emotion, which only shows how much I underappreciated our situation. He replied, "Fuck yeah, it was, Sir," through a raspy voice that reflected a similar lack of appreciation for our predicament.

That burst immediately heated things up, but the Marines had now begun to dig into improvised fighting positions and had started using their weapons with the grace and discipline of artists. I knew that my battalion was known to be good under fire, but this was something else. The Marines in the battalion moved with uncompromising speed, bravery, and efficiency that was the result of exceptional small-unit leadership. Each time the units completed a road march or entered a new forward-operating base, the fire team leaders would gather their Marines and conduct "I'm up, they see me, I'm down" drills for approximately a hundred meters out and back, without instruction from a squad leader or platoon sergeant and before a break or gear adjustment. This was a common and arduous drill that was much more about individual fire team cohesion than actual combat tactics.

Back in Karma, later nicknamed "Bad Karma," we had shifted the enemy's momentum and begun moving through the city, preventing the insurgents from gaining an advantageous position. My platoon and the fourth vehicle of the LAV platoon were tasked with securing our route out of the city, to where the disabled vehicle had fallen into the canal. The exit route was being inundated with enemy fighters attempting to trap us in the city.

As the sun began to rise, the day got busy with episodes of enemy fighters popping up on rooftops and sporadic firefights throughout the city. At one point, seven high-value targets retreated into the town's mosque and transformed it into a fighting position. It is against the Geneva Conventions to use religious facilities or hospitals for enemy positions, but this didn't stop the insurgents. We had enough intelligence that authority was given for an Air Force F-16 to flatten the mosque into a new soccer field for the town.

That was the event that broke the enemy's back. As we moved out of the town, the order was given to blow the vehicle in the canal. Enemy sharpshooters were still in the area, and as my platoon had also been taking sporadic RPG fire, it wasn't worth it to tow the damaged machine with us. In hindsight, we shouldn't have left the city after having gained control or left a damaged vehicle behind, but this was 2004, and we still had many lessons to add to our knowledge bank. The trail tank put a high-explosive round into the vehicle, and we made our way back to base. The enemy killed during the operation was estimated to be close to a hundred, and no Marines or sailors had been lost.

★ ★ ★

Over the next week we returned to Fallujah, holding our line in the city while the politicians debated a course of action. Complacency and flies became our biggest adversaries until we were ordered to return to Bad Karma. Late into the night, Knox and his LAV Marines entered the city ahead of the main body and engaged an enemy observation position, killing a handful of insurgents and leaving one badly wounded.

We were at the southern end of the town when I got the call to take the wounded insurgent out of the city, down a dangerous route known for heavy contact. We were to meet a regimental aid unit that wanted to attempt to save the insurgent in the hope of gathering intelligence. I gave slight protest, believing that the guy was expectant, meaning death was imminent, and that it wasn't worth the risk to leave the company's rear trace unguarded. I was quickly silenced.

As we moved toward the linkup, a truck with four headlights mounted on the top pulled out from behind a building and directly faced my lead vehicle. Our night vision was immediately washed out, and I could feel our vehicle veer off the road. I yelled for my driver, Corporal Jordan, to come to the right, but it was too late. I could feel us take to the air as we jettisoned off the side of the bridge and into the canal below.

Regonini was in the second vehicle stopped before the canal, engaging and destroying the enemy vehicle. My vehicle was suspended in the air, wedged against the bridge and the bank, flipped 90 degrees to the driver's side. I suffered the least, with a bloody lip and slight haze. The machine gunner, Sgt. Sean Austin, was unconscious, having hit his head on the machine gun. Corporal Jordan was responsive enough that I knew he was not badly injured, and the two Marines in the back were completely fine until the door they were supported by broke open, causing them to fall into the canal, along with the extra ammunition, claymore mines, and various weapon systems.

I pushed open my door above me and helped pull Jordan and Austin from the vehicle and onto the bridge. The Marines in the canal had worked their way to the side and were coming up the bank. Regonini was immediately on the scene, always the adroit and disciplined Marine. He had coordinated one of the LAVs to provide overwatch, and I instructed him to link up with the regimental aid team that had moved north enough to be in view, adding Sergeant Austin to his medical evacuation.

We spent the next hour pulling weapons and other gear from the canal. Once we had finished, the LAVs helped tow our vehicle from the canal and get us back into fighting shape. I then walked around the bridge to conduct a final inspection with a flashlight to make sure we had not left any equipment behind for the enemy. At that point, I noticed a 155 mm improvised explosive device half buried between my feet. A quick "holy shit" moment for the Marines was followed by a crime scene–like investigation. I could see that the tape and wires around the device were new, so it obviously wasn't an old bomb that had failed and been left behind. It had also had many opportunities over the past hour to have been employed. I backed my Marines up and followed the wires toward the detonator setup beside the bridge. On the spot just before the detonator, the wire had been severed, and there was a piece of glass from our vehicle's headlight along with an impression from the front of the Humvee.

Wes Pass and his team of Marines after a failed IED attack in Fallujah, Iraq. (Courtesy Wes Pass)

The enemy had set up the IED for a strike on the bridge. Knowing we would be operating with night vision, they used the truck with the headlights to fix our position on the bridge, so they could detonate the IED on a parked and vulnerable target. When our vehicle hit the opposite side of the canal wall, we cut the line to the detonator and deactivated the IED. Once this became apparent, I looked at my Marines and said, "If this isn't God saying 'Here's one more day for you,' I don't know what is." Coincidentally, Sergeant Austin, never a religious man, had chosen that night to say a prayer for the first time in his life.

We did not immediately pack up and leave the town after recovering the vehicle. Throughout the morning, I watched my mechanic, Sgt. Travis Hill-McBride, disassemble my vehicle's leaky radiator, which had cracked upon impact with the canal. He found the source of the leak and collected some goo and water bugs from a puddle, mashed them up in his hands, and used it as a paste along with some other additive to fill the crack. Once the makeshift paste dried, he refilled the radiator with water, and we drove home that afternoon.

In combat, success is as much a product of luck as it is of skill. Simple things, such as putting a foot outside a vehicle without looking at the deck first, or flipping over an obstacle without checking for a trap, have claimed the lives of some exceptional war fighters. I am humbled by the things I have seen, and grateful for the sacrifices of my fellow Marines. The combat environment is often a crapshoot, and all you can do is train hard, prepare your Marines well, and make every possible effort to keep complacency at bay. Semper.

We Serve Where We're Needed

Johnathan Van Meter

"I'm trained for this." I had been repeating these words for twenty-four hours like a mantra, trying to shut out the cold. While lying rigid and prone facing north, I stared down a long road stretching through a breathtaking, moonlit desert landscape. The rain that had begun falling the night before was now a frozen, muddy slush covering my four-man team. The intelligence guys had told us that the weather was going to be typical for Iraq, which meant hot and dry. They failed, unfortunately, to mention the freezing rainstorm that would be moving in on our position.

With each of us observing a cardinal direction, there was nothing protecting us from the elements but the clothes on our backs and the camouflage face paint we had applied more than two days ago. Our muscles were so sore that shivering actually hurt. Bleary eyed from the lack of sleep, I was having trouble focusing on the red crosshairs in the scope of my rifle. It hurt to keep my eyes open, but just as I was about to fall asleep, I felt a tap on my right boot. Just like we had trained, my teammates and I were keeping each other alert by tapping our heels against each other. It's a good way to communicate and stay awake on clandestine missions; plus, it just feels good knowing that you have a teammate nearby when you're feeling so exposed.

We were lying in a concealed position, camouflaged to blend into the desert landscape five hundred yards west of the intersection of two main roads near insurgent strongholds south of Ramadi, Iraq. The lateral road is a dirt corridor frequented by dilapidated transport vehicles commonly referred to as "bongo trucks." The dirt road leads east, out to a village of small huts and farms. No U.S. forces had dared operate there since the war began. We were literally lying in al-Qaeda's backyard. The other road, running north-south, is asphalt. This road is why we were there. This piece of blacktop was a main supply route for coalition forces operating in and around Ramadi.

Dozens of convoys crossed this intersection every week, delivering supplies and transporting personnel. Sadly, in the preceding month, five U.S. soldiers had died in this intersection as a result of roadside bombs. The Army unit in charge of the area had been unsuccessful in capturing the insurgents responsible for burying the explosives. That is the simple reason my team was there—to conduct a clandestine insertion into the area, observe the intersection, and capture or kill the IED emplacers. The mission was originally planned to last one to two days. We were freezing and tired on the morning of day four.

My radio earpiece crackled to life. My team chief's muffled voice whispered over the circuit, "Headlights approaching from the east." I took a moment to stop my teeth from chattering and then calmly pressed Talk on my radio: "Here we go." A bongo truck approached the intersection and began to slow down. I clicked the selector switch on my M-4 rifle to fire and pulled my night vision goggles over my eyes. I quickly glanced at my watch: it was 0323, Christmas morning.

★ ★ ★

I had entered the Naval Academy with the singular goal of becoming a Navy SEAL. I failed. I gave everything I had for four years to earn one of sixteen coveted slots and join the SEAL community. When selection time came, the Navy saw fit to send me another way. The night before graduation, while other midshipmen were celebrating with their families, I was alone in my room feeling like a complete failure. For me, graduating the Academy without entering the SEAL community was the equivalent of washing out. I felt like I had been run over by a train. At first, I was angry and felt sorry for myself. It would take a few years before those emotions completely went away.

I was sent instead to surface warfare officer school in Newport, Rhode Island, where I was trained in the arts of seamanship and navigation to serve in the world's most advanced warships. My first assignment was as a division officer on board a guided missile frigate. I deployed to the Mediterranean and the Middle East, where my ship conducted boardings of foreign vessels to inspect for contraband cargo and the smuggling of possible terrorists.

In 2003, I was patrolling the northern Persian Gulf when the U.S. Navy launched a barrage of Tomahawk cruise missiles that started a war that would last for the next seven years. A dozen warships floated quietly in the dark waiting for the predetermined hour to launch. When the time came, the ocean lit up like it was daytime, as all the missiles screamed high into the air. Their rocket boosters slowly disappeared as they flew toward their targets and day became night again. CNN was on in the ship's wardroom, and we watched as the cameras observed downtown Baghdad. We knew the missile flight times and waited to see the explosions rip through the Iraqi city hundreds of miles away.

It's strange watching the beginning of a real war on television. It's even stranger knowing you're one of the people who started it. There's an empowering feeling knowing that you're watching history in the making. It was clear in my mind that what was happening was a lot bigger than I was and that I was witnessing what the rest of the world would be reading about in tomorrow's newspaper. It's the closest thing to seeing the future that I can imagine. This momentary exhilaration was tempered, however, by the humbling knowledge that those missiles would eventually explode into their targets and people would be killed. Because I would never see the faces of those killed that night, the consequences of our actions seemed vague and distant. It was like watching a movie, only we got to decide how it ended. It was real, but happening to someone else. In a few short months, my perspective would shift significantly.

After I finished my first tour on a ship, all I wanted was a second tour on the ground. I was tired of being so far removed from the action. I wanted to be closer to the sound of the guns. I heard about an opportunity to work with the Marine Corps as a naval gunfire liaison officer, planning surface-fire support missions for Marines conducting opposed amphibious landings. I volunteered for the job because it meant stepping off the ship and into a combat zone. While waiting to transfer, I received a call from the Bureau of Naval Personnel. The voice on the other end of the line informed me that the Marine Corps was standing up a new unit that needed qualified naval officers.

My record showed that I had at one time asked to be a SEAL and that I might be a good candidate for the new training. Although the detailer did not have many specifics, he told me that the new unit would be referred to as "ANGLICO" and that it would definitely see frontline combat in Iraq. He gave me forty-eight hours to decide whether I wanted to modify my orders, but I gave my answer without hesitation. Six months later, I was on the ground in Iraq with a contingent of highly trained Marines that comprised the 1st Air Naval Gunfire Liaison Company (ANGLICO) based out of Camp Pendleton, California.

Our mission was to work closely with the Iraqi military, U.S. Army, and Special Operations forces. We were trained to call in close air-support missions on insurgent positions during firefights. We were also trained as forward observers to scout out enemy positions and call for fire from naval guns and mortar and artillery batteries. During this deployment, I experienced my first firefight, my first time killing someone up close, and my first time seeing a friend get killed. I was so close to hundreds of explosions from IEDs that I still imagine feeling the shock waves pushing me off balance.

I also saw Iraq's first free, democratic elections. Thousands of Iraqis risked their lives going to polling stations to vote while we stood on street corners and rooftops providing security. It was amazing to watch as people came out smiling and holding up their stained index finger to show everyone that they had voted. Even though it was scorching hot, the people still danced around the streets in

Johnathan Van Meter deployed to Iraq with his Marine ANGLICO unit. (Courtesy John Van Meter)

celebration. There's a special pride in getting to witness history in the making. People who read about it in the papers can tell you what it looked like, and maybe those who watched CNN or BBC can tell you what it sounded like, but I can tell you how it smelled and how the heat and excitement filled the air.

My next assignment took me from the scorching sands of Iraq to the beautiful, pristine beaches of Miami, Florida. As a staff officer in the headquarters of the U.S. Southern Command (SOUTHCOM), I was in charge of coordinating maritime operations throughout the Caribbean and the Americas. During this tour, I traveled to more countries in two years than I thought possible in two lifetimes. I trained foreign military officers in Ecuador, worked with international disaster relief agencies in El Salvador, and toured the military prisons in Guantanamo Bay, Cuba. I landed in Cuba in the early morning hours of February 19, 2008. As my team of SOUTHCOM officers and I disembarked a small propjet into a humid hangar, we were greeted by the commanding officer of Naval Base Guantanamo Bay. He informed us that Cuban president Fidel Castro had just resigned, after fifty years in power, and had ceded control over the government to his brother, Raul.

In the wake of Hurricanes Hanna and Ike, I was deployed to Haiti to coordinate humanitarian relief efforts from the U.S. embassy. The country had been devastated by torrential downpours, destructive winds, and mudslides. There were times when the job entailed sitting on the floor surrounded by ten phones coordinating supply flights from USS *Kearsarge*. Sometimes it involved going out into the villages with engineers to survey damaged roads and bridges. When travel was restricted and logistics were a challenge, it meant flying in helicopters to isolated regions to drop off food, water, and medical supplies. We identified American citizens requesting evacuation and facilitated their extraction. Sometimes this was as simple as driving a car to a prearranged rendezvous and picking them up. Other times, it meant landing a helicopter in a soccer stadium and crossing a washed out bridge on foot while avoiding local gangs to arrive at their front door.

After my tour at SOUTHCOM, I volunteered to be a financial reform officer for the government of Afghanistan in Kabul. I started to realize that the military, in addition to its ability to destroy, also had an ability to build. After some basic infantry training with the U.S. Army in South Carolina, I deployed to Afghanistan and went to work creating financial reform initiatives for the Afghan Ministry of the Interior, which was plagued by widespread internal corruption. The national police force, still in its infancy, was experiencing major problems with paying personnel. The organization was still using archaic processes to deliver payroll monies to the provinces and relying on questionable accountability forms, stuffed into the socks of couriers. As a result, many policemen went months without pay. Corruption was rampant, with large numbers of police officers deserting their posts or supporting the efforts of al-Qaeda.

Working with a team of financial experts, I and other members of the coalition went about installing a national banking system. It was our goal to create an electronic system, similar to that in the United States, that automatically deposits money into an electronic bank account. This was a hard sell to the government as change is a slow process in Afghanistan. We worked through many obstacles, including language barriers, tribal differences, and legal hurdles. Oftentimes the process required loading up an armored SUV and traveling around the country on IED-laden roads to pay police officers directly or to educate them on the new pay system. We developed pay-incentive programs that cost millions of dollars, made possible by coalition donations through the Law and Order Trust Fund of Afghanistan. We even established a new payment system through which police officers in remote regions could be paid through their cell phones by going into a participating merchant's store à la Western Union. This last program was a revolutionary solution to the problem of paying police officers in the more remote regions of the country. I felt very fortunate to have a part in the implementation of these initiatives, which helped strengthen the security and legitimacy of the Afghan government.

Above the door leading into the Naval Academy's chapel is inscribed the Latin phrase *Non sibi sed patriae*, which translates as "Not for self, but for country." Graduating the Academy is the end of four years of preparation and the beginning of a lifetime of service to the nation. No one can tell you what that service will entail or where it will take you. For me, it has meant a journey through the streets of Iraq and Haiti, into the jungles of South America, the Arctic Circle, over the mountains of Afghanistan, and through the steamy waters of the Persian Gulf. One thing is certain, however: I could never have foreseen what was ahead as I walked across the stage on May 24, 2002, in my choker whites and graduated with my classmates.

★ ★ ★

That Christmas morning in Iraq was the last time that the insurgent in my cross-hairs ever buried a bomb. As soon as he began lifting an artillery shell from the back of his truck, my team accomplished our mission. I radioed for an extraction as soon as the dust settled and waited for the vehicles to arrive. As the convoy approached our position, I walked toward the first vehicle, slowly waving my arms above my head so they wouldn't mistake us for the enemy. A young Army sergeant hopped out of the passenger side door and ran up to me. He looked at my Marine Corps fatigues. My last name was written in black thread on one side with "U.S. Navy" on the other. It must have been quite a confusing sight: a sailor dressed like a Marine in the middle of the desert.

"There isn't an ocean around for miles," he joked. "You must've gotten lost."

I just smiled and replied, "We serve where we're needed."

The Real Hurt Locker

Eric Jewell

L ike an alarm, the phone rang in our detachment's tactical operations center. Having operated in Iraq for two months with more than a hundred
missions in the rearview mirror, one might think that we'd become desen-
sitized to the rush of adrenaline. That would be wrong. I still felt it every time the
phone rang.

On this particular day, it was an urgent 911 call, delivered in the standard nine-
line format. According to line four, there had been a car bomb, or vehicle-borne
improvised explosive device (VBIED). The suicide bomber had driven onto the
grounds of an Iraqi police headquarters and recruiting station. My explosive ordnance disposal (EOD) teammates, Richie and Adam, looked over at me with the
loyal resolve born of countless hours of working together under incredible pressure. I knew I could trust them with my life.

We double-checked our gear and then checked it again. I donned my body
armor, hefting the familiar weight onto my shoulders, glancing down at my
chest to quickly survey the ceramic bullet-stopping material secured within
the chest pouch of the vest. This part of my routine was so familiar, it almost
felt like a cadence as I opened and closed the Velcro strips around the super-
hardened ceramic plates. Patting the vest twice with confidence, I looked up to
see my teammates standing ready. We mounted up in the Humvee, yanking the
heavy armored doors shut and immediately conducting standard communications checks. Part of me felt invincible; the other part shut off for a while, because
whatever that part was, it wouldn't be useful for the mission at hand. I focused my
thoughts, playing through scenarios in my mind, running mental simulations in
preparation for the moment of action that was quickly approaching.

We linked up with our security element and headed off the base, "outside the
wire." The whine of the Humvee's engines was piercing as we accelerated, driving
in a tight convoy. Local civilian drivers were familiar with the sight of our military formation flying down highways en route to various objectives. They pulled

off to the side of the road just as we would if we heard an ambulance approaching back home.

The Iraqi police station was four kilometers away. As we navigated the streets we'd previously cleared of improvised explosive devices, I cautiously scanned the road for anything suspicious. We listened attentively for the periodic beep cuing us into the lead vehicle's tactical updates. We were thinking about the threat ahead, but also imagining the very real possibility of an unseen IED along the way.

We arrived on the scene unscathed and immediately saw the Iraqi police buzzing with activity. A crowd of twenty to thirty men had gathered as casual spectators. We had no idea who among them might be friendly and who might be hostile. A handful of the police spread out to stabilize the area. A white police truck was parked in front of what looked like a high-ranking police officer's office. Next to the building, twenty meters away, was a dilapidated, white sedan. I kept asking myself, "What could kill me right now? How do I take control of this scene?"

I directed our Army security element to set up a perimeter on opposite sides of the suspect vehicle. As they spread out to arrange for our protection, several of the Iraqi police approached my vehicle, obviously agitated and panicked. One of them explained through my interpreter that he was the chief of police and a newly assigned "bomb expert." I asked him where the device was located, and he replied that the suspected VBIED was the same white sedan I had observed no more than twenty meters from the group of spectators. We had no way to safely detonate the explosive device without endangering the civilians. "BIPing it," or "blow-in-place," was not an option. As the leader on the scene, it was my responsibility to somehow disperse the crowd, set a proper perimeter, and deal with the device.

Experience had eroded my trust in the generally corrupt Iraqi police. Nevertheless, I had to get people out of the way and somehow go to work on this deadly weapon. Thoughts of what might happen if the bomb detonated near the crowd were too tragic to consider in this moment. I cordoned the thought off in a part of my mind for later consideration. I had a mission to complete. The language barrier exacerbated the stress level exponentially as I attempted to maintain a clear and calm line of communication through the interpreter. As I spoke with the so-called bomb expert representing the Iraqi police, something didn't feel quite right. Sweat was pouring off his brow in the 115-degree July heat, but it seemed to be the cold sweat of nervousness. He also seemed to have a stutter in his voice. The translator conveyed to me, with a measure of concern all his own, the message, "I took it apart . . . I took it apart."

Richie prepared the iRobot PackBot to investigate the sedan, and Adam built up a bootbanger water disruption charge for our option of last resort—a remote disruption attempt and the possible high-order detonation of the device (and vehicle). Part of me wanted to go straight to plan B and blow the car sky high. I didn't trust the police "chief." The tension kept building. An Iraqi army-police recruiting station was an attractive target for the insurgency. How could I know whether this "bomb tech" had put the VBIED there to target potential new recruits and my team?

Suddenly Adam's voice piped in on comms, "Lieutenant, I've got at least a half-dozen one-five-five projos daisy chained with det cord in the trunk. The det cord doesn't have an initiator that I can see, but I've got separate wires going into the backseat." In the vernacular, he said that in the back of the car there were at least six 155 mm projectiles, each carrying a heavy metal fragmenting shell with approximately twenty-five pounds of explosives, connected with explosive cord. He was viewing the device via the camera on the PackBot. He maneuvered it to view the backseat but couldn't trace the wires with 100 percent certainty. Meanwhile, I continued to question the Iraqi police chief, who conceded that the vehicle hadn't been searched from bumper to bumper, only in the trunk. I sensed his embarrassment of contradicting his earlier statement as I stared him down with disdain and continued to stay vigilant for signs of deception.

My team and I concluded that the potential for a high-order detonation would not be feasible, and 100 percent clearance could only be achieved by sending an operator downrange. I directed Richie to take charge uprange, and we talked through the emergency procedures. This would be the first time that I would wear the bomb suit on a live IED.

The forest green EOD VIII Med-Eng bomb suit went on piece by piece. My feet slid into the toe cups, and the flexible front armor wrapped around my legs, as Richie and Adam zipped up the trousers on the backside of my calves. The trouser suspenders slid over my shoulders like a bulky but comfortable pair of overalls. The additional armor groin-pad "diaper" Velcroed into place and the turtle shell–type spine armor completed my lower half of protection. The heavily padded and armored top half was donned from the front, arms in first. With armor, seams create a point of failure, and the EOD bomb suit was designed to absorb a forward facing blast. All the closures attached in the rear. The bulky neck dam flowed around the underside of my chin, designed to deflect a blast wave up and away from my vital grey matter upstairs. Last came the helmet and visor, completing my security cocoon.

I had a clear understanding of the objective and even had a sense of peace as I donned each article of the bomb suit. Richie and Adam double-checked me. The scene was certainly similar to several in the movie *The Hurt Locker*, yet it was also unique. I wasn't about to rush recklessly downrange to cut the blue wire, like some character in a movie. Everything had a process, and the process would work, as my training had led me to believe. My heart raced, but I refused to think of anything but complete success. Adam attached my facemask, and the world went quiet. I could hear myself breathing and that was all.

A pull line trailed me as I approached the vehicle on foot. My teammates would use the pull line to yank me back if an explosion occurred. The line unwound from a wheel, slowly spinning as I closed in on the car. I saw the robot camera turn to look at me. I knew that my boys were behind its eyes, keeping watch on every move I made. If I made a mistake, they would quickly take my place to complete the mission. "Initial Success or Total Failure," the EOD motto, was branded in my mind, and I trusted my team to complete what we'd started, no matter the cost.

Twenty feet out. Ten feet away. On target. Doing my best to search the interior of the vehicle, I felt a bit like a little kid dressed by mom in a bulky snowsuit . . . in the middle of a 115-degree desert. The trunk was filled with ordnance, just as Adam had indicated. I determined that it was safe to continue and did a systematic assessment of the threat while trying to assume the perspective of the bomb maker. I found the wires Adam had mentioned and traced them under the backseats to more projectiles. With every moment I spent there and with every action I took, I felt like the IED got a little more pissed off. In our line of work, an EOD tech tends to personify the IED as he faces it one on one. The more one has to manipulate the device, the more one thinks it will defy one. After a quick snip and the tie of a "bowline" knot, however, I was ready to return to the boys uprange. I backed away carefully and felt as though I were dropping a two-ton elephant off my back. I had deactivated the bomb, and the stress was streaming out of my pores.

Adam and Richie welcomed me back to the world and greeted me with a bottle of water. My chest was pounding as they helped strip off the bomb suit, piece by piece. We shared a quick laugh as we moved to the final steps of rendering the device safe and tying up the operation. It was another one of the many events that cemented my love for those guys.

We were able to extract more than two hundred pounds of explosives from the sedan along with a lot of forensic evidence. From the rearview mirror, we were able to recover latent fingerprints that later led to an important intelligence development, a targeting package, and the capture of an insurgent bomb-making cell in the area. We found additional electrical components that helped us identify new bomb-making trends in the region. The icing on the cake was taking the ordnance to a remote location to make it disappear in the loudest and most violent way possible.

Our unit, EOD Mobile Unit 6, Detachment 12, accomplished 426 missions supporting the U.S. and Iraqi armies in and around Baghdad from January through July 2007, during the height of the troop surge. Our tasks were to identify, neutralize, and render safe any explosive hazards and make the battle-field accessible to our troops while also protecting the local populace. When I returned home, some of this mission further crystallized as the locked corners of my mind opened and began examining it. There were feelings there that I'd locked away, such as fearful "what-ifs," and bottled-up tensions. In truth, adjusting to normal life was difficult after living and conducting operations in a culture of war. I worked at accepting that life goes on and summoned the courage to continue serving in my old environment with a forever-changed perspective.

I have learned so much from the men on my team, from the Iraqi people, from every breath counted in the brief silence of a moment downrange. I have learned that my alma mater's ideals—duty, honor, and loyalty—are more than worth fighting for. For this knowledge, those values, and the wonderful gift of freedom, I feel truly blessed by the grace of God.

Eric Jewell , front row, far left, with his EOD team in Baghdad. (Courtesy Eric Jewell)

Evacuating the Injured

Rocky Checca

After graduation from the Naval Academy and commissioning as a Marine Corps pilot, I went to flight school and selected the CH-46E Sea Knight out of Marine Corps Base Camp Pendleton, California. The CH-46 is the Marine Corps' medium-lift assault support platform. I was detailed to join Marine Medium Helicopter Squadron 364 (HMM-364), the "Purple Foxes," deploying to Iraq. Combat operations had supposedly concluded in May 2003 while I was still in flight school, well before I arrived on station. After I arrived, however, the insurgency began, and the situation in Iraq rapidly deteriorated. From early 2004 to February 2010, HMM-364, HMM-268, and HMM-161 operated on a continuous eighteen-month rotation at al-Taqaddum Air Base in Iraq.

Al-Taqaddum Air Base was located in the heart of the insurgency, halfway between the cities of Fallujah and Ramadi, in the infamous Sunni Triangle in al-Anbar province, in western Iraq. The primary role and mission of our squadron was casualty evacuations, CASEVAC. We also flew hard-hit raids, insertions, extractions, snap vehicle checkpoints, and night external resupply missions. The commanding general considered CASEVAC the "no-fail" mission in Iraq, making it clear to us that there would be no dropped CASEVAC missions for any reason. Although CASEVAC were flown on a daily basis, multiple times a day, there was absolutely nothing routine about any of them. Each one presented unique challenges and problems. The pilots, aircrew, maintainers, and corpsmen prepared for the known task, but with ample contingencies for the "fog of war." We had to be prepared to fly through any and all weather conditions, at any time, and into all kinds of enemy situations to save the lives of the people we were called on to evacuate.

The CASEVAC process was important to everyone in theater. If an individual can be provided medical treatment within one hour of an incident, the chances of survival increase exponentially. This is known as the "golden hour," and that is why the entire CASEVAC process, from start to finish, is standardized, efficient, and quick.

Being on standby for CASEVAC was physically and mentally exhausting. It created feelings of anxiety 24/7; you couldn't relax. Being a CASEVAC pilot was like being a fireman. We couldn't leave the squadron area; food was brought to us; and if we had to use the bathroom, we hoped that the bell wouldn't ring while we were sitting on the can. When the bell rang, we sprinted to the helicopters and would have a primary, a secondary, and a backup aircraft up and spinning four minutes after the CASEVAC bell rang. Many times we would be in the aircraft ready to taxi for takeoff having no idea where we were flying to or exactly what situation we would find once we got there. On many days the bell seemed to ring constantly, and we would fly CASEVAC after CASEVAC. Even on slow days, including days when no CASEVACs were flown, we would still be exhausted by the end of the shift because of the constant state of anticipation.

We flew CASEVACs for all coalition personnel, Iraqi civilians, and even insurgents. The lives of our forces took priority over the insurgents', but if an insurgent's life could be saved, he potentially could provide valuable intelligence that might save American lives. There were times when we would pick up insurgents and Marines who had just been fighting each other and would load them together into the back of the helicopter. Sounds crazy, but it's true.

I experienced several close calls while flying. During my first deployment, on one of my first flights at night in Iraq, we received multiple RPG (rocket-propelled grenade) shots and small-arms fire while flying on final approach and on departure for a mass casualty call at Combat Outpost in Ramadi. The first RPG was shot from directly in front of us on final approach and passed ten or fifteen feet above our rotors. Another was fired from behind us on departure and passed the left side of the aircraft. RPGs and small arms were shot at our aircraft numerous times, and on several occasions aircraft took battle damage or were shot down. HMM-268 even had an incident where an RPG entered the bottom of the aircraft while it was flying, hit the crew chief in his back on his SAPI protective plate and helmet—knocking him out—and then exited through the top of the aircraft, miraculously missing all the vital flight components and never detonating.

I distinctly remember evacuating a Navy SEAL on my second deployment in 2006 from the very same zone. He was the first SEAL killed in action in Iraq. One of his fellow SEALs came with him on the flight when we picked him up. He had a severe gunshot wound to the head and face but was alive during the transit. He succumbed to his injuries after we dropped him off. It became clear early on that no one was invincible here, not even a SEAL.

Mass casualties were the worst because improvised explosive devices and car bombs were usually the culprits. The odor of burned flesh is something I hope to never again smell. Lots of times, people with missing limbs were bleeding to death in the back of the aircraft. If it weren't for the Navy corpsmen, who worked tirelessly to keep the wounded alive while in transit, many more would have died. They did the dirty work to keep everyone breathing or from losing that extra pint of blood that might cost the individual his or her life. They stopped bleeding from massive wounds or held someone's guts in during the flight to keep them alive.

One of the worst things to hear a corpsmen say to a pilot is "Fly faster," because that means the patient is slipping away. During CASEVAC, the pilots already fly as fast as the aircraft can go, so to get such a request from a corpsman leaves one with a helpless feeling. There were times when patients would expire in the aircraft en route. Those are some of the longest and quietest flights a pilot experiences. No matter what the situation is regarding the enemy or what is occurring in the back of the aircraft, you must force yourself to compartmentalize what you are seeing and hearing, separating it from the task at hand, which is to get everyone out of there as quickly as possible.

★ ★ ★

It was about two months into my second deployment in 2006 when I was assigned to fly a mission to al-Qa'im, near the Syrian border. I had been so glad when I learned I was flying to this desolate outpost, because I had heard a rumor that I could hardly believe. I had endured numerous months of compartmentalizing what I saw and only focusing on the task at hand. When we arrived and shut down the aircraft, I headed straight to the chow hall. As I approached the door to the small, rickety wooden structure, I saw the words "Winchester Hall" above the entrance. It made me smile ear to ear. I was nervous though, wondering about the rumor. I walked in the front door and looked around. There, just inside and to the upper left of the main entrance, was a glass case. Inside it, there it was—a big, bright-blue football jersey with white block letters on the chest: NAVY 73.

It was the Navy football jersey of Ron Winchester (USNA 2001). He had been a teammate, killed in action in Iraq in September 2004, a few months prior to my first deployment. Navy football is a brotherhood, built through strong bonds among teammates. Ron was the first person I knew who had given his life during the conflict. His death was shocking; I had a hard time absorbing that he was actually gone. It was one of those things that people never think will happen to someone they know. Two months later, J. P. Blecksmith (USNA 2003), another teammate, was killed in action. Other teammates, Bryce McDonald (USNA 2003) and Scott Swantner (USNA 2001), suffered injuries. I received telephone calls about all of them. My reaction to seeing Ron's jersey was immediate and uncontrollable. I turned away and walked outside so the other pilots and crew chiefs wouldn't see me.

Here, in this God-forsaken shithole of a place that looks like the surface of the moon, was the most beautiful thing I had seen in a long time. I pulled myself together by focusing my eyes on the metallic band around my left wrist that bears Ron's name. I wore the band during all three of my deployments to Iraq. Every time it was hot, things were shitty, or I didn't think I could do another day of the grind, I'd look at my wrist and be reminded of the numerous people, like Ronnie and J.P., who had counted on us on a daily basis.

Once I had pulled myself together, I walked back in, had a little something to eat, and then walked over to the glass case. I left Ronnie a note on the glass thanking him for his sacrifice and letting him know it had not been in vain. I also left him one of the squadron patches that we wear on our flight suits. At some point, he had been in the back of a CH-46 being CASEVAC'd while mortally wounded or his remains were transported via an "angel" transport to al-Taqaddum, where Mortuary Affairs was located.

Angel transport was a routine part of my squadron's mission, so I knew that there was absolutely no delay in getting the remains of coalition personnel killed in action to al-Taqaddum. On the day they perished, the deceased were transported there and prepped for the return home. These missions were flown nightly, and like CASEVACs, I had to learn to compartmentalize and focus on the task at hand. One mission in particular, though, momentarily broke through the compartment.

I had been assigned to transport five Marines out of Ramadi who died in an IED blast. As we flew in, the entire Marine battalion that operated out of Ramadi was off to the right of the landing zone, standing in formation, at attention. After they brought four of the remains to the aircraft on stretchers, someone hand-carried the remains of the fifth Marine in two body bags to the helicopter. When we had landed, the battalion's commanding officer had come on board the aircraft to tell us that one of his Marines was going to accompany the remains back to al-Taqaddum. Passengers and "angels" were never on the same aircraft together, but in this case an exception was made. The Marine accompanying one of the bodies back was the deceased Marine's twin brother.

Several months after seeing Ronnie's football jersey in the chow hall at al-Qa'im, disaster struck within my squadron: Morphine 1-2, one of the call signs of our aircraft, was shot down by a man-portable air defense shoulder-fired missile near Karma while returning from a CASEVAC mission on February 7, 2007. Capt. Jennifer Harris (USNA 2000), 1st Lt. Jared Landaker, Sgt. Travis Pfister, Sgt. James Tijerina, Cpl. Thomas Saba, HM1 Gilbert Minjares, and HM3 Manuel Ruiz all perished. These individuals had saved hundreds of other people's lives flying CASEVAC missions before giving up their own.

As I considered my time as a member of the Purple Foxes, I realized that the hardest part was the mental aftermath. I would lie in bed after a mission, alone with my thoughts. I recalled everything in detail—the sights, smells, radio calls, and what the weather was like. I felt somewhat responsible for any deaths although there wasn't anything else I could have done. I thought about the fact that that person had a mom and dad who did not yet know what horrible thing had happened to their son or daughter. I wondered about the person who had just made the ultimate sacrifice.

It's a mixture of emotions. I felt great about what we were doing, because we were saving lives, yet there were times when I knew that those who survived an incident were at the beginning of a painful postwar life. I often wondered about those whom we flew out of harm's way because we never saw them again. Were they upset about their situation? Did they wish that they had not lived because their life from that point on would be so different and difficult? Were they glad they had survived despite their injuries? Were any of them like Lieutenant Dan from the movie *Forrest Gump*, who hated Tom Hanks's character for rescuing him, forcing him to live life in a wheelchair instead of letting him die on the battlefield?

These thoughts weighed on my conscious for a long time, and then on October 21, 2008, I received the answer to some of the questions that I had been afraid to share with anyone. On that day, I received an email from another pilot with whom I had done the first two deployments to Iraq. He said that he had received an email from one of the Navy nurses who had flown with us during the second deployment. An Army sergeant by the name of John Kriesel was trying to get in touch with the squadron. Our squadron had CASEVAC'd him on December 2, 2006, in Zaidon, south of Fallujah, after the vehicle he was in struck a pressure-plate IED wired with two hundred pounds of explosives. It left a crater seven feet wide and four-and-a-half feet deep. One person died at the scene, and another died in the helicopter, but Sgt. Kriesel survived. Now, two years later, Sgt. Kriesel was searching for the crew, flown by a USNA 2000 grad, that had picked up him and his men that day. He wanted to tell us the following:

> I know that you said I don't have to thank you, but I will always have an appreciation for you guys at TQ and the military medical system as a whole. Both of my sons know the story and always ask about you guys and even at 6 and 7 say that they thank God that you guys were there for me and my men. They know and understand that I wouldn't be alive without you guys. My seven year old built a CH-46E Sea Knight with Legos and it looks pretty good. Take care and thanks again.

I remember reading that and bursting into tears. I got on my knees and thanked God that he and his family were grateful that he was alive, despite his

The Purple Foxes, saving passengers and transporting angels. (Courtesy Rocky Checca)

having lost both his legs. Not only was he grateful that he had survived, but his kids were so glad to have their dad back with them. His email was an unexpected gift that helped relieve the weight I had felt about the missions we had flown. Sgt. Kriesel was grateful, and so was I.

That is what Marine Air is about—supporting the guy on the ground, whether through assault support or close air support. It certainly is not about us. It always has been and always will be about supporting the guy on the ground. It is clearly understood that when a pilot screws up—whether because of a bad decision, lack of attention to detail, poor planning, headwork, or situational awareness—many times it is the Marines on the ground who pay the price for the pilot's mistakes. The driving force is the fear of failure and the thought of possibly letting someone down. People are relying on you to protect or save their life. Failure is simply not an option. If that doesn't motivate a pilot, then Marine Air is not the business that person should be in.

Now, years later, I can say with certainty that the challenges of serving in Iraq combined with the lessons learned at the Naval Academy—along with the accompanying hurt, pain, adversity, and emotions—have built me into a much better person. I would not trade these experiences, the good and the bad, for anything. It was a gut check and trial by fire, a life experience that I will never forget. The lessons I learned are applied to every facet of my life every day.

The American way of life is not possible without the sacrifice of the few. Edmund Burke wrote, "All that is necessary for the triumph of evil is for good men to do nothing." Those that sacrificed did something and are some of America's bravest sons and daughters. I can only hope that the families of Ron and J.P., the crew of Morphine 1-2, and others that made the sacrifice knew that when things sucked over there, they were the ones that I thought of, that kept me going. I know that there is nothing I can say or do to make their families' pain go away, but I hope and want them to know that there were people over there who found strength and drive in themselves at the very thought of their son's and daughter's sacrifice. I will forever remember what my passengers in the back of the CH-46 did for our nation and how humbling it was to have served them.

From the Cradle to the Grave

Anonymous

I will never forget the first time I saw Lt. Col. Kevin Shea. It was the spring semester of our junior year at the Academy, and I was walking between Chauvenet and Michelson in the underground hallway that connects many of the academic buildings on the Yard. He trod by like the Jolly Green Giant, an imposing six-foot-four, 220-pound Marine. He sported the "dual cool" insignia, having been certified in both advanced parachuting and combat scuba. He strode confidently down the hallway with a clear sense of purpose. As I walked in the opposite direction, I thought to myself, "I sure am glad he is on our side." I would have reason to think this again in the future.

Born on September 14, 1966, Kevin Shea was destined to be a Marine Corps officer from an early age, characterized by his determination and dedication. Upon graduating from high school in Seattle, Washington, he received an appointment to the United States Air Force Academy Preparatory School. After successfully completing studies there, Kevin Shea received an appointment to the United States Air Force Academy (USAFA). While at USAFA, he lettered in varsity football and was a member of the 1987 Freedom Bowl team. He also played rugby on the club team that won the 1989 collegiate national championship. In May 1989, he received a rare interservice transfer and a commission as a United States Marine Corps second lieutenant.

By the time those of us in the Class of 2002 met him at the United States Naval Academy as a Marine Corps major and systems engineering professor, he was a decorated combat veteran of Operation Desert Storm and had participated in numerous other overseas missions. He had held positions as a platoon commander, company commander, operations officer, and executive officer. He also had received his master's degree in electrical engineering from the Naval Postgraduate School.

In the summer of 2001, those members of the Class of 2002 who wanted to pursue a commission in the Marine Corps participated in the Leatherneck program, which entails four weeks at Quantico, Virginia, learning the basic skills of an infantry officer. Major Shea, among others, served as an instructor and mentor there. Following four weeks of training in land navigation and tactics, and some moments of extreme discomfort, we participated in a final exercise meant to test us on the skills we had hopefully learned. During this exercise, we were divided into offensive and defensive units and directed to attack each other.

My platoon was assigned the task of establishing a defense in a cinderblock town in the woods of Quantico. We had thirty minutes to prepare before an aggressor platoon would attack. Both sides were armed with paintball guns; they weren't the high-speed, professional type that work with flawless precision, but the Marine Corps' finest, which had been broken and fixed too many times to count. We wore protective masks that covered the forehead, eyes, and mouth and inevitably started to fog at the worst possible moments. We also had simple two-way radios that pretty accurately mimicked the frustrations of communication in combat; notably, they never worked when you needed them.

With minimal time to prepare for the attack, our designated platoon commander decided to defend the tallest building in the village, a four-story structure at the edge of the town with an excellent view of the woods from where our attackers would arrive. We established our positions less than a minute before the attack commenced. I had the fortune, or misfortune, of being on the ground floor of the building with my motivated fire team. Major Shea maintained an observer position in the middle of the room.

The attack kicked off, and we observed the aggressors tactically bounding in the woods as they drew closer to our building. As might be expected of anxious newcomers to the art of war, we began to fire our weapons well before their effective range, and so began a brilliant display of the chaos of conflict. With the sound of paintballs smacking concrete, so began the scattering in all directions of midshipmen in the woods and in the building.

While I cannot recall much of this doomed, ten-minute mock attack, I do remember with great clarity seeing Major Shea through my fogged mask as the paintballs flew by. He simply stood there in the midst of the chaos and smiled, a teacher proudly watching his students taking their final exam. Though he wore a mask similar to ours that covered his mouth, his huge grin was unmistakable. Not once did he duck, even as paintballs hit the walls behind him and smacked his uniform. When the battle was over—who knows who won or who lost— I came away with a better sense of Major Shea's character. He was a rock. Our rock. While this battle was only an exercise, I knew that Major Shea would stand firm in the face of a real enemy and inspire confidence in his Marines. At that moment, he became the face, the picture for me, of the character, strength, and physical courage required of a Marine Corps officer in combat.

During our final semester at the Academy, one of our classmates—we'll call him Joseph Smith—experienced a series of life-changing events that left him distraught, depressed, and distracted from his schoolwork. Major Shea, one of Joseph's teachers, almost immediately recognized that there was something amiss. While Major Shea's only job was to teach and evaluate Joseph, he took the time to talk to Joseph and arrange the care he needed to recover from the events affecting him. Furthermore, Major Shea served as an advocate for Joseph, who, if not for Major Shea's actions, may not have graduated from the Academy. While perhaps an easily forgettable episode, I was struck by Major Shea's leadership and moral courage in taking care of one of his own in a way that was above and beyond his responsibility.

As I raised my hand on May 24, 2002, and accepted my commission as a Marine Corps officer, I could not have known that I would have the honor and privilege of witnessing Major Shea's leadership in combat. When I stepped foot on Iraqi soil in August 2004 for my first combat experience, there he was. He greeted me with his warm, trademark smile and a huge handshake. Seeing his face, I instantly felt relieved, recalling fondly the image of him standing in that paintball-filled room with a smile on his face. The very strength of his presence conveyed that he would continue to watch over us, even in the face of real gunfire.

After settling into Camp Fallujah, a military outpost to the east of the most dreaded city in Iraq at that time, I quickly caught up with the rhythm of battle. From my interactions with the Marines of the 1st Marine Regiment, where Major Shea served as the communications officer, I learned firsthand of his sterling reputation. Although Major Shea had been selected for promotion to the rank of lieutenant colonel, had been chosen to command the 9th Communications Battalion, and was scheduled to return to the United States early, he elected to extend his tour in Iraq to complete the mission and look after his Marines. Every Marine looked up to him for this decision, and all of us asked ourselves if we would have done the same if given the opportunity to return home early. Without hesitation, most of us decided we would have boarded the earliest bird to the States.

During one of my first missions off base, Major Shea served as the patrol leader. From the moment our mission brief began, I relaxed knowing he was in charge. The mission was a tank feint at the northeast corner of Fallujah. The tanks would proceed toward the city with the intent of drawing insurgent fire. The tanks would return fire until enemy fire ceased and then withdraw to base. Major Shea was responsible for directing friendly forces from a position to the rear of the tanks, and I would be one of the Marines in his command post.

As the feint got under way, our mobile command post stood a good distance from the front lines, where the tanks were located, and behind a one-story sand berm, far away from the action for my liking. As the enemy fire began and the tank counterfire roared, I paced at the edge of the berm with my rifle at the ready, even though we were well outside of my M-16's effective range. Behind me, I heard the voice of Major Shea, "Lieutenant, don't worry, you will get your chance at combat." Major Shea smiled, a radio handset to his ear as he stood over a tactical map spread out on the hood of a Humvee. Without a word, I returned the smile and then instantly relaxed, lowered my rifle, and returned to my Humvee and the radio.

Two days later, on September 14, 2004, the day began like any other in Iraq, which is to say cloudless and hot. There was a change of command scheduled, and the roving Catholic chaplain would say a mass that evening. It also happened to be Major Shea's thirty-eighth birthday, but I only learned about that later.

I attended the mass with approximately forty other Marines. It was a solemn occasion, as all masses are in a combat zone. As I exited the auditorium, I greeted and thanked the priest and walked down the stairs toward the command center. Without warning, there was a *BOOM!* . . . and then quiet. Approximately fifty meters to our left, at the command headquarters, a cloud billowed toward the sky. Several of us ran toward the noise. As we faced the cloud of dust, someone called, "Marines with flashlights forward." Being one of the few Marines with a flashlight, I was the second to enter the room, which vaguely resembled the office of the commanding officer of 1st Marines. My flashlight cut through the thick smoke. The faint twilight of the setting sun was shining through a window that had previously been covered by sandbags. Furniture and cinderblocks were sprawled all over the room, and a faint groan could be heard under the now exposed window. Time stood still.

There, at my feet, lay the man I so deeply respected and admired. I can't describe what I felt at that moment. Shock? Disbelief? While the body did not resemble that of Major Shea, the face was certainly his. He was smiling, his eyes partially opened as he faced the open window to the west, toward the city of Fallujah, toward the enemy, and toward his wife and two children living in the United States. He was dead. I covered him with blankets I found in an adjacent room and then watched as his body was carried away. I also watched as his body was placed in a body bag and moved to a transport vehicle. I saluted my teacher—our teacher, our leader. I wiped the smoke debris from around my nostrils and mouth with a tissue and then went back to work, back to war, back to the insanity.

I would later learn that Major Shea had been killed by a 122-mm rocket fired from the west side of Fallujah, approximately twelve to fifteen kilometers away. It was a lucky shot—the perfect shot—a shot that took our teacher away on his birthday. He was posthumously promoted to lieutenant colonel, and at the time of his death, he was the most senior-ranking officer to have been killed in action in Operation Iraqi Freedom. He was buried at Arlington National Cemetery, section 60, site 8002.

As I reflect on his life and on the moment of his death, I realize that the Naval Academy and Lieutenant Colonel Shea prepared me, us, for war as best they could. They taught us tactics and strategy. They taught us leadership in the face of adversity and ethics without clearly drawn lines. They taught us the poetry and philosophy of those who had experienced war before us. The Naval Academy could never prepare us, however, for the essence of war, the violence of war, the cruelty of war. Ironically, and sadly, it was the smiling, unflappable Lieutenant Colonel Shea who taught me the true nature of war by his death. He also taught me physical and moral courage through the manner in which he lived his life and stood firm in the face of the enemy.

I visit Lieutenant Colonel Shea's gravesite twice a year, on Memorial Day and on his birthday, the day of his death. He continues to teach me, to lead me. Even now, I can hear his voice and see his smile, which still causes me to relax, lower my guard, and return to life.

(Courtesy of author)

Dhow in Distress

Patrick McConnell

USS Bulkeley *(DDG 84), central Persian Gulf, June 13, 2004,*
approximately thirty minutes after sunset:

"Red deck, red deck! Wave off the helo! Boats, on the 1MC:
Commanding officer to the pilot house! Rescue swimmer to the
boat deck!" The orders flew from my mouth as fast as I could get
them out.

The captain was soon behind me, offering calm reassurance.
"I'm here, Pat," he said.

"Captain's on the bridge, aye. Conning officer, get us there,
twenty knots. Boats, get the translator back up here! Call away
the low-visibility detail, Gold section. And find us some lights!"

A round 1745 that evening, I had taken charge of USS *Bulkeley* as officer of
the deck, the captain's direct representative in charge of navigation and
safety of the ship. Earlier that afternoon, our helicopter had overflown
a seventy-five-foot cargo dhow that appeared to be in distress, its crew waving a
large orange tarp to signal for help. A dhow is a traditional wooden vessel used to
make commercial journeys in the Persian Gulf and Indian Ocean. Cargo dhows,
as opposed to fishing dhows, are relatively long and narrow and have a striking
resemblance, as funny as it sounds, to a Twinkie sliced in half lengthwise. It is
a law of the sea that mariners provide assistance to those in need, so our commanding officer ordered us to make best speed for them. We couldn't get them
on the radio to know exactly what was wrong, but after ninety minutes at thirty
knots, we were about to find out.

The first part of the operation went smoothly. Our chief engineer and his sailors had a chance to pre-stage their equipment and brief the rescue and assistance
detail. The boat engineer was on station with an M-60 machine gun for the boat's

bow mount, and the bow hookman and coxswain were reviewing the underway checklist. The boat officer stood by, armed with a 9-mm pistol, overseeing the preparations. In the back of everyone's mind was a similar operation that had gone bad, so we took extra precautions. Less than two months before, a team from USS *Firebolt*, a crew with which we had interacted several times while on deployment, had two sailors and a coastguardsman killed while boarding a dhow not unlike this one.

Our boat covered the last hundred yards to the drifting vessel in seconds. Once on board, the assistance detail discovered that the dhow, *al-Rashid Mum 131*, had in its holds more than eight feet of water, which is enough to completely cover the engine and explained why it was dead in the water. Though our translator didn't speak the same dialect as the Arab crew, we were able to determine that they'd been drifting for two days. There were eleven men on board, and they looked typical of the seafarers in the region: young, fit, and accustomed to hard work in an incredibly harsh environment. We gave them food, water, life preservers, and medical aid (one of them had a gash on his foot) while our assistance detail started de-watering. Using a pump, we were able to remove about two hundred gallons per minute. We anticipated remaining on the scene for several hours pumping, patching the leak, and fixing the engine. From the pilothouse, I had our ship continue a lazy circle around the dhow.

After about two hours, an Iranian tugboat, which had been called many hours prior by the dhow to help, finally arrived. The rescue and assistance team had lowered the water level in the dhow significantly, and it was in no immediate danger of sinking. Our captain, Cdr. Bob Barwis, was more than happy to give responsibility to the tugboat, pull our team off station, and move on to the next day's scheduled multinational exercise. The dhow's crew couldn't stop thanking our team as they made their way back to *Bulkeley*.

We set off and prepared to land the helicopter, but we were less than ten minutes from the dhow when the quietness in the pilothouse was shattered by a piercing scream in a language I'd never heard. I still don't know if there were words in the transmission, but I know the sound of terror. Any mariner who has traveled in the Middle East can tell you the radio is rarely quiet, and often chaotic—with yelling, calls to prayer, and music at all hours—but everyone on the bridge knew this was different. The transmission was clear and strong, which meant it was close. I directed the Combat Information Center to slew an infrared camera back to the dhow and the tugboat.

The tugboat came into view first. The camera continued on, well past where the dhow had just been. The camera swept back and forth, searching for another boat that couldn't be found. Within the few seconds it took to slew the camera, the dhow had slipped beneath the murky surface of the Gulf. What about the crew—the same men we'd just helped with food, water, and medical assistance?

The crew of a warship at sea is a team of teams, capable of drawing upon great resources of people, equipment, and ideas. Officers and crew from each division and every department of the ship sprang to action, relying on their training and knowledge of their shipmates' skills and abilities. There was no specific procedure or checklist to follow in this scenario, but we were prepared. We had conducted countless man-overboard drills and practiced noncompliant boardings and boat operations. We had exercised our topside communications for numerous events, from antiterrorism and force protection to rendering honors for visiting dignitaries. Drawing from this menu of capabilities, we responded quickly.

As *Bulkeley* changed direction, the bridge team was a study in organized chaos. The boatswain's mate of the watch relayed orders via the ship's announcing circuit and took reports from the lookouts as they manned their stations. The conning officer, thankfully, was Ens. Steve Philabaum, an outstanding mariner who required little oversight. The quartermaster of the watch plotted the dhow's last position on the chart while his assistant attempted to keep the deck log current with the constant stream of orders and reports.

The most important report we were seeking was from the boat deck. Having been at flight quarters, the boat-deck detail and boat crew were nearby and sprang into action immediately. During the brief wait for the first boat to be launched, the gruesome reality struck home: we saw the body of a man, face down, floating in the inky darkness off the port bow. I faced a decision with which I had never been confronted: Do I order the rescue swimmer over the side of the ship to save a man who might already be dead or do I wait for the boat to be launched and send the swimmer to aid three men, very much alive, who were now coming into view under the piercing glare of the helicopter's spotlight? Ensign Philabaum could maneuver the ship for a recovery using the davit, a steel structure used to lower people and equipment over the edge of the ship, but it would take several minutes to ready, and the boatswain's mates were already engaged in launching the boats. It felt like time was slipping away too quickly.

Somewhere in the middle of this thought process, I had a flashback to an ethics class I'd taken back at the Naval Academy. In the third deck of Luce Hall, we had studied Jeremy Bentham's theory of utilitarianism—the greatest good for the greatest number. I pointed out the body to the captain a few seconds later and told him what I thought we should do; he concurred. The rescue swimmer would go with the boat, and we would continue toward the site of the sinking. A petty officer with a powerful spotlight was sent to the aft missile deck, atop the helicopter hangars, to try to keep the body in view.

The helicopter pilots steered their aircraft to the area of the tugboat and hovered less than fifty feet from the ocean's surface, their spotlight casting a stark beam of light into the growing darkness. They quickly located the site where the dhow had sunk. In the spotlight, we saw three crewmen clinging to a decrepit refrigerator, one of the few remaining pieces of their ship capable of supporting a man's weight. *Bulkeley* arrived faster than the pilots anticipated, so we had to sound the ship's whistle to alert them that we were there.

As the helicopter cleared, the three men and their makeshift life raft came closer still; we slowed as the first of our small boats sped away. Standing on the bridge wing, we could clearly hear their terrified screams over the cacophony of the helicopter and our own gas turbine engines. The diesel fumes were so thick they were *felt* as much as they were smelled; we used the relative strength of these fumes to judge our proximity to the wreckage for the rest of the night. Within seconds, the rescue swimmer was in the oily water, bringing the men to the safety of the boat one at a time.

Convinced that the boat crew had the situation in hand, the captain and I discussed our next moves. The body that had floated down the port side of the ship was no longer in view, and no other crewmen were in sight. With much difficulty, our interpreter established that the Iranian tugboat had picked up only one crewman; we had three. Where were the other seven of the eleven we had counted earlier?

Five minutes after the first boat launched, the second boat set off. Manned with a corpsman and a second rescue swimmer, it was dispatched to recover the first man we had seen and passed by. They found him within minutes, and performed CPR while returning to the ship, but it was too late. After about half an hour, the three surviving crewmen were transferred to the Iranian tugboat, but the tugboat's captain refused to take the body of the fourth crewman.

We landed the helicopter for a refueling and then relaunched it to aid the search. We stayed with the debris field for the next several hours, making pass after pass, searching with night vision goggles and spotlights. I stationed the boats about 250 yards on either side of the ship. A few times our hopes were lifted by what we thought we had seen; each time we were disappointed. The boat crews began picking up the life jackets we found strewn over the site. Our final count: eleven life jackets. Not one of the crewmen had put on the life jackets we had provided. I couldn't decide whether to be saddened by the tragedy or angered by their stupidity.

At midnight we made one last pass through what was left of the debris, landed the helicopter, and headed west. The next day we flew the body we'd recovered to a nearby U.S. warship, which then delivered it to the deceased's home city of Basra. To our knowledge, the bodies of the remaining crewmen were never recovered. For many of us that night, normal watch relief times came and went without notice. Most of my team was on watch for nearly ten hours, almost double the regular shift. When I look back on that operation, I'm struck by how quickly events can turn. In one moment, the men on board the dhow were yelling their grateful thanks, and in the next, they were gone. The professionalism displayed at all levels by our team confirmed what I already knew to be true: *Bulkeley*'s officers and crew were ready, willing, and able to perform whatever was required.

From Fallujah to Now Zad

Benjamin Wagner

I watched through night vision goggles as Marines scrambled over the wall surrounding the cemetery. Our company commander, Capt. Doug Zembiec, had wanted us in position before the 0530 call to Muslim prayer. We were almost there, almost ready just as the prayer began to be broadcast from a loud-speaker atop a minaret. My radio hissed, and Captain Zembiec's voice bellowed over the transceiver. We weren't in position in time, and he was pissed.

What had I done wrong in preparing our assault? The infantry lieutenant's greatest fear is missing the time appointed to cross the line of departure. "Never miss the LOD!" had been drilled into me during my training, yet here I was just a month into my first combat experience, and I was falling behind. I was trained for this mission, but for some reason this assault was different. I was different. I was no longer a junior enlisted Marine Corps grunt. Now I was the officer in charge—a position I had always dreamed of assuming—with all the trepidations and rewards of command.

We were part of a thirty-day marathon battle dubbed Fallujah One. The insurgents' numbers were strong, with probably more than a thousand men spread out over several key posts across the city. The U.S. Marine battalions gathered, accompanied by Army and Navy air support, to seek out and defeat the enemy. I was a platoon commander, and it was my job to lead twenty-seven strong and disciplined Marines through this field of battle. Everyone had a role, but there were three men I relied on most. The first was SSgt. Willie Gresham, who was meticulous about everything and had had enough wartime experience to warrant the respect of the others. Next, Sgt. Terry Fullerton, who was capable and dependable and never let his guard down as first squad leader, which made him the perfect candidate to lead tailored missions. After them, I counted on my company commander, Captain Zembiec, for his strength and steadfast courage, although he didn't know it. He had been an all-star wrestler at the Naval Academy and had mentored me during my sophomore year. I remember that during my first firefight, I had looked across the line of fire, and Captain Zembiec stared back at me and smiled—a reminder that everything was going to be okay. We were all scared in combat. Anyone who says that fear is not part of combat is lying. Captain Zembiec had a confidence that calmed the storms.

My platoon and company had a simple but important role in Captain Zembiec's opinion: "Go pick a fight." On March 28, 2004, just a week after arriving in Iraq and relieving an Army battalion, we set out on our first patrol of Fallujah and took our first casualties. Eric Elrod and Juan Fernandez were wounded in an ambush crossing a large courtyard. We'd been too hesitant with our actions and uncertain about how aggressive to be. The rules of engagement are well defined back at headquarters, but protocol sometimes gets blurred in the field. We hesitated to fire at buildings or bring full combat power to bear because we had been following the counterinsurgency doctrine—"do no harm" to the population. Our mindset was to preserve the infrastructure and to limit the impact we had on the people of Iraq. We went days without sleep, but the men showed greater confidence with each contact.

On April 12, our platoon experienced its first Marine KIA, killed in action. That evening was one of the longest of my life. In a firefight that had begun at dusk, Robert Zurheide and Brad Shuder were mortally wounded. We had evacuated them without knowing if they would live or die. After the assault, I walked the lines checking on the remaining Marines. It wasn't too long before the report came from headquarters that the two men had died. My platoon sergeant took the message. He knew I was exhausted and wasn't sure how I would tell the others. As their leader, I felt this huge weight on my shoulders. I reminded myself that I wasn't the first platoon commander faced with telling his troops that some of their brothers had died.

I pulled my platoon into a huddle and told them that Rob and Brad had been killed. The men mourned, walked away, and continued the mission. As their leader, I couldn't shake the question, Were their deaths my fault? Communicating such a tragedy is not something one learns at the Academy, and it wasn't something I had practiced as a junior officer. I remained stoic in front of the platoon, but I was quickly learning that although leadership is an honor, it is also a great burden, and there's always room to become better at it.

★ ★ ★

My path to becoming a Marine officer was not a straight one. As high school was ending, I didn't feel ready to enter college life. I was used to my Southern California lifestyle of ska music and tattoos. Another four years of school didn't interest me. I wanted freedom, opportunity, and the ability to go places and do things. I was an athlete, but not good enough to be recruited, and I had little interest in school, books, and homework.

College didn't seem "big enough" for me at the time. I didn't want to wait four years to do something tangible with my life, so I decided to join the Marine Corps. My parents were wonderfully supportive, and although they would have preferred that I enter university right away, they encouraged me to succeed in whatever I chose to do. I was seventeen. My mother agreed to sign my enlistment papers for the Marine Corps Reserve, as long as it wasn't for the infantry, so I could attend college courses full time. After my eighteenth birthday, shortly before graduation, I changed my contract to active duty and requested an assignment in infantry. This change in direction was not a sign of rebelliousness; it was simply what I felt called to do.

As a young Marine stationed in Camp Pendleton, California, in the mid-1990s, life was good. I earned $350 per paycheck twice a month. I had a place to sleep, food to eat, and best of all, our barracks were literally five minutes from the beach. I met great guys during that phase of my life. We worked hard, played hard, and took being grunts seriously. We were proud of our heritage and jealous of those who had fought in Vietnam, Desert Storm, and Somalia. Our squad leaders told us stories about the 1991 Persian Gulf War, after Iraq invaded Kuwait.

After a couple of years, I realized that I wanted more than an enlisted man's life. I had respect for those I worked with, but I was more intrigued by our platoon commanders. The way they interacted with one another and with the upper chain of command was different; they exhibited a level of knowledge and responsibility that I craved. I wanted the camaraderie and bonds of the officer corps. The seeds of leadership had been planted. In particular, I noticed the lieutenant in charge of my platoon. He seemed to have it together, and I wanted to know if I could handle that level of responsibility, too.

I had applied to the Naval Academy as a senior in high school but was rejected. Over the years, I had thought about applying again, but I had no idea how to do so as an enlisted Marine. When I got a new platoon commander who was a USNA grad, I saw an opportunity to get the advice I was looking for. My second lieutenant found out that I'd once applied and encouraged me to try again. I did and was accepted; fifteen months later, after a year at the Naval Academy Preparatory School, I was inducted into the Class of 2002. The Academy had afforded 150 billets in each class to prior-enlisted men and women. The reason for admitting students with Fleet experience was to add diversity to the learning environment. Regardless of the reason, I was in. I finished my tour in California, was given ten months of preparatory education in Newport, Rhode Island, and arrived in Annapolis on July 1, 1998. I had gone from a corporal in the Marine Corps to a Naval Academy plebe, probably one of the biggest demotions in the history of the military.

As a prior-enlisted man, I had more ribbons and real-world experiences than many of those senior to me walking around Bancroft Hall, the USNA dormitory. I was twenty-two years old when I entered USNA, and I immediately earned the respect of my peers and seniors. That respect was also mine to lose. I felt a responsibility to lead by example because I knew what enlisted personnel expected from officers. For four years, my shoes were the shiniest, my haircut was tight, and I had a pressed uniform when others let the standards drop. My personal daily routine was a source of pride.

Mentors at USNA come in all forms. I met Doug Zembiec during my youngster year. Little did I know that four years later, he would be my company commander and one of my most important mentors. He was a Force Recon Marine and all-star wrestler from the Class of 1995. Capt. Richard Gannon was another one of my closest advisors, as we both participated in the extracurricular Semper Fi Society. Both Zembiec and Gannon would be killed in combat in Iraq. They were giants to me, true heroes.

I quickly transformed from a Marine infantryman with a narrow focus into a quirky history student influenced by some of the most adroit leaders in naval service. Professors Mary Decredico and Ernie Tucker, who taught my military history courses, were mentors in their own way, showing me the gateway into the minds of the American military's finest leaders. Even Woody in the barbershop made an impact on me; he was one of the most dedicated people I met in my four years at the Academy. A loving father and a humble veteran, he instilled wisdom in us midshipmen and made those twelve-minute haircuts count for something.

My senior year, I was selected to be Brigade commander, the highest-ranking midshipman, and gained access to some of the military's finest leaders. General Peter Pace and Colonel John Allen were my early mentors. They taught me about the personal side of leadership in combat and about the importance of leading with honor. As Brigade commander, I was the conduit for the administration and was charged with leading my peers and the Brigade in the aftermath of 9/11. This experience helped me understand the pressures on general officers, something that would help years later on the front lines.

★ ★ ★

No amount of schooling could have prepared me for the emotions I experienced when Rob and Brad were killed under my command. During my second combat tour in Iraq, I was again faced with casualties. Although I was just one year removed from the Marines I had lost in Fallujah, this time I felt like a different person. I remember talking on the radio to my company commander while watching my corpsman try to resuscitate a mortally injured Marine. Although I still felt compassion for the tragedy before my eyes, I was callous to the magnitude of it all; this was war after all.

The pain of losing men in combat weighs heavily on a leader's heart. It's more than a lump in the throat or a pang of hurt; it's like a car parked on one's chest. I thought back to the lessons I'd learned from my mentors while at the Naval Academy. I remembered General Pace, then chairman of the Joint Chiefs of Staff, speaking to a group of midshipmen about his experiences during the Tet Offensive regarding the moral imperative of the officer. I thought back to the lessons delivered by Colonel Allen, our Commandant of Midshipmen, about the importance of character and the influence of the officer on his or her Marines and sailors. I thought about the way Captain Gannon, 13th Company officer, trained me to influence the lives and character of my Marines. Dealing with death as a military officer is the product of leadership lessons I learned from mentors, books, and personal involvement.

Much of my experience at the Naval Academy, and in some ways my philosophy of life, had been shaped by Sen. Jim Webb's *A Sense of Honor*. As a plebe, I empathized with the Midshipman Dean's frustration over foolish Bancroft Hall traditions and the brainwashing that plebes received. As a firstie, I understood Midshipman Bill Fogerty's desire to serve and live out his destiny as a combat leader. As a combat veteran, I empathized with Captain Ted Lenahan's pain. Captain Lenahan, a company commander in Vietnam, had lost many good men. Each of these men reflected a stage of development that mirrored my own journey.

In Fallujah, Ubaydi, and Hit, in Iraq, and Helmand, in Afghanistan, I suffered losses under my command. I knew what Captain Lenahan felt when he visited wounded Marines in Bethesda. I understood the depth of his pain and his commitment to "doing it right." All of this became clear when I cried with Brad Shuders's parents at their home. It was understandable when I visited my Marines in the hospital and saw their broken bodies, but I didn't really understand it until I'd cried with widows and parents and hugged Marines who were missing limbs, possibly unable to ever run or walk again. There is no desire on my part to seek pity for myself or those wounded. It's simply a fact that only those who have devoted their lives to guarding their country in a time of war can truly grasp the depth of these lessons.

★ ★ ★

A lot changed after my platoon commander days in Iraq. During my shore billet, between tours in Iraq and Afghanistan, I'd spent three years as an instructor at the Basic School and the Infantry Officer Basic Course in Quantico, Virginia. My experiences at Basic School were profound. Along with twenty other combat veterans, I trained the Marine Corps' up-and-coming generation of infantry officers.

I demanded that the rising infantry officers be ready to lead in combat. In doing so, I refined my own skills and technically sharpened my understanding of wartime doctrine. Would I be ready to lead like Doug Zembiec had?

The next time I was in harm's way was as a company commander in Helmand province, Afghanistan, in 2010. The number of men under my charge was triple what it had been during my first fight. My company had been assigned to secure the Now Zad district in Helmand, an area where some of the fiercest Taliban took refuge. Our mission was to prevent the insurgents from moving from the central mountainous areas into the southern districts to sell weapons, opium, and other contraband.

On October 17, 2010, my company was engaged in a firefight. We moved south by vehicle and helicopter to trap the insurgents in an area the enemy knew. As we searched buildings and talked to local farmers, I got a call that one of my blocking forces was engaged with enemy fire three kilometers away. We loaded up and moved to their position. In transit, I heard a report of a casualty. An unforgiving lump began to develop in my throat, and I expected to hear the worst.

My initial reaction had always been to ask who had been wounded. I had to be especially cautious now because any emotion I showed over the radio would

Former Naval Academy Brigade commander Ben Wagner (far right) stands with his junior officers in Helmand, Afghanistan. (Courtesy Ben Wagner)

affect the men around me. The report came that one of our corpsmen, Doc Speed, had been shot. As we arrived on the scene, I sent two vehicles to cordon off a nearby farmhouse. I couldn't think about Doc. I was amped for a fight and eager to kill those who put my men in danger. Despite the fear, heat, and pain felt by me and my men, everything felt right. We were in the crucible of war, but I felt strangely in control, after my days as a corporal in Pendleton, hours of midshipman training, and intense battlefield scares in Iraq. Thankfully, Doc survived, and we pressed on.

My tour in Afghanistan was one of the true honors and highlights of my many years of service. I can honestly say that the Marines in Charlie Company, 1st Battalion, 8th Marine Regiment, served with honor, dignity, and grace. They ruthlessly hunted a determined enemy, and when necessary they killed with skill and precision. We guarded and secured the people of Now Zad, and we made the district a safer and more successful community than it had been when we first encountered it. It was an honor to lead this group of Marines as their company commander. My greatest hope as I continue in the Marine Corps is that I am able to pass along the many leadership lessons from my mentors to men who, just like myself, are learning to live the highs and lows of combat leadership.

Part IV

★ ★ ★

Beyond Battlefield Bullets

Leadership is intangible, and therefore no weapon ever designed can replace it.

GEN. OMAR BRADLEY, 1967

Exactly what type of education equips the twenty-first-century Navy or Marine officer to do well in this complex and often uncertain world? Carl von Clausewitz wrote about what he called the "fog of war"—all the things one can't possibly plan or prepare for in battle. There will always be the X-factor, the "fog" that requires a leader to remain adaptable and flexible, or "Semper Gumby" as we naval officers sometimes call it.

During the wars in Iraq, Afghanistan, and beyond, we had to adapt to constant change. Armor Marines served as house-to-house security forces; bluewater sailors operated along the coast (in the "littorals") and often went ashore to defend important outposts. Both the Marine Corps and the Navy sent personnel to sit down with Shia and Pashtu district leaders to develop infrastructure strategies for improving the lives of their communities. We planned and certainly followed through on many of these efforts, but along the way we encountered Clausewitz's fog of war, which demanded creativity and flexibility.

In order to do both things—accomplish the mission and remain flexible—we had to keep in mind the "commander's intent." Joint Publication 3-0, the bible for all military services, defines "commander's intent" as "The desired end state . . . a concise expression of the purpose of the operation, not a summary of the concept of operations." Having a clear understanding of the overarching purpose of each mission allows us as leaders to be more flexible and creative in our approaches to getting the job done.

Great leaders make their intent clear and then rely on the initiatives of those they lead to carry the day. Adm. Arleigh Burke, as commander of Destroyer Squadron 23 during World War II, told his ship captains, "If you encounter the Japanese, you know what to do." Simple and succinct, Burke provided the guidance and a strategic way forward and then allowed his men the opportunity to use their ingenuity and experience to accomplish the mission.

This has been the heritage of the Navy. Each ship pulling away from the pier is left to its own devices when confronting danger. Knowing the commander's intent, a young Navy ensign instinctively steers the ship with enough separation from hostile forces, but keeps a wartime footing with increased lookouts. A Marine second lieutenant knows to position his troops in a staggered formation to avoid threatening local villagers, and also to maintain a strong perimeter. With the commander's intent in mind, the military officers who operated on the ground in Iraq and Afghanistan wrote the instructions on civilian-military operations and problem solving when no how-to manual was available.

Trust up and down the chain of command and through rigorous training has fostered a culture of flexibility and adaptability within the ranks of the Navy and Marine Corps. It is a unique characteristic that enables America's military success at sea and forward from the sea.

Military Diplomats

Graham Plaster

Dispatch: From the Journal of a Navy Foreign Area Officer

It's an hour until midnight on September 11, 2010, and I am on board a plane bound for Jordan. The small monitor embedded in the headrest of the seat in front of me displays a GPS map of the East Coast of the United States. Location names are written in yellow Arabic script, making the familiar geography seem like a foreign land. After a few seconds the screen switches over to a graphic of the plane with an arrow pointing toward Mecca, to aid the observant with their prayers. Mothers in hijab are trying to keep restless children happy during the red-eye, but there will be some crying through the night; it can't be helped. As I recall my multiple Navy-mandated moves, flying and driving across the country with children in tow, my heart goes out to the parents.

I'm a foreign area officer now, one of fewer than 250 naval officers who specialize in foreign languages, culture, and history. This subspecialty was created in the wake of 9/11 because the admirals and generals who advise political leaders couldn't find a junior officer who spoke two languages, much less one who possessed the cultural awareness necessary to counsel decision makers. Although my ticket into the community was specialization in Iranian social media, the needs of the Navy summoned me to an Army desk in Rosslyn, Virginia, as an operations officer for United Nations Peacekeeping. There aren't many U.S. military members involved in UN peacekeeping. In fact, there are only slightly more than thirty. I handle administration and support for the officers sent on one-year IA (individual augmentation) assignments to Israel, Iraq, and Egypt.

Amman is an intermediate stop en route to Iraq, where I'll be visiting two of the four U.S. military members serving as UN peacekeepers there. The previous day marked the end of Ramadan, which could have been a more dangerous time to fly. On the other hand, flying to the Middle East on a September 11 feels a bit surreal, especially since the flight had originated in Washington, D.C., and laid over in New York. On the TV in the lounge, President Barack Obama was trying to smooth over the tensions caused by a pastor in Florida threatening to burn a Quran.

Despite news reports of unrest in New York City and Afghanistan, JFK airport was quiet, and security was relatively pain free. Dinner on the plane was good—some kind of spiced chicken. I couldn't quite place the flavor, but washed it down with a free Corona. I spoke at length in broken Arabic with the guy in the seat next to me about Jordanian weather, the job market in America, the difficulties for him making money as a mechanic, and the sacrifices we make for our children. I have four; he has five. We both congratulate each other with "Alf mabrook!" (a thousand congratulations). As our conversation wanes and the night deepens, I can't help but reflect on the September 11 nine years before and marvel at the course my life had since taken.

I had been on my way to a creative writing class, one of my favorites as an English major at the Naval Academy. I'd finished breakfast early with my squad and was making a beeline down Stribling Walk, headed for Mahan Hall. The weather, as I recall, was typical Annapolis fall fare—beautiful and crisp. A youngster walked past me. I didn't know him, but he called out to me, "Hey, a plane just flew into the World Trade Center." I assumed he was referring to a low, slow flyer of some kind, a freak accident, but his alarmed tone also gave me the sense that this might be more than news casually passed along at the breakfast table. He obviously felt compelled to share it with me, a stranger, for a reason.

A few minutes later, I arrived at the classroom in the basement of Mahan. I was the first one there and the room was still quiet. The new classrooms had pull-down screens with projectors hooked up to cable TV. I extended the screen and cued up the live news feed just as a few other students came in. They asked what was going on, and I explained what little I knew: A plane had flown into one of the Twin Towers. The professor arrived and then the rest of the students a moment later. We all stood and watched in silence as news commentators reported on things they could not see and things that we could see happening live behind them. We watched the impact on the second tower, the fires, the people jumping, and the cascade of smoke and ash as the towers collapsed. We saw confused and grieving news anchors. The hour passed without any discussion, and we wandered to the next class with a vague sense of purpose. A few rooms down the hall, I took my seat in another English class. By then everyone knew. The professor walked in. We opened *In Memoriam*, Tennyson's classic poem wrestling with pain and death. She began to read and then stopped as tears came. She left the room. I tore the pages from the book and tucked them away to keep.

Turning toward our final descent into Jordan, I note the bleached landscape. I would later learn that Jordan has the fourth lowest supply of fresh water among all countries. Without massive reserves of oil or gas, indeed, even without enough water, Jordan manages to get by as a safe place to do business. It is the crossroads between several points of commerce and stands to gain the most by supplying one of the world's most valuable commodities, security.

After a thirty-minute shuttle ride, and another "Alf mabrook" from the driver on hearing of my progeny, I arrive at Le Méridien Hotel in Amman. It is beautiful inside, with turbaned men smoking and talking in the lobby, women in expensive-looking hijabs pushing strollers and corralling large families. When I get to my room, I unpack my laptop and set up Skype. The broadband connection is excellent, and I quickly find myself connected to the world I know. An Army friend of mine, another foreign affairs officer, is in Pakistan at the war college there. We bring up the video and chat about our kids, learning foreign languages, and nuances of Middle Eastern culture. Over Skype, I can hear the call to evening prayer beginning to crescendo. We say goodbye so he can have a virtual date with his wife and five kids, who are in Monterey, California.

★ ★ ★

My time in Jordan, while filled with valuable experiences, seemed insignificant next to the import of my meetings in Iraq. I was able to sit in on discussions among key leaders at the United Nations' headquarters in Iraq and the U.S. embassy and with other operational planners plotting the withdrawal of U.S. troops from the country. Our chief concern during the course of that week was to connect the dots between the United Nations, the U.S. embassy, and the military as responsibility and authority was shifting away from the military and toward the State Department. It became clear that the United Nations would be changing its security posture in ways that would make it increasingly difficult to send U.S. military members along on missions. I returned to the States with a number of items to monitor. The situation reports from the field began to carry much more meaning in the context of my visit.

Not long after my return from Iraq, tragedy struck, but from an unexpected quarter. A U.S. Army Reservist serving in Liberia as a UN peacekeeper had tripped and fallen to his death from a rooftop deck. He had been only weeks away from coming home to his career, wife, and children. He had survived tours in Iraq and Afghanistan only to fall prey to the asymmetrical warfare of chance. His fellow peacekeepers returned to the States soon after, shaken not only by the tragedy of his death but also by the heart-wrenching conditions in Liberia. In their debriefing, one of them explained to me how much the rule of law had been degraded since the civil war. The infrastructure for education and governance had been destroyed, but even more tragic, the social fabric had begun to unravel in ways that made progress seem Sisyphean. If you could imagine a state of nature, one of them said, it would be like Liberia. "Lord of the Flies?" I asked. "Of course there are two visions of the state of nature—Hobbes and Rousseau—one is nasty and brutish while the other is noble and good," I said. I was assured that regarding the Liberian situation, Hobbes would be closer to the reality. I couldn't help but think back to Tennyson's analysis of the human condition, as had Hobbes, as "red in tooth and claw" (*In Memoriam*, section LV).

The many pointless tragedies of life, pummeling us from every side in the news and via social media, raise our awareness certainly, our compassion hopefully, and our defenses inevitably. Bad news cascades like floors of the Twin Towers falling upon themselves, and yet we find a way to survive and even, on good days, to thrive. That is where Tennyson leaves. Like Hobbes, he sees the human condition as lacking something. But by the end of *In Memoriam*, he has consoled himself with his faith:

> I stretch lame hands of faith, and grope,
> And gather dust and chaff, and call
> To what I feel is Lord of all,
> And faintly trust the larger hope.

As I look east in anticipation of a career at the crossroads of culture and language, I continually search for common denominators. I think the Navy, and the Naval Academy, helped develop this personal philosophy. Whatever the human condition may be, and whatever one might think about it, we certainly share it. In addition, I agree with Tennyson that we share in a larger hope, and that in the end the cascade of bad news will not be the end of the story.

Shaking the Hand of Fate

Courtney Senini

As I stepped off the C-130, I was shocked by the intensity of the heat. Hot air rippled up from the tarmac, and the desert wind whipped around my face and over my fatigues. It was 2007, and we had just been flown over the Hindu Kush into the Afghan capital, Kabul. We were there to take part in a U.S. military assistance mission with the Afghanistan National Army. I shifted the heavy gear I was carrying, and as I did, I looked around at the arid landscape. Maybe at that moment I should have been thinking about the honor of my mission, the men and women standing beside me, or the people I loved who were back home. Instead, I found myself wondering, How in the hell did I end up here?

I am not a Marine or Army officer. I wasn't trained in the ways of counterinsurgency. I'm no ground pounder or Special Forces officer. The Navy had made me a surface warfare officer (SWO), whose job is to lead ships and sailors at sea. I could not have been more out of my element. As I stood there on my first day in Afghanistan, I remember thinking that fate had forgotten me. I thought back to the path I'd taken in life that led me there and hoped I would get through this alive and without posttraumatic stress disorder.

MONTANA TO ANNAPOLIS

The hospital where I was born is the same hospital where my father was born, in the small agricultural town of Yuma, Arizona. Years later, we moved to another small town, this time in Montana. When I was a junior in high school, my parents sat me down and told me that they couldn't afford to send me to college. Coming from a family with a strong military background, the natural next step was to apply to a Reserve Officers' Training Corps (ROTC) program that would pay my way through school. Instead, my father pushed me to apply to the Naval Academy. I did so, but blindly. What the hell, I thought. It never hurts to try.

One day, months after my application had been submitted, I was pulled out of class by the dean of my high school and brought to the front office. I thought I was in trouble for cutting class, but then I saw my mother standing there. She was crying when she pulled me into her arms and told me I had been accepted to the Naval Academy. I wouldn't understand why she was crying until ten years later, when she shed those same tears as I boarded a plane that would take me from Montana en route to Afghanistan. She knew there was a distinct possibility that I would be sent into harm's way. Military moms are special in that they dread every moment of deployment, but still have great admiration for their children serving in the military. Meanwhile, my dad was just happy that my tuition was free!

The night before I flew to Annapolis for Induction Day, I was terrified that I might be making the worst decision of my life. I didn't know why I was signing up for a military education and giving up everything I knew back home. College *was* an option. I could have taken out loans and gone to Montana State, picked a safe major with good job prospects, and married a high school sweetheart. That seemed like happily ever after, but something deep down said it wasn't for me. I would follow a different path into the unknown.

Despite my ignorance, I flourished in the land of winter working blues. During plebe summer, I excelled at time management and waxing floors. Yes, there is an art to stripping, waxing, and shining Bancroft's decks. My company mates and I faced challenges, academic and physical, as a thirty-five-unit family. I felt myself getting smarter and stronger every day. Of importance, the leadership classes forced me to challenge core assumptions about right and wrong. I actually read Aristotle, Kant, and Rousseau in the process! I felt like the small-town girl who'd made it big.

I thought often about my fear of the unknown and about being away from my family. Some nights I would go running along the seawall hoping to find a little clarity about where my life was headed. By the end of my four years at the Naval Academy, I couldn't say that I knew where I was going, but I did feel ready for a commission and ready to lead. One other thing I knew was that I wanted to be a pilot. I'm fairly certain I wasn't the only one of my classmates who was swayed by the speed and excitement of flying planes. On top of that, Hollywood's version of a pilot was *Top Gun*'s Maverick or Ice Man, and who wouldn't want to work with them? Academics were tough for me, however, and I was up against stiff competition for the coveted aviation billets. When service selection night came, I not only discovered that I wasn't going to be a pilot, I also found out I had been appointed a SWO. "Really?" I asked myself. Not very many people wanted this appointment, least of all me. I was angry and devastated, and I cursed fate for not giving me what I had wanted.

On Board USS *Tarawa* and 463 Days in Afghanistan

It was March 2003, and I was twenty-three years old when I arrived on USS *Tarawa* (LHA 1) in the northern Persian Gulf just days before the U.S.-led invasion of Iraq. I was lucky enough to have one of the best chiefs in the U.S. Navy, Richard Schwartzman. He taught me to lead by example, put my sailors first, and only accept excellence. I came to appreciate the deck plate leadership— being physically there with my shipmates—that you can only find as a SWO. I was handed responsibility and the power to direct operations at sea from the start. Not bad for a Montana girl who had a tendency to get sea sick! My counterparts in other communities would have to wait years in some cases for such opportunities.

In the fall of 2006, I was fortunate enough to be assigned to the Surface Warfare Officer School in Newport, Rhode Island, as an instructor to young division officers. My job was to teach ship handling and seamanship. After three and a half years at sea, I was on shore duty and loving feeling the earth beneath my feet. I had two whole years of not being deployed ahead of me. Just as quickly as I had begun to think that fate was on my side, things changed. I found out I had been selected for a 463-day deployment to Afghanistan in support of Operation Enduring Freedom.

My first day working hand-in-hand with Afghans and with the U.S. Army sent me into immediate culture shock. The environment was fast-paced, confusing, and frustrating. At Camp Blackhorse, the commonsense approach of purpose that circulated throughout the command was inspiring and impressive given the presence of four different services—Marine Corps, Navy, Air Force, and Army— as well as civilians and foreign forces. We may have come from different backgrounds and approached goals from different perspectives, but in Afghanistan there was one team, one fight. It made me proud to watch the branches come together, each using its strengths to support the others.

Being a woman in Afghanistan was an unusual experience. It was strange having Afghan men openly gawk at me. I wore a full uniform at all times, my hair was uncovered, and my face was visible. These men had never seen a woman who wasn't traditionally dressed and therefore covered. It took months for me to stop feeling like I was on display every time I left the camp. Afghan women have no voice in society, and in some cases they're nothing more than second-class citizens traded like chattel. One of the Afghan majors I advised was Major Nador. One day at the garrison, he said to me, "You are not a woman; you are a soldier, and that is how we look at you." I argued with him that I was a woman and that I was as capable as he and his soldiers. He laughed and said, "No, you are not a woman, again, you are American, different, and a soldier to us." I never could understand this rationale, but it was my job to work with these men for the purpose of progress, and so that is what I did. Most were uneducated and unwilling to think differently from the way they had been raised. It inspired me even more to perform well and show them that women are meaningful members of society. I hoped that with time they would come to treat their wives and daughters differently.

During my Afghanistan deployment, I was an adviser to a small group of women called family support officers in the Afghan National Army. Most of the women were nurses and midwives; one had even been a practicing doctor before the Taliban forced her to seek refuge in neighboring Pakistan. There were only six women in a garrison of more than 6,000 soldiers. I have never met a group of stronger women. Forced to endure hardship and social restraints, they did what they could with minimal resources to educate Afghans on staying healthy and avoiding communicable diseases. As part of their job, these women visited families of slain Afghan soldiers and did what little they could to help ease the pain of having lost loved ones. I found myself admiring their compassion and genuine care of the Afghan soldiers with whom they worked. It was fascinating to watch them operate with little to no medical resources.

The atrocities and abuses women endure in Afghanistan are heart wrenching and continue today. I observed many incidents firsthand and heard of many more from my colleagues. A family support officer told me the story of her youngest sister, Najeeba, who had been accused of being unfaithful to her fiancé under Taliban's rule. The truth of the story was that the fiancé didn't want to marry Najeeba, but his family insisted on the match. He therefore accused her of infidelity, and as a result, she was stoned to death on a dirt road in front of the people of her village. I will also never forget the woman from Kabul who had acid thrown on her face for pursuing an education against her family's wishes. This was a common practice of the Taliban.

During a routine convoy operation some seven months into my deployment, soldiers from my camp came across a horrendous multivehicle accident. Four cars filled with Afghan civilians were involved in a collision, leaving at least three dead and three more in critical condition. All were immediately rushed to my camp, where they could receive trauma care. Because of the cultural restraints on women in Afghanistan, I was assigned the female victim. If a man other than a husband or direct blood relative were to see her without the burka, she would be disgraced and her family would be dishonored. She frantically screamed and resisted the male medics but calmed down when I arrived. My presence would preserve her honor.

With an interpreter, I took her to a private area and was able to convince her that she needed to be examined. Her white burka was covered in blood, and the medics needed to know if it was her own or from another victim. With the interpreter doing his job from behind a screen, she took off her burka and let me examine the extent of her injuries. Inside this makeshift infirmary, I was giving aid while communicating to the unseen interpreter. She was so scared, yet we had a connection, woman-to-woman, and I believe that provided her some relief.

She had minor cuts and bruises but while examining her, I noticed a bulge around her belly as well as some bleeding down her leg. She was pregnant! I now realized her condition was much more serious than originally thought. We rushed her to a nearby French medical facility. I accompanied her because I did not want her to be frightened and alone with strange men. I assisted a female physician with a sonogram, and we were able to tell her that she and her child would be fine. I was with the woman from the time she came to the camp to the time she was told she would be all right. Consequently, a strong bond was established. I felt strange and sad when I left her in the care of the female French medics, and I wondered what would happen to her and her family. More than anything, I felt I was fully participating in the operation, as a soldier and as a woman.

Courtney Senini interacting with Afghan children during a routine patrol in 2007. (Courtesy Courtney Senini)

★ ★ ★

Although I had cursed fate the day I learned I'd been deployed to Afghanistan, it would come to be the greatest experience and adventure of my life. It caused me to grow as an individual and allowed me to defend my country in a way most naval officers would never experience. My time in Afghanistan made me realize what it was that I would do next in my life. In essence, it was the adventure that defined who I was. On the day I spent with the pregnant Afghan woman, in Afghanistan's nastiest terrain, I realized I wanted to be a trauma nurse. I am now pursuing a career in nursing.

Does everything happen for a reason? I think so. My appointment to the Naval Academy, the designation as a SWO, and the individual augmentation to Afghanistan were milestones pivotal to my success and achievement as a leader, sailor, soldier, and citizen. I continue to be humble and proud in the service of my country. Going ahead, I know fate will have a plan for me whether I like it or not. With the confidence in myself as a woman and a leader, developed at the Academy and beyond, I know I can do anything.

Visit, Board, Search, and Seizure: Unsung Heroes

Jason Jackson

N avy sailors and Marines teamed up to defeat Mediterranean threats as far back as the 1790s; they partnered to conquer the Confederate Army in New Orleans in the 1860s; and they fought side-by-side in World Wars I and II. The Marines have needed the Navy to get to the fight first, and the Navy has needed the Marines to extend its reach on to shores. It's not like Jack Nicholson's character berating Tom Cruise's character in *A Few Good Men*. Marines and Navy sailors can and do play nice together. Sometimes it takes personal experience to understand that. As a Navy man, my first tour at sea gave me a newfound respect for the Marines when I found myself leading a squad of sailors into harm's way.

On August 22, 2003, the 1st Expeditionary Strike Group set sail from San Diego en route to the Persian Gulf to fight the global war on terror in support of Operations Enduring Freedom and Iraqi Freedom. The strike group consisted of 3 amphibious assault ships, a cruiser, a destroyer, a frigate, a submarine, 2,200 Marines, and 3,000 sailors. We sailors navigated the ocean, and the Marines hit the weight room; we shared chow lines, shower facilities , and Internet services. Conceptually the group represented an innovation in maritime strategy: Every element of the Navy's power was being brought into one cohesive, deployable force, giving the president a spectrum of assets ready to respond to any regional threat.

Over the course of six months of operations in the Persian Gulf, we flexed our capabilities. We conducted amphibious operations putting more than a thousand troops to shore, provided point defense for offshore oil platforms, and patrolled the region looking for smugglers. One of my duties on board USS *Germantown* was as the assistant boarding officer for the visit, board, search, and seizure (VBSS) team. Our team had almost contradictory missions. One was to aggressively patrol, identify, and interdict smugglers violating UN embargoes on Iraq, the other was to provide humanitarian relief in the form of food and supplies to vessels that had been detained for violations. This philosophical dichotomy required us to have a unique preparedness and mindset. On one hand, my team was fierce and ready to extinguish any threat to the ship; on the other hand, we had to provide humanitarian resources because some of the ships we searched were honest brokers obstructed by U.S. forces by circumstance. My team had to be ready to kill or protect within a split second of shifting events.

The first time I led one of these missions, I felt as close to the fight as any of my Marine classmates. We were patrolling the central Gulf when we were tasked to board a six-hundred-foot freighter en route to Iraq that was suspected of smuggling. While *Germantown* changed course and sped to intercept the ship, my team began our preparations.

We changed into desert fatigues, strapped on utility vests and gloves, and headed down to the armory to get weapons. Officers carried 9 mm handguns, but the rest of the team had M16 rifles or shotguns. Our gear was unique because we had to have flotation capability but also enough tactical space for extra ammunition, a flashlight, a medical kit, and a camelback for water. It was my responsibility to make sure we were equipped, prepared, and safe. We rendezvoused on the boat deck for muster. I quickly surveyed the men to make sure everyone was present. I asked them to check their weapons and make sure they could remain hydrated since the mission could last up to ten hours. I ordered everyone into a weapons posture—round chambered, clip inserted, and safety on—that would give us the most readiness with a needed level of security.

With the whole team accounted for, we tested our communications with one another and with our bridge crew. We quickly reviewed what we knew of the vessel: name, next port of call, last port of call, number of occupants, basic layout, cargo, and any other details available. This information was important and documented by our officers. If anything was found to be inconsistent once we were on board, we would know the ship's crew was lying. Finally, we reviewed our tactics and reminded each other of our roles. We hadn't had a lot of training for this before our departure, so quick huddles were essential for maintaining unit cohesiveness once we boarded the suspect ship. Confusion can increase on board another ship because there is no familiar frame of reference. We quickly reviewed our plan. Two security teams of three men each would sweep the vessel and secure the crew. The boarding officer and I, with a petty officer for extra security, would proceed to the pilothouse to interview the master, while a fourth team with an engineer would inspect spaces and holds and take soundings in tanks.

Once we were clear on our assignments, we were ready to disembark USS *Germantown* and proceed to the vessel we were intercepting. The eleven-meter rubber-hulled inflatable boat, "rhib" for short, was lowered into the water, and my team climbed down two stories on a rope ladder to board the boat. Once on board, we made our approach to the suspect vessel at high speed. With nothing to do but wait as the rhib traversed the gap between *Germantown* and the suspect vessel, my mind contemplated the potential hazards we might encounter. I felt anxiety like never before.

Questions flooded my mind. What if they opposed the boarding? What if they were trafficking in illicit cargo? Was I prepared for the mission? Would I be able to do my duty? While these thoughts were going through my head I knew I could never let the men see my uncertainty or fear. Many of them were even younger than I was and probably feeling similar anxieties. I had spent years at the Naval Academy learning the importance of confident leadership, so even though I felt plenty of fear, I tried to project the image of a stoic leader as the rhib bounced through the swells toward our target.

The Navy's protocol for approaching another vessel respects the United Nations' Law of the Sea. The United States does not have the right to obstruct foreign vessels on the high seas without reason, but within the northern Persian Gulf and Gulf of Oman, we had authority to search. The suspect vessel was expecting us because *Germantown*'s bridge crew had already established contact with them by radio and had directed them to a safe course and speed in anticipation of our boarding.

Once alongside the merchant vessel, we began to make our ascent on board. By this time, it was easier to put my fears aside and focus on the mission. I would quickly discover that just getting on board the other ship was often the scariest aspect of a mission. While *Germantown*, with its deep draft, sturdy ladders, and expert seamanship, made boarding the rhib easy, the rickety rope ladder of the suspect vessel was far less steady. Waves swelled treacherously and tossed us about as we tried to grab the rungs of the ladder. My team finally made it on board and hurried to carry out our assignments.

As soon as my feet hit the deck, I began to survey my surroundings. My eyes were immediately drawn to the bow and dozens of gas masks strewn about on the deck. In my anxiety, my overly imaginative mind went to a worst-case scenario, and I wondered if the ship might be carrying weaponized gases. Prepared for anything, our security teams began their sweeps down the port and starboard sides of the ship as the boarding officer and I made our way to the pilothouse. We moved tactically and quickly, aware that danger might lie around any corner of the unfamiliar ship. We also had to trust our teammates, as they proceeded to secure the rest of the ship.

When we arrived at the pilothouse, the boarding officer began interviewing the ship's master, and I took reports from the rest of the team. Because I was at the highest point of the ship, I could maintain better command and control. Both teams reported all secure, and the whole crew was accounted for. Our engineer began taking soundings in their fuel tanks as the interview with the master proceeded. Fuel tanks could hold illegal substances, and it was a place weapons could be hidden.

The pilot master spoke English, which was pretty common, and he confirmed their cargo and destination. When asked about the gas masks, he offered a very plausible explanation—they were used for hazardous materials handling. The engineer's inspection took about thirty minutes, and as it progressed *Germantown* steamed on a parallel course to provide cover for us and the rhib; we frequently radioed them on the bridge-to-bridge radio to update them on our status and progress. Finally the engineer reported that he had completed his soundings and hadn't discovered anything unusual. We thanked the master for his compliance and headed back to the ship.

Such search missions were only half of our duties. Other times we clearly offered charity, which required an entirely different leadership mindset. Quarantined in a ten-by-ten-mile grid of ocean, affectionately known as the "smug box" (as in smuggler), some ships sat at anchor for months at a time while authorities ashore made determinations as to their status. While the ships' owners and masters might have been smuggling illicit cargo, their crews were impoverished victims. They were often third world citizens that had signed on with a ship to make a meager wage to support their families.

We still approached charitable boarding with the same preparation as for uncooperative vessels—weapons ready. One time as we approached the coordinates of a vessel for which we were providing provisions, I was struck by the putrid odor in the air. As the vessel became visible through the polluted haze of the northern Persian Gulf, the odor became stronger. I realized with shock that it was emanating from the ship we were about to board. Sanitation standards are not the same in the Middle East as in the United States. We had to follow strict environmental laws as part of our seagoing practices, but it was not uncommon for some foreign vessels to dump sewage and food waste, or slaughter a calf on the deck of a boat, leaving its remains to float in the gulf's waters.

Coming alongside the vessel, we had our first glimpse of its dire circumstance, as the ship wallowed in spilled oil and human waste in the stagnant water. Braving the noxious odors, we boarded the vessel with flour, fresh water, and some other meager supplies. An appreciative crew of six men greeted us. They were a sad sight, completely emaciated and wearing torn and stained clothing. They obviously had not bathed in months, choosing instead to drink the precious little water that was provided to them. As was our practice, we inspected the vessel to ensure their safety and ours.

Once we were certain there were no weapons or other hazards on board, we proceeded with distributing supplies. We conducted health and wellness checks on the crew members if they wished. They lined up, and our corpsman listened for symptoms they might have, while also visually assessing if they needed treatment. As the doc attended to the crew, and members of my team unloaded the supplies, a gunner's mate who was providing my security briefly surveyed the ship. Our visit was during the holy month of Ramadan, and we had boarded in the late afternoon, so we saw the cook preparing their evening meal to break their fast. With the flour and water we had provided, the cook made unleavened bread in a fly-infested kitchen. It was nothing short of filthy, and the food was meager.

I had never seen poverty of that kind before. I realized that these men were guilty of nothing, just hoping to make fifty cents a day to send to their families. Theirs was a simple case of bad luck—signing up to serve on a vessel whose proprietor was smuggling oil. It occurred to me at that moment that what separated my relative wealth from their poverty was not any ability or work ethic, but our circumstances of birth. I had the good fortune to have been born in the United States. I didn't fully appreciate it at the time, but I have since come to regard those charitable missions, providing food and comfort to the world's underprivileged, as one of the most rewarding aspects of my naval service. Further, that our nation and naval service continued to focus energy and resources on benevolent charitable missions—and that I had the opportunity to serve in this capacity—imbued me with a sense of purpose and pride.

While leading fellow sailors under arms into potentially dangerous situations on VBSS missions, I had to call upon my Naval Academy training to overcome the unique leadership challenges, anxieties, and uncertainties that came with the

Jason Jackson preparing to debark a rhib from the USS Germantown *for boarding operations.* (Courtesy Jason Jackson)

diverse missions we were assigned. Inspections of suspect vessels forced us to focus on preparedness and judgment, while the charitable aspects of the mission imbued us with empathy and led to a newfound appreciation for the blessings we enjoyed because of the missions our Marines were performing. This perspective furthered the partnerships of the sailors and Marines of the 1st Expeditionary Strike Group and led to mutual respect between the Marines embarked on board ship and the VBSS sailors of *Germantown*.

Lending a Hand in Tsunami Relief

John Cauthen

O
n December 26, 2004, a massive earthquake ruptured the sea floor of the Indian Ocean, triggering a devastating tsunami that struck the shores of India, Indonesia, Sri Lanka, Thailand, and countless other islands and atolls. The U.S. Navy responded, arriving on the scene within days to assist with relief efforts for nearly a month. This is one junior officer's story of flying nearly one hundred hours, delivering thousands of pounds of supplies, witnessing the rescue of hundreds of injured people, and grappling with the destruction of one of the Navy's aircraft as part of Operation Unified Assistance.

In September 2004, I departed San Diego on board USS *Abraham Lincoln* on a deployment to the Western Pacific that was scheduled to return to port by January. On Christmas Day, my squadronmates and I found ourselves waiting out the remainder of our deployment in Hong Kong. We all would have rather been home for the holidays, but we tried to make the best of the situation and celebrated together late into the night in our hotel room. The next day, I awoke to the familiar odor of stale tobacco smoke, the sight of my sleeping fellow officers scattered around the room, and the sound of the television someone had left on the night before. The television was turned to an English news channel, which was reporting an earthquake and tsunami in the Indian Ocean. Having grown up in the San Francisco area and experienced the 1989 World Series earthquake, I wondered how bad it could be. At that moment, a more experienced officer muttered, "Shit, so much for going home on time." When I realized what he was saying, it felt as if a crushing weight had been placed on my shoulders. Would the carrier really be ordered westward? Why would anyone think that the Navy could be of any use in this situation? The United States was a nation at war. Why would we distract ourselves with this additional burden?

Each of these questions would be answered in time, and my conception not only of the Navy's capabilities but America's benevolence as well would be forever altered. The tsunami killed nearly 200,000 people throughout the Indian Ocean region from Indonesia to East Africa. My squadron was one of the first American air assets on the scene to render assistance and hope to those still clinging to life on the northern tip of Sumatra. The U.S. Navy occupied the world's stage for nearly a month as it entered Indonesian waters, and by the end of the mission it had become clear that the efforts of so few would be the salvation of many.

★ ★ ★

USS *Abraham Lincoln* and Carrier Strike Group Two (CVW-2) arrived on New Year's Eve just off the coast of Banda Aceh, the capital of Aceh province on the Indonesian island of Sumatra. The seas were calm, the air clear, warm, and humid; from a distance the island looked peaceful and idyllic. There was no indication that a monstrous hundred-foot wave had torn into the unsuspecting population just days earlier. The only hint that something terrible had occurred was the flotsam passing the ship as it meandered to and fro, awaiting the vagaries of diplomacy and politics to be agreed to by military and civilian officials. Aceh province had been in active revolt against the Indonesian central government at the time, and following the earthquake and tsunami, a tense peace had to be brokered. As the hours passed, we began to see and smell the bloated remains of people washed out to sea along with shattered timbers from houses, palm thatching, plastic bottles, clothing, and so many objects we couldn't begin to identify. As I took in all the destruction, I wondered again what the Navy's mission would be here.

Indonesia, the fourth largest nation in the world, consists of 17,506 islands, of which Sumatra is one of the biggest. Bounding the Strait of Malacca, Sumatra also has one of the busiest sea routes in the world. Islam is the dominant religion in this vast archipelagic nation with a population of 230 million people who speak three hundred different languages. To say that Indonesia is a diverse nation would be an understatement. With so many languages and peoples separated by seas and volcanic mountain ranges, influenced by Europeans, and joined loosely by Islam, it should come as no surprise that the identity of Indonesia is difficult to comprehend at a glance. The area is truly a crossroads of old, new, European, Islamic, and modernizing forces and traditional, indigenous cultures.

The juxtaposition of recent devastation and nature's new calm struck us as our two-aircraft section approached terra firma at a cautious three hundred feet and seventy-five knots to survey Aceh's landscape for the first time. The stark beauty of the verdant province and its coastal turquoise waters were contrasted by the destruction wrought by the tsunami. Lush green jungle abruptly met the denuded western coastline of Sumatra for hundreds of miles. Brown rot and decay replaced vibrant greens, and blue waters were sullied by mud and debris. Concrete pads marked where homes and buildings once stood; almost nothing remained. The singular north-south highway that once linked villages along this coastline was shattered and in some areas had been completely swallowed by the sea.

Banda Aceh's infrastructure was in ruins; in addition to the problems on land, there was no air traffic control. I was assigned co-pilot in the trail aircraft of a two-aircraft section on the first sortie of the start of operations. Beginning our flight brief at 0430 on January 2, 2005, we decided to locate the airport and ask what help they needed. The flight crew made its way to the flight deck and began preflight checks on the aircraft as the sun began to break the horizon. The Air Boss—the ship's air traffic control—cleared our section to depart, and within seconds we were clear of the aircraft carrier and on our way to land.

All the flight crews were briefed on the mission, but none of us was given instructions for how it would be accomplished. Aviation training prepared pilots to operate helicopters technically and tactically, but it was anyone's guess how this would translate during an unorthodox mission. It turned out that the unknown allowed us the freedom of action necessary for a dynamic and constantly changing mission. We learned by doing, and we cataloged and passed down these lessons to the crews that came after us. Mission objectives became clearer with each passing day, and the efficiency of operations took on a rhythm all its own. Operation Unified Assistance was truly a massive team effort; we were simply one part of a larger machine. Every level of the Navy was involved in the operation, from the coordination between regional flag and general officers to the sailors who were ferried from ship to shore to load our helicopters.

Within days of the 2004 tsunami, John Cauthen and a squadron of rotary-wing aircraft brought massive quantities of supplies to the needy citizens of Indonesia. (Courtesy John Cauthen)

We often had to descend into a sea of people who would slowly part to accommodate the heft of our aircraft. As soon as we touched down, we would be mobbed like celebrities. We distributed the food and water in a matter of minutes; the most able-bodied grabbed as much as they could carry and fled the scene. This process improved over time, as Indonesian soldiers began to make their way to villages and set up distribution points. What never changed, however, was the cheerful exuberance of the children, no matter where we went. A helicopter to them was not only a savior appearing from the skies, but also an opportunity to be playful. As we prepared to depart, children would gather under the rotor arc and time a collective jump with our liftoff. The downwash would throw their small frames backward and down to the ground. Their smiles and laughter were reminders that hope and optimism remained very much a part of the individual communities we visited.

Within days, the chaos and confusion we encountered the first few days began to take on order. Fixed-wing aircraft brought massive quantities of supplies to the airport. Their cargo was marshaled, sorted, and then staged to be loaded onto awaiting helicopters at a soccer field that doubled as a landing site. Within a week of the start of operations, the Navy had created a system reminiscent of a factory assembly line. Helicopters would land, be loaded, be given tasking, and take off. All of this occurred in a matter of minutes and continued during daylight hours for the remainder of January.

★ ★ ★

The pilots of Helicopter Anti-Submarine Squadron Two flew continuously for nearly a month, amassing so many hours that we were required to get waivers to continue flying during January. (A hundred hours a month is typically the maximum allowed.) This took a toll not only on the pilots and mechanics but also on the machines we operated. Our procedures and manuals help us avoid making mistakes, but because humans are fallible, some mistakes are inevitable. For me, one of the most eye-opening mistakes was when one of our helicopters, side number 613, crashed in a rice paddy near the staging area. It was one of the longest days of my Navy career. Due to a combination of luck and pilot skill, all crew and passengers survived, but the aircraft was destroyed. Standard operating procedure mandates stopping flight operations in the event of aircraft loss, but on that day, I logged ten hours. Our mission continued; these were extraordinary times, and we were required to continue flying and deliver aid.

I remember arriving the morning of the crash to a frenzied ready room: the phone was ringing, the computer was flooded with emails and chat messages, people milled about offering speculation to fact, blurring the reality we desperately sought to find. We began our flight around mid-morning and headed straight to the staging area at the airport in Banda Aceh. We cleared the beach, and in a few short minutes we passed over a ground checkpoint in preparation to enter the makeshift helicopter pattern that had been created to regulate entry into the soccer field. The pattern was controlled by Australians operating from a makeshift location on a portable radio. I remember the controllers being competent and humorous, but on this day they were dour.

As we entered the pattern, we were met with a full view of the crash scene: The helicopter was on its side covered in mud and filth; the tail boom was cracked in half and barely attached to the main fuselage; the windscreen and chin bubble were shattered; and the four blades, upon impact, were flung hundreds of yards away from the site. People were perched atop the fuselage, and a great many more were in waist-deep mud surveying the rest of the crash site. I remember thinking that the aircraft, having crashed from more than three hundred feet, looked remarkably intact.

At that moment a number of thoughts were competing for my focus. What would I have done had I been at the controls? Would I have managed to crash-land the helicopter as well as the pilots of 613 had? Would we have lived? How was our aircraft going to perform today and would I make any mistakes? My thoughts snapped back to the present—I had a helicopter to land and a mission to complete. We landed on our designated spot in the soccer field and began preparations to load food and water onto our stripped-down aircraft. All tactical gear and unnecessary equipment had been removed in order to carry as much as possible, whether it be people, water, or foodstuffs. We took on about 5,000 pounds of goods and were on our way again.

For the remainder of the day, we made our way up and down the coastline and ventured inland where villages once stood. Makeshift camps supplanted pre-tsunami communities, most of which had already been cataloged and marked for regular resupply over the coming days. On this particular day, we sought out inland communities and villages that had been spared from inundation but were isolated from assistance because the only road, their sole lifeline, had been consumed by the tsunami's waves. These communities, in dire straits, desperately needed water and food. Many also needed medical assistance. Our one helicopter could only bring so much, but over the course of the day, we made multiple sorties and found a number of isolated villages in distress. We dropped off our load, marked the locations, and evacuated the injured or sick.

We refueled three times: aboard the carrier, on an amphibious ship, and on a cruiser. The only food we had was Pop Tarts, and I ate three packs. (I could gladly go my whole life without eating another Pop Tart!) We made multiple deliveries to villages along the coast and inland, and we evacuated dozens of people to the triage tent at the airport at Banda Aceh. In many ways, my ten-hour day captured precisely the intent of our leaders for the mission. Over time, the mission took on a clarity all its own with each flight and successful supply drop and evacuation. Our utility as a helicopter squadron was proven consistently over that long day and during the entire month we provided assistance to the people of Sumatra.

★ ★ ★

The panoramic view of devastation we had seen on our first day began to be built up and added to with every flight. Each village and makeshift camp was marked for continued resupply. As the weeks passed, we got a more comprehensive picture of the post-tsunami landscape, both human and geographic. People migrated to areas near the coastline where food, water, and medical assistance existed. We established ground checkpoints—often named after familiarities or derived from local names, one of the more memorable being PB&J—air routing, and altitude separation for aircraft heading up the coast and those transiting down the coast, and established common operating frequencies. All of this served to lay the foundation for successful flight operations as well as the overall mission.

The men and women of CVW-2, USS *Abraham Lincoln*, and HS-2 proved they were adaptable and could discharge any duty to which they were assigned. This mission was an unknown to all personnel but would in many ways set the precedent for future humanitarian assistance in disaster relief operations. Amid the ever-evolving landscape of conflict, threat, and natural disaster, the Navy will continue to adapt and bring to bear its assets in support of any mission it is assigned. It was proven in Sumatra, validated in New Orleans, and employed most recently in Japan. It will continue to be an integral component not only for advancing U.S. interests and national security, but also for showcasing the nation's beneficence.

Training with the Enemy:
Iraq and U.S. Naval Partnerships

Travis Bode

I n 2006, I was assigned to a *Tarawa*-class assault ship called USS *Peleliu*—a "motorized island" stationed off the coast of Iraq and temporary home to more than two thousand sailors and Marines. I had always dreamt of being closer to the fight, so when the opportunity presented itself, I jumped at the chance to work with Combined Task Force 158. I would be a liaison officer for a U.K.-led group of Royal Navy and U.S. Navy personnel charged with training the Iraqi Navy. Maritime security in the northern Persian Gulf was anything but stable at the time, and we knew we had a challenge ahead of us in trying to build a strong and effective force in Iraq.

I would be based out of Umm Qasr, a major port facility. My responsibilities included going on patrols with the Iraqi Navy to nearby oil platforms and the Khawr Abd Allah River, the main waterway between the Persian Gulf and the port. This area had been a hotbed of contention between Iraq and Iran for decades, and as a result sunken ships litter the riverbed to this day. Another river, the Shatt al-Arab, serves as a maritime border between the two countries, forming Iraq's southeastern border, and drains out into the Persian Gulf. The 1975 Algiers Accord between Iran and Iraq attempted to settle a border dispute between the two countries by designating the border at the thalweg, or median deep-water line. The thalweg, however, has shifted over time, and with no survey having been completed since the accord was signed, the exact border remains unclear and therefore contested.

Iran's Revolutionary Guard Corps aggressively enforces what it perceives to be Iran's rightful territorial waters. On two occasions prior to 2006, coalition military personnel were taken hostage by Iranian naval forces in the general area. There was potentially imminent danger because the Iraqi government and military were in their infancy and vulnerable to attack. As I embarked on my new mission, foremost in my mind were the reports of American coalition advisers being killed by turncoat Iraqi soldiers. Here I was, about to be a senior Navy adviser and the only American on board a seventy-five-foot Iraqi Navy patrol boat. Just the thought of it made me instinctively reach down to check my side-arm in its holster—loaded, round chambered, safety on. I'd volunteered for this, but not without apprehension.

When the time came for me to be dropped off at the patrol boat, I was nothing but nerves. I tried to take in as many details as I could: The patrol boat was covered in black soot and tar from the vessel's engine exhaust, and Iraqi sailors ran around on deck in all directions and dressed in all different kinds of uniforms. The scene reminded me of something out of the movie *McHale's Navy*.

I was experiencing my own version of culture shock. This wouldn't be like training plebes in King Hall; that was something I knew I could do. This felt different because of the cultural chasm between the Iraqi sailors and myself. I wondered how I would ever fit in with these sailors. I was raised in Scottsdale, Arizona—not exactly the roughest town in America; I was trained in Annapolis, the most structured college in the country; and I was a Judeo-Christian with only a limited understanding of the Islamic faith.

I thought back to the numerous statements by senior U.S. officials about what our mission was supposed to be: help the Iraqi military stand on its own feet. I heaved my bag on board the Iraqi boat feeling that the mission—to turn this ragtag bunch of Iraqis into a modern navy—was beyond my capabilities. Despite my reservations, since I was a surface warfare officer (SWO), and my seniors must have felt I was multitalented enough to make this happen, I was determined to prove them right. That was the SWO ethos. SWOs are flexible, quick thinkers, and willing to take on any challenge no matter how futile it might appear to be.

On board the Iraqi patrol boat, I was pleasantly surprised to learn that the captain had attended Dartmouth Royal Naval College (the United Kingdom's naval academy) and spoke excellent English. Over Pepsis and Twinkies during the transit to Umm Qasr, the captain and I discussed life in our respective countries. It was evident from talking to him that he loved Iraq, but he was also envious of America's wealth and democratic way of life. We found common ground in our love of the sea and knowledge of nautical rules of the road, the cornerstone of any mariner's profession. It was a simple conversation, but already I was starting to feel some hope for our mission.

Early on, I had the opportunity to participate in Operation United River Dragon, a joint operation between Iraq, Kuwait, and the United States to provide security along the Khawr Abd Allah and the extreme northern Persian Gulf near Kuwaiti and Iraqi waters. My job was to help the Iraqi captain coordinate his operations with the Kuwaiti and U.S. elements. This wouldn't be easy. First, the Kuwaitis harbored a deep-seated resentment toward the Iraqis because of the 1990 Iraqi invasion and subsequent plundering of Kuwait. Their nationalistic distaste for one another was palatable. Second, the Kuwait Navy and Kuwait Coast

Guard did not get along, because they were subordinate to two rival ministries—defense and interior. Thankfully, on board the Kuwait Navy patrol boat would be Joe Hooper, one of my Naval Academy classmates.

Prior to the commencement of the exercise, the participants rendezvoused on board the Kuwait Navy boat for a coordination meeting. In private, Joe and I discussed our concerns about the meeting and the overall operation. We knew we'd be the only real sounding board for one another's ideas and that we'd need to work together to get through this in one piece. In my speech in front of the whole group, I reminded the separate factions that we had a singular goal—to bring security to the river and provide a better place for people to live. I tried to say it with confidence, although the Iraqis and Kuwaitis would not speak to each other, and the Kuwait Navy and coast guard representatives wouldn't either. As we were leaving the conference room, Joe and I exchanged looks of doubt; we both knew from the first meeting that this operation would be fraught with complications. Whatever lessons I had drawn from my political science classes and from reading Tom Clancy novels were being put to the test. The plan was for each of the different elements to patrol a specific sector of the Khawr Abd Allah—God willing, or *insha'Allah,* as my Arabic-speaking comrades would say.

Those of us on the Iraqi patrol boat proceeded to our assigned sector. One of the long-term objectives for the Iraqi Navy was for it to assert itself as the primary security provider along the Iraqi part of the Shatt al-Arab. After the fall of Saddam Hussein's government and the disintegration of the Iraqi military as a security provider, pirates—*ali babas* in Arabic—had free reign along the river for smuggling and robbery. It was the job of the nascent Iraqi Navy to reclaim the local waters from the ali babas and provide a secure environment for fisherman and merchant traffic. It was particularly important for local fishermen and merchants to see the Iraqi Navy actively patrolling the local waters. To accomplish this, I encouraged the Iraqi captain to approach and interact with various fishing vessels (dhows) to reinforce the presence of the Iraqi Navy and to ask questions regarding the presence of ali babas. The Iraqi captain was skeptical of the practice. The first time we came alongside one of the dhows, he didn't know what to do, so he chose to remain inside the pilothouse.

The crew of the dhow looked at us like we were crazy. "What are you doing here? Do you need something?" their looks seemed to ask. The Naval Academy had taught me to make decisions and take swift action, and it was difficult for me to let the Iraqis take the lead. The Academy had also taught me patience, so I waited. (It helped to think back to what it had been like standing at attention on the parade ground in Annapolis, sweating on a hot Maryland day waiting for the next command from the Brigade adjutant.) As much as I wanted to, I didn't leave the pilothouse, and I didn't take charge. It was important to let the Iraqis do this themselves.

I did, however, coach the Iraqi captain through a series of questions, such as, Have you seen any ali babas in the area? If so, when? Which direction do they normally come from? We also told the crew to contact us over bridge-to-bridge radio if they saw any ali babas. As we executed several of these approaches and visits, the Iraqi captain's confidence grew, and I could tell that he was feeling more sure of himself and enjoying the work.

It didn't take long, however, for the tensions I had witnessed in the coordination meeting to resurface. My first indication of a problem came over the bridge-to-bridge radio in the form of yelling in Arabic and a look of alarm from the captain. He immediately got on the radio and began conversing with someone in Arabic. He told me that a Kuwaiti patrol boat was harassing an Iraqi merchant ship transiting the Khawr Abd Allah to Umm Qasr, ordering the vessel to lower its Iraqi flag and strike up a Kuwaiti flag while it was in Kuwaiti waters. (Parts of the Khawr Abd Allah are Kuwaiti, but vessels of all flags are allowed to transit this area in accordance with international law.) The Iraqi merchant had refused to comply, and the Kuwaitis threatened to open fire. As we rushed to the scene, I radioed Joe to get an explanation from him and figure out how to diffuse the situation.

We were right in the middle of a potentially serious international incident, and as we sped along, I worried that one of our patrol boats would open fire on the other, putting me and Joe on opposing sides. Joe told me that he didn't know why the Kuwaitis were doing what they were doing and that he had thus far been unsuccessful in getting them to back off. As we tried to come up with a plan, a U.S. Coast Guard patrol boat came to the rescue. Its captain contacted the Kuwaitis, citing specific articles of international law that supported the Iraqi merchant's insistence that he was not obligated to follow the Kuwaitis' demands. After several minutes of discussion between the Kuwaitis and Coast Guard captain, the Kuwaitis backed down, barely avoiding an international incident.

That same night, we proceeded out to sea to patrol the area just northwest of the offshore Iraqi oil terminals. An estimated 90 percent of Iraq's oil is exported through the two oil terminals we were visiting, and as a result they are closely guarded by the Iraqi Navy and a coalition naval task force. As we drew closer to the terminals, the ship went dark, and we lost all power. No propulsion, no radio, and no lights. I knew that if I didn't remain calm, the Iraqis around me might panic. As we drifted to the southeast, I was concerned about two things: being fired upon by the coalition naval task force as we drifted into the security sectors around the oil terminals, and drifting into Iranian territorial waters, which were about a mile or two away.

With no way to call for help, I urged the Iraqi captain to fix the problem as soon as possible. If we drifted into Iranian waters and an Iranian patrol identified us, we would almost certainly be taken into custody. Much to my surprise, he responded quickly this time and went into the engine room and personally helped the crew rectify the problem. After several hours, and before drifting into Iranian waters or the security zone around the oil platforms, the engineers were able to fix the problem, and we resumed our patrol. Less than a year after my deployment, fifteen British sailors and marines were detained by Iranian military personnel in this same area, allegedly for violating Iranian territorial waters.

Being an adviser in a complex joint environment was both empowering and humbling for me. I was proud to wear the American uniform and could tell it was respected by the foreign militaries, but as an adviser my authority was limited. It was a powerful lesson in respecting the mission and supporting the host nation with patient, steadfast leadership. With each successful day, trust grew between me and the Iraqi captain. I began to think there was real hope for Iraq's reconstituted navy. When I left Iraq, I felt confident that my contribution, albeit quite small in the grand scheme of things, helped the Iraqi Navy stand on its own two feet and eventually turn the tide in that country.

Travis Bode at sea in the Persian Gulf mentoring an Iraqi naval officer. (Courtesy Travis Bode)

UN Peacekeeping in Practice

Dave Augustin

The dirt roads leading out of the city of Voinjama were some of the worst in all of Liberia. It took almost an hour for our UN patrol vehicle to travel the short distance from the city to the village of Masabulahun. Thankfully it was January and the beginning of the dry season, otherwise the roads would have been impassable trails of red mud. Occasionally we passed a pickup truck overflowing with people and supplies headed toward Sierra Leone or Guinea, but otherwise the roads were clear, and it was a lonely journey. I had plenty of time to reflect on how I had gotten there and what a unique deployment I was entering.

As a submarine officer, I never imagined my career path would bring me to the jungles of West Africa. A Navy officer's career progression is generally rigid and does not allow for opportunities outside the submarine community, so when I was offered the opportunity to serve with the UN mission in Liberia I jumped at the chance. At the time, I didn't even realize that the United States sent officers to UN missions.

Many of the countries that support UN missions do not have large militaries, therefore sending fifty or one hundred soldiers to a UN peacekeeping mission is significant, and only the best and brightest are chosen. Presently there are twenty deployed U.S. military members supporting several UN missions. This is a small number and will remain small because the United States provides so much financial assistance to the United Nations. In our compound, I was the most junior officer and the youngest, but I was the team's operations officer, a senior position, because I am an American, and Americans are considered to be particularly capable and hard working. It was an honor for me.

That first trip from Voinjama had left me tired and thirsty from inhaling dust and dirt kicked up by our vehicle. I was also nervous. I had only been working in Liberia as a UN peacekeeper a few days prior to heading out on my first patrol. I barely knew my teammate, a friendly Nigerian named Nehemiah, and now we would be on a patrol together to an isolated village in the Liberian countryside for the rest of the day. Our task was to enter a village of complete strangers and assess health conditions, education, economic development, and crime in the community. The first village we visited was one of nearly one thousand towns and villages under our jurisdiction. We were unarmed peacekeepers, each wearing our national military uniform and a light blue and white armband to signify our mandate. I didn't really know what I was supposed to be doing or how the villagers would react to our presence. Arriving at the town, I grabbed my camera and clipboard and got out of the patrol vehicle.

As soon as we entered the village of Masabulahun, we were greeted by young, cheering Liberians. I had pens, pencils, and candy for them. The flag on my uniform instantly put people at ease and let them know that I was there to help. The children truly enjoyed seeing a *tubabu* (white man) and wanted to pose for pictures. When the excitement died down, several women and children took us to see the town chief. He was the only man in the village at the time since all the others were out working the fields.

We sat down in a palava hut, the town meeting place, and started discussing conditions in the village. We covered some heavy issues, including security, education, human rights, and the treatment of women and ex-combatants. The town chief asked for more resources. It was a town with no running water or electricity, but he wanted computers. It was a town miles away from an economic hub, but he wanted machinery to process grain and corn. Even though I felt they were ridiculous requests, I wrote them all down as "needs" in my notebook. I didn't know what else to do. Then my Nigerian teammate sat down and began asking questions. He asked when the town had last pooled its resources to earn extra income for a processor. Did they hold a meeting with the young men about their work ethic and their contribution to the town's food supply? Why hadn't they developed a program for the girls to help in the fields?

My teammate was African, and he was trying to impart a sense of responsibility to the villagers. It was an awkward feeling for me. I felt bad for the locals. Their huts were made of clay, the children had mismatched shoes, and their food was served out of unsanitary pots. One potential drawback of international peace operations is that the host nation can become dependent on the United Nations and non-governmental organizations for food, security, and a myriad of other services. Instead of perpetuating this dependency, it is better to teach the villagers the skills to sustain UN and NGO efforts long after these organizations leave. It is a painful but necessary lesson for them to learn.

Not every village was the same. Some made the best of the United Nations and NGOs operating in their country. They took pride in their villages and were excited to show the progress they had made. Whether it was a clean-water initiative or some other community health measure, survival was only possible with hard work and collaboration among the tribal leaders—often a town chief, a women's leader, and a youth leader. When there was a rule of law dispute, the community of elders made a decision and a ruling. It was a defined structure based on norms, not laws.

Although the overwhelming majority of developments in northern Liberia were positive, we did experience a serious problem during my time there. World food prices skyrocketed in the spring of 2008, and the effects of this could be seen in the local markets. Many people in northern Liberia traveled across the border to Guinea and Sierra Leone in search of cheaper food prices. Families dramatically cut back on their food consumption, and there were concerns that many young children would begin to starve. Ultimately, the World Food Program intervened and distributed rice and other goods to help stabilize prices. It was certainly a tense period during my tenure in Voinjama; the worst of the food shortage seemed to be over by the time I left.

My deployment went far beyond patrolling villages in the Liberian countryside. It also gave me the opportunity to live and work with people from all over the world. I lived with a team of international military officers from more than fifteen different countries. I was the only native English speaker, and thus I felt an obligation to help my teammates gain proficiency with the language. I knew I was having an impact when I heard my Ukrainian teammate using slang and curse words he had picked up from me after hours on patrol together. In addition to the time spent with my teammates, I had the opportunity to work with numerous UN agencies, such as the UN Development Programme, UN High Commissioner for Refugees, and UN Police, as well as several NGOs, including the International Committee of the Red Cross, International Rescue Committee, and the Right to Play. Collectively, the UN agencies, NGOs, and military units saw tangible results in northern Liberia. Improved roads, new government facilities, and a new hospital are just a few of the projects completed while I lived there.

In addition to living and working with international officers and NGO workers, I also spent a great deal of time with a Pakistani infantry battalion (Pak Bat) providing security throughout my area of responsibility. As military observers we were unarmed to provide governance and structure, but the Pak Bat provided the consistent physical security in the region. The Pakistanis also provided our team with food, clean drinking water, and fuel.

Pak Bat was a gracious host and helped make my stay in Liberia enjoyable. The Pakistani commander frequently hosted formal lunches and dinners for our team; his contingent served the most delicious chicken, rice, chapati (a type of pita bread), paneer, and sanagalu (chickpeas) I've ever had. I developed a good working rapport with the Pakistani soldiers and was constantly impressed by their knowledge of U.S. current events. The presidential primary campaigns of 2008 were in full swing while I was in Liberia, and the Pakistani officers were

Dave Augustin with Liberian partners. (Courtesy Dave Augustin)

familiar with all the main issues. Each day I joined them for lunch, they wanted me to explain something about how the American system of government works and how we elect the president. I was impressed by their knowledge of our government and their desire to learn more about our democracy. It certainly made me feel good knowing that other countries were impressed and respectful of our government even at a time when many Americans seemed frustrated by it. Some headlines indicated that the Pakistani military could not be trusted and claimed that there was evidence that the Inter-Services Intelligence directorate was collaborating with the Taliban. To me, however, these men were my only protection, and we became great friends.

I spent a great deal of time working with the Pakistani officers coordinating air and ground patrols and documenting the disposal of unexploded ordnance (UXO). The area saw a great deal of fighting during Liberia's fifteen-year civil war, and remnants of the hostilities constantly turned up in villages. UXO was the biggest problem in the country; each week my team accompanied the Pakistani explosive ordnance disposal detachment to a new village to destroy weapons. Rocket-propelled and hand grenades accounted for the vast majority of UXOs discovered, but occasionally villagers found buried automatic weapons and ammunition. During the construction of a hospital right next to my team's residence, a worker unexpectedly detonated a UXO while burning some trash. Fortunately, he was unharmed, but it reinforced that UXOs were all over the country.

I was never more proud to be an American than while serving in Liberia. Seeing the joy on the faces of Liberian children when I entered a town, teaching my teammates English while on long patrols, and discussing politics with the Pakistani wardroom reinforced my belief that the United States is widely respected around the world. At a time when negative media coverage of U.S. operations in Iraq and Afghanistan had many Americans questioning our role in the world community, my experience proved that Americans still had a responsibility to lead.

When it came time for me to leave Voinjama, I felt conflicting emotions. I was excited to go home and see my wife and family, but I knew there was so much more that could be done if I were to stay there longer. When I boarded the Ukrainian Mi-8 helicopter for my last trip back to the capital, Monrovia, I looked out the window at the pristine, unmolested forests that cover the beautiful Liberian countryside and thought about what a unique opportunity I'd been given to represent my country and the United Nations. My time in Liberia left a lasting impression on me, and I will never stop hoping and praying for lasting peace and prosperity for that country and its people.

Casey vs. the Volcano

Casey Bruce

"Navy Rescue Two, Portland approach."

"Go ahead for Rescue Two."

"Yeah, Rescue Two, understand you want flight following?"

"That's affirmative for Rescue Two."

"We can provide that for the next one-five miles or so. Then we're going to lose you."

"Roger. We'll take it as long as we can get it, Portland."

"Rescue Two, understand you intend to fly inside the Mount St. Helens crater?"

"Portland Approach, Navy Rescue Two, that's affirmative. We'll call you when we are out."

I n the wilderness, there's a threshold where communications between home base and rescue crew fail—the signature falls off the radar, there's silence on both ends of the radio, and the crew is reminded that the mission is theirs alone. Past that point, if mistakes are made and they need help, it could take hours for someone to notice. And so I was taught not to make mistakes, as were the members of my search and rescue (SAR) crew. Like so many others at the Naval Academy, I had yearned to be part of something great for a long time. I could not have known at the time that a flight into the crater of a volcano would play a pivotal role in defining my career for me.

★ ★ ★

I grew up an all-American boy who was powerfully drawn to the military. I thrived on discipline and learned at a young age that hard work wields the greatest and most enjoyable returns in life. I couldn't picture myself sitting in an office all day. During my years at the Naval Academy, I drew strength from the litany of stories about the heroism and sacrifice of the grads who had come before me, and I made it through. The Academy was not a normal college, and I knew after five minutes of standing in long lines, all the while getting yelled at for no apparent reason, that it was not a stepping stone to a normal, average life.

I was getting ready for a career in aviation when the United States went to war in Afghanistan in 2001 and Iraq in 2003. I assumed my path to something great would include flying in combat. I finally got my wings in the spring of 2004 and headed to San Diego to be a helicopter pilot. I made two deployments to the Persian Gulf in three years, flying mostly logistics missions or search and rescue. Although I loved flying and was proud of my accomplishments, I was disappointed that I'd never flown a single combat mission. Hell, I'd never even been *in* the combat zone. Near, but never in; never close enough to feel any real danger. I knew that this was nothing to be ashamed of, but I still felt like I was getting off easy. I began to weigh the merits of my contribution against the other sacrifices I was making in my life.

I thought about how I had spent seventeen out of the first twenty-four months of my marriage at sea and forever lost that precious period with my bride, Amy. At the time, I could see only two options: Do something in this war to validate my name and my education or return home to be with my family. I made the decision to do something for my family and took orders to my home state of Washington to fly as a SAR helicopter pilot. Everyone warned that this would kill my career, but I was beyond caring. It sounded like a fulfilling job in an awesome place. If I was going to coast through my navy career, at least I could do so with family nearby.

★ ★ ★

Back in Washington, February 16, 2010, was like any other day to me. I was up before the sun cracked the timberline, readying for my day of SAR duty and savoring another breakfast in a string of great breakfasts with my wife and little girl. I was half listening to the TV in the background when a news story caught my attention. The day before, a hiker at the summit of Mount St. Helens had been standing on an ice cornice when it broke, sending him into a 1,500-foot free-fall into the snowy crater below. Rescue crews spent the afternoon attempting to get to him via helicopter, but poor weather and harsh conditions had hindered progress. The report said that rescue efforts were to continue at first light.

I listened to news radio as I dashed to work, hoping for updates and knowing where our entire outfit would be spending its resources that day. As soon as I stepped foot in my office, I got a call from my boss. He briefed me on the situation and the previous attempts our unit had made. The night SAR crew had flown down the previous evening but couldn't get within three miles of the stranded man's position because of the bad weather. All the news networks were reporting that the search had been suspended the previous afternoon, so I was encouraged to learn my unit had pushed forward, working through the night to continue the rescue effort. My boss asked me bluntly, "Do you think this is something you can do?" "Yes, Sir, absolutely," I responded without even thinking. "I know exactly where it is. I've climbed that mountain twice before. My crew is briefed, and we're ready to fly." "Ok," he said, "I'll get approval again from the Air Force Rescue Center, but we'll get you guys a new mission number and get you headed down there."

I hung up the phone and thought to myself, Holy shit, I'm about to fly inside Mount St. Helens. I immediately began to think about everything needed to make this a safe, successful day when my phone rang again and interrupted my thoughts.

"Hello."

"Is this Lieutenant Bruce?"

"It is."

"Lieutenant, I'm Sheriff Brown with the Skamania County Sheriff's office. I wanted to cover a couple things before you head down this way."

"Good morning, Sheriff. No problem. What's up?"

"Well, lieutenant, I'm sure you know what the situation is. If you get down there and find a dead body, I just want to have a plan in place. News reporters swarm around these stories, and I don't want that information to get out through the wrong channels."

I casually sent the conversation back to him, thinking he was going to want to brief me on the working frequencies, location of the victim, and details about ground support as in a typical rescue call. This guy was all business. He continued, "I've got a lat/long where we'd like him dropped if he is deceased," he pressed on. "You got a pen? You ready to write?"

I need another cup of coffee, was the only thing going through my mind as I jotted down the coordinates. It wasn't even eight o'clock in the morning. Before the conversation wrapped up, I asked, "Sheriff, what are the odds this guy is alive?" He answered, "This man fell 1,500 feet and spent the night in the freezing cold. Probably not good."

There was a cold wind gusting in from Puget Sound that morning and a blanket of gray clouds as far as the eye could see. My copilot recommended we try to climb through the clouds to hopefully "pop out" on top. Our victim was at a relatively high altitude, and arriving at his position from above the clouds would likely be our only chance for a successful rescue. I took his advice and climbed, emerging into sunny skies over a broken layer of moisture-laden clouds. Scanning south, I saw the snow-covered tops of Mt. Hood in Oregon, Mt. Adams in Southwest Washington, and finally my bull's-eye. The jagged, snow-covered top of Mount St. Helens barely emerged above the layer of winter weather. My copilot and I both knew immediately that the only way we were getting into the rescue zone was from the top down.

This massive volcano stands 8,365 feet with a horseshoe-shaped crater a mile wide in its center. The crater floor lies at about 7,100 feet, opening to the north a massive area of desolation that thirty years ago had been the blast path of the most memorable eruption to shake the Pacific Northwest. At almost the exact center of the crater floor lay a massive dome of igneous rock. The dome, at three hundred feet tall, is the telltale sign that this behemoth is still alive and churning with fire and magma far beneath the surface.

Arriving from the north, we found ourselves flying directly toward the mouth of the open crater, like fishermen drifting out to sea directly into the open jaws of a great white. The weather gods were cooperating, appearing to allow us a way in, but I wasn't sure we would be allowed a way out by such kind fortune. The cloud tops led right into the crater, but another small patch of clouds and fog loomed just above the lava dome, which meant we'd be sandwiched inside the crater, unable to make a rapid ascent or descent. Although our search area would be small and well defined, I knew we would be extremely limited in our ability to safely maneuver. This mission would be the practical exam on everything I had learned in my career and how well I could fly this aircraft.

I read my instruments to check winds and saw 30-35 knots from the southwest. I remembered reading that a flight should not be conducted in mountainous terrain if winds of 30 knots or more exist because of possible severe instability, turbulence, and extreme down-flowing winds. I knew we'd be able to pull it off if we did everything perfectly, but we were flirting with danger. Prior to entering the crater, my copilot and I briefed our search patterns, checked our available power, and determined the exact routes we'd use if we had to execute a quick escape. Once my preliminary terrain readings were complete and assessed, I made orbital passes one hundred feet above the crater's floor. With our cabin doors and windows open for visibility, the blowing snow and crystalline ice ripped its way into the helicopter, collecting in our noses, mouths, and every crevice in the plane. There was great temptation to turn on the heat for the cabin, but the risk of it robbing the engines of power could mean the difference between flying and crashing.

The sloping terrain below revealed hundreds of snow fractures, enormous slabs of snowpack that can break off and start an avalanche from essentially any direction inside the crater. The fractured land inside the volcano was the most desolate and unforgiving I'd ever seen and revealed nothing conducive to supporting current or future life. The helicopter bucked and strained against the high winds but was steady enough to keep going. Its jerky movements indicated that it wanted to go into the caldera even less than we did.

I was losing count of how many laps we had made when two dark objects caught my eye. One of the news reports had mentioned that the fallen climber's partner had hurled his own pack into the crater, hoping that it would land near his friend and provide extra supplies. Knowing this, I identified the first object as the partner's pack, which was mostly buried in a low drift. Fifty yards away, the second object was a set of unmoving arms sticking up out of the snow.

The chatter inside the aircraft intensified immediately. As we circled back, the fear expanded inside my chest at the thought of what our SAR medic would discover when he was lowered into the basin to investigate. We entered a hover over the second object, tucked up tightly against the inside wall of the crater. As expected, our rotor immediately went to work on all that beautiful, soft, fresh snow. Visibility went to zero in a matter of seconds. In overland SAR, the pilot nearest the terrain usually manipulates the controls since he or she has terrain to see and can keep a hover position alongside. On this day, my copilot was the man who had to make it happen. Once established in the hover, my copilot began asking to deploy smoke grenades, all three of which were thrown down immediately by the rescue crewmen.

"What the hell are you doing, man?" I shouted. Expending all of our smoke grenades at once was not normal practice. He answered, "I've got *nothing* to look at over here! I need some contrast on the snow!" Amidst the hurricane cloud of snow engulfing us, the low cloud layer directly above us, and the near vertical wall of white thirty feet beyond his window, my copilot was fighting with everything he had to maintain our position.

My copilot and the crewmen at the back of the aircraft were extremely skilled and experienced, but we were struggling with every nugget of information we had, and I could hear panic rising in everyone's voices; it was easy to see we were in a bad spot. To add insult to injury, a news helicopter now hovered in a patch of clear sky near the mouth of the crater, undoubtedly filming and photographing our every move. Great, I thought. Now if we crash, the entire world will get to watch it on the news tonight.

The smoke grenades weren't enough to give my copilot the references he was scouting for. The oscillating grew worse, panic continued to escalate, and we were quickly edging toward a loss of all control. As much as I wanted to get this person on board and put this whole story to rest, my better judgment prevailed. We stayed in that hover until the absolute last second that it was safe to do so, although thinking back, it was probably ten seconds longer than we should have. "Stop right, Sir!" the crewmen shouted. "Stop right, stop right!"

I glanced out my window to the left, away from the terrain, and saw a small hole under the clouds that had since crept down and was basically sitting on top of us. It was time to get the hell out of there, and this might be our only opportunity.

I didn't think twice, grabbed the controls, and began to slide the aircraft directly toward the blue opening. "I have controls! We're waving off!" I said. Out we flew, barely skirting the lava dome and sneaking out under the billowing clouds.

I was collected, but scared. My arms and hands had a violent tremor to them as I guided us away. That particular incident was one of only two times in my flying career that I truly thought I might crash in a matter of seconds. We exited the crater, reevaluated our situation, and talked about what had just happened. I was secretly relieved to find out that everyone in the crew agreed that my decision was the correct one. With fuel low, a shaky crew, and poor weather conditions, we decided to depart the scene for a refuel and hopefully give the clouds in the crater a chance to disperse.

After we landed in Portland, I called and briefed my boss on what we had seen and done. He now assumed what only my crew had observed: Our rescue mission had just become a recovery mission. Holding this information, we faced a tough decision. Do we tell the news stations what we saw and that we'd be sticking to our policy of not picking up dead bodies? Could we even say for sure that he was dead? Do we try to be heroes and get him on board? Was it worth the risk to my aircraft and crew? It wasn't entirely my decision, but I told my boss, "Sir, I'm 99 percent sure this guy is dead. If we don't get him today, though, he'll never be found. As soon as it snows another six inches, he's gone forever."

I was sure he'd tell me to head home as body recoveries are not in our playbook, but he surprised me. "Do you think you can safely get him out of there?" he asked. "Only if the clouds clear, Sir," I answered. "I need some visibility to make this work, which we didn't have last time." He snorted, then said, "Recharge your batteries and head back up there if you're comfortable. Don't do anything stupid trying to get this mission done. And as far as you know, he's still alive. Roger?" "Yes, Sir," I replied, understanding that a gentlemen's agreement had just been made.

My crew hid out and recouped in a back room at the airport, away from the throngs of reporters. I had briefed the crew upon landing that they were to talk to no one and assume nothing about the outcome. We debriefed on what we had experienced, focusing on how each crew member felt about continuing. The overwhelming response was to charge back into the fray and get the mission done. We constructed our approach, debated what needed to be done differently, and lastly, discussed our comfort limits.

When we returned to the crater, by the grace of God we found clear skies. We flew right to the victim's position, and the hover was not a problem now that we had solid ground reference. We deployed our SAR medic to proceed to the victim and evaluate his condition. We orbited above for mere moments before the crackle on the radio confirmed what we had thought. "Rescue Two, Rescue

Ground. We have an angel here. Ready for hoist pickup in ten," came the medic's report. There was silence in the aircraft. We had struggled as a crew for six hours to hopefully save this man's life, and now we knew for sure we wouldn't be doing that. We delivered the body to the local sheriff at the predetermined location, shielded from media coverage. The sheriff and his deputies expressed their profuse thanks for the assist and took custody of the body.

★ ★ ★

On every clear day of my childhood, I looked up at the south side of Mount St. Helens and thought what an amazing sight it was: snow-covered in the winter, bare in the summer, but jagged and broken all the time. At eleven years old, I watched as a large steam vent shot into the sky and created a flurry of rumor and mystery around town. During college, I climbed Mount St. Helens twice. Both times I stood on the summit staring down from exactly 1,500 feet above where I'd one day be hovering in a $20 million helicopter. What a view.

It will always be upsetting to our crew that the man we were sent to save was dead before we had a chance to save him. I didn't walk away from this feeling like a hero, but I didn't feel like a failure either. What I do know is that my decisions and the razor-sharp skills of my crew returned this man's body to his family and answered questions that otherwise they might have wrestled with for the rest of their lives.

I'm not a war hero. I haven't saved hundreds of lives in a massive, coordinated humanitarian effort, but I have been part of something powerful for a few and that justifies the investment I've made. Humanitarian service impacts people on a personal level. Although this was only one of hundreds of missions I will fly as a naval aviator, I know this man's family will remember this single mission forever. I used my education, military training, and an expensive piece of hardware to get the job done on my home turf. Not many people ever get that opportunity, and I know I'll cherish if forever.

Inland Sailor

Joshua Welle

———— ★ **★** ★ ————

"Wheels up!" the air crewman yelled. He was nineteen years old, with a blond streak of hair trimmed high and tight. Only his accent revealed the cowboy beneath the shine and polish of military professionalism. The C-130 Hercules roared at 440 mph. It was able to go into dangerous terrain night or day, making it the workhorse of the U.S. military logistics network.

This was my third visit to Afghanistan in six months, and although it was getting to be routine, it wasn't any less of a marathon. It was a sweaty and claustrophobic commute. I was thirsty, crammed inside with 125 other soldiers departing Ali al-Salem Air Base in Kuwait en route to Kandahar, Afghanistan. The 1,300-mile journey skirts Iranian air space and circles the shockingly beautiful Hindu Kush, a region most Americans will never see.

I was returning from an all-too-brief R&R at home with friends and family on a mid-deployment leave. At my departure, my mother cried as if I were going away for plebe summer while my dad maintained his typically stoic exterior even though he too was upset. I was returning to Afghanistan for another five months to support the International Security Assistance Force (ISAF), an international coalition formed and maintained in response to the 9/11 al-Qaeda attacks and in defense of other terrorist attacks in Madrid, London, and India. NATO had a UN mandate to establish good governance, internal security, and to sow the seeds of a democratic nation.

The touchdown at Kandahar Airfield was the culmination of a fancy combat landing. It felt like we were on a rollercoaster as the C-130 screamed high into the sky and then dropped low, finally swerving to a landing position. It is considered a combat maneuver because the plane shoots flares off the wings to distract any RPG strikes.

After helping unload the duffle bags, pallets of bullets, and rations, I called Maj. Fred Tanner, my best friend in country, to pick me up. As I waited with my body armor, an extra thirty pounds, I leaned against a protective barrier and thought back to the many unexpected twists and turns that had brought me, a Navy surface warfare officer, to this strange, remote place.

The opportunity had presented itself in July 2008. During a military fellowship at a think tank in Washington, D.C., I participated in a counterinsurgency (COIN) conference in which Afghanistan experts discussed U.S. policy. The guest of honor, Brig. Gen. John "Mick" Nicholson, presented lessons learned and battlefield perspectives from his recent command tour in eastern Afghanistan's Kunar and Nuristan provinces. General Nicholson captivated the audience with tactical insights and a genuine compassion for the Afghanistan mission and purpose. He believed that the only way to win over the Afghan people was to fight side-by-side with them against the Taliban. The warrior spirit and trust are at the center of the Pashtu culture, and the people deeply respect their elders who survived the war with the Russians and later the mujahidin. In General Nicholson's view, the best way to establish that trust was to fight, sometimes die, and soldier on with Afghan partners.

After the general's talk, I approached him at the roast beef buffet line and introduced myself. General Nicholson stood 6 feet 3 inches and looked like he could run a mile in a respectable 6:00. He had salt and pepper hair, a weathered and tanned face, and piercing blue eyes.

"Your talk was outstanding, Sir. I understand you're going to southern Afghanistan this fall. I'm going to Afghanistan in November. To Bagram," I said.

"That's great, Josh, what's your mission?" he asked, speaking to me as though he had a personal interest in me. I was elated to think that he might actually want to know about my small part of the Afghanistan mission.

"I am going to be the public affairs officer for CTF-101, serving as a visitor's officer," I said. This admission was a bit embarrassing for me considering that Nicholson had just served fifteen months as a battlefield commander. In essence, I was going to Afghanistan as a travel agent, albeit one facing high risks. Serving as a visitor's officer is not exactly Rambo duty, but it was closer to the fight, which was where I wanted to be. I sheepishly followed up: "It's not great, but the best I could get as a Navy guy, and I want to be in Afghanistan."

He could probably sense my dissatisfaction with the job. My best friends had already served two or three tours in Iraq and Afghanistan, and I was anxious to get closer to the conflict. Still, I was caught off guard when he asked, "Wanna join my team?" Even though I had half imagined that approaching him might lead to some kind of opportunity, I never assumed it actually would. I stuttered, "Uh . . . My tour is six months, Sir, how long will you be going?" I was a little worried that he would say fifteen months. The time commitment was a constraining variable because there was only a twelve-month window in my career "pipeline" in which I could detour from my surface warfare trajectory. At the time I didn't know that General Nicholson's "team" consisted of only four other officers. This number seemed insubstantial relative to the task they were assigned to accomplish. As I would discover, General Nicholson had been given special tasking from the senior levels of the Pentagon to usher incoming forces to the southern region should U.S. combat operations surge in Afghanistan.

"At least a year. Are you in?" he responded in a way that implied that anything less than a year would be short. In that moment I felt as though I was being asked a fairly straightforward question: "Josh, do you, or do you not, have a spine?" This was my Rubicon, a moment that would undoubtedly change my life, but I took mere seconds to respond: "Sir, I'm in. Let's do it, Sir." It was the only correct response.

"Outstanding," General Nicholson replied.

The time was August 2008, and although Barack Obama had not yet been elected president, the Department of Defense had already begun to focus more on Afghanistan than on Iraq, especially Afghanistan's southern region. The new president, Republican or Democrat, would need to decide whether to send 17,000 more troops to Kandahar and Helmand provinces.

At the COIN conference, I had told General Nicholson about my experience as a military fellow and about the master's degrees I had earned from the University of Maryland. I talked of my experience teaching political science at the Naval Academy and how I had proven myself as a capable communicator and staff officer. I'd also been at sea and had accumulated some "salt" as a surface warfare officer, particularly as an engineer officer in Yokosuka, Japan, managing the propulsion plant of a Navy cruiser. I was comfortable working in dynamic environments, and I had no problem doing grunt work. Maybe I *would* be a good fit to join his band of strategic planners.

General Nicholson filled me in on my new position. "Josh, you will have an important task. I want you to work in a SECDEF-endorsed Civil-Military Cell. It's brand-new. You will operate side-by-side with other nations' civilians and military officers and create a framework for economic development in southern Afghanistan. We start training with the NATO staff in Germany next month. I'll work to get your orders changed. We need you there." His small team consisted of three Army officers, a Marine lieutenant colonel, and now, me.

During the Afghanistan tour, I served as the CivMil Cell operation's boss, energy analyst, agricultural adviser, general's aide, infrastructure engineer, and strategic planner. With a tidal wave of soldiers and Marines inbound to Afghanistan, everyone, from the White House to congressional staffers, wanted to know more: What are the troops going to do? Where are they going to stay? How would we measure coalition success?

Joshua Welle conducts engagements with Afghan leaders, a key component of counterinsurgency operations in Afghanistan. (Courtesy Joshua Welle)

The team was General Nicholson's brain trust, and he was the voice back to Washington on daily operations in Kandahar and Helmand. The CivMil Cell became the node for information flowing up to coalition headquarters and the U.S. embassy and outward to provincial reconstruction teams, those responsible for rebuilding civil society. We were not rugged combat arms officers on patrol, but we had an important mission: We were interlocutors for senior officials who needed to know how to allocate assets for the president's renewed commitment to Afghanistan.

Australia, Canada, Denmark, Great Britain, the Netherlands, and Romania were all key stakeholders and had participants in the CivMil Cell. During our NATO training in Germany months prior to deployment, we met experienced Afghanistan experts responsible for teaching inbound troops the social and economic dynamics of the region. Rodney Cocks, a former Australian army veteran working for the British government in Kabul, was a crucial link for General Nicholson as he established the first joint interoperability task force to address the nexus of crime, narcotics, and corrupt government officials. Sarah Chayes was also an irreplaceable adviser in Kabul. A former National Public Radio correspondent, she moved to ISAF headquarters to help advance good governance throughout the provinces. Both Rodney and Sarah would become close friends in-country and my knowledge-link to Kabul.

In ten months' time, the U.S. secretary of defense and chairman of the Joint Chiefs, the British prime minister, and the NATO secretary general all made trips to meet General Nicholson. In some of these meetings, I was a fly on the wall; in others I was a briefer and participant. My job put me face-to-face with congressional representatives and had me playing email tag with colonels in Kabul and Washington. Everyone wanted to know the plan, and we were the "subject matter experts." We did not, however, limit our communications to only senators, representatives, and colonels. We also talked to pomegranate farmers, grocers, Afghan contractors, foreign military staff officers, and non-governmental organizations to explain the tactical dynamics on the ground. Knowing the supply chain of the farmers or the value chain of exported goods fed into the detailed regional economic strategy that would enable a physical corridor, bringing goods to market to and from Pakistan.

Early in my tour, we befriended a U.S.-Canadian contractor working to improve pomegranate farming in rural areas outside Kandahar City. He worked with brave men who had been hardened by the elements and were desperate to have their contracts renewed by the U.S. Agency for International Development (USAID). At one meeting in the RC-South Compound, I took notes as the growers briefed General Nicholson. Their pictures showed Afghans working on farms, nurturing and packaging pomegranates for export to Dubai. These men seemed genuine, but they were a few of hundreds trying to tap into the flood of aid provided by the U.S. government.

In some ways, my job was a bit like an MBA case study analysis combined with Hollywood event planning and a layer of danger to boot; we typically had to fly at low levels in a UH-60 Blackhawk to support off-base missions. We were always trying to further General Nicholson's vision and affect positive Afghan-led change. Our focus areas were power generation, water development, and agriculture value chains. In addition, whenever a visitor was expected from abroad, oftentimes a well-known news anchor or columnist, the CivMil Cell would be asked to brief him or her on the "southern strategy," which was a comprehensive approach to stability operations and unified military and economic operations— shape, clear, hold, build.

As the workload increased for General Nicholson and my experienced British civilian boss, Philip Hatton, so did the output of the team. I frequently depended on skills I'd acquired at the Naval Academy for travel to remote outposts, dangerous convoys, and facilitating dialogue between Afghans and the coalition. When faced with a question at the Academy, we'd only been allowed five basic responses: "Yes, Sir." "No, Sir." "Aye, aye, Sir." "No excuse, Sir." "I'll find out, Sir." The most important lessons I'd learned as a plebe were resourcefulness and gumption, and they served me well on this tour.

The CivMil Cell's mandate allowed the creation of a strategy that exceeded the boundaries of the formerly dominant provincial mindset. Helmand's provincial strategy had been controlled by the British prior to 2009, and their counter-narcotics, agriculture, and security strategy had stopped at a border that most Afghan tribes did not in any case recognize. Kandahar province was managed by the Canadians, whose country had a tailored approach to reconstruction. Uruzgon and Zabul were controlled by the Dutch and Romanians, respectively. Meeting with key provincial civilian leaders, we brought together coalition partners at every turn and began to reap the benefits. Our coalition team developed detailed energy and agricultural analyses used to formulate President Obama's Afghan strategy documents, which would later unleash economic opportunities in Helmand and Kandahar and all the way to Spin Boldak, the cross-border town and economic center linked to Pakistan.

As part of our analysis of the region's resources, we took a closer look at the Kajaki dam, a strategic node for economic development in southern Afghanistan, but one that had had problems keeping the water flowing. Taliban fighters had planted improvised explosive devices along the roads leading toward the facility, and the Afghan government only had control of a five-mile radius of the facility. Our task was to assess the economic viability of the dam and prioritize its rehabilitation within the broader southern strategy.

Our post-Soviet helicopter circled the dam and began its descent into Kajaki. Andrew Scyner, a Canadian development specialist, 1st Lt. Russ Grant, an Army reservist handpicked by General Nicholson from IBM Strategy, and Marcus Knuth, a Danish civil affairs officer, were all part of the project team. Upon landing, we were picked up by a convoy of dilapidated trucks and driven a mile to the generator facility. Defense contractors lined the helicopter pad and were perched on the back of pickup trucks, ever vigilant of Taliban fighters, who were no fewer than three miles away.

For six hours we toured the facility. We went deep into the caverns of the sluicing system, along the bottoms of the fifty-foot generator consoles, and to the island tower eight hundred feet inward of the lake where the valve controls are managed. We were told that USAID had built the Kajaki dam in the 1950s and that a massive, electrical turbine generator had been installed in 1972. The foreman was Asad Fisulla, a fifty-six-year-old engineer who had been living and working around the plant since he was a teenager and could tell us what it had been like in the 1970s.

The facility was showing its age, but I could tell it was still highly functional. With only one turbine online, generator output was at fifty megawatts for all of

Helmand's and Kandahar's 1.4 million residents. If the Taliban could be stopped from siphoning off power and destroying power lines, output could be tripled. Power was needed for economic growth, and economic growth was needed to get young Afghan men away from the madrasas where they were training to be Taliban fighters. The NATO generals had to decide whether high casualties were worth the risk to escort the remaining material up to Kajaki to repair the dam.

I realized that I was inspecting more than just a dam; I was inspecting the potential of a society to reinvent itself. Our team knew that reconstruction was desperately needed for the area to sustain any industrial development. In the end, we advised that the coalition subsidize generators rather than risk lives trying to clear the area leading to Kajaki.

In the final days of my time in Afghanistan, when our team needed more troops, I was reminded of the real sacrifices of military service. General Nicholson often said, "Things in the South will get worse before they get better. There will be more casualties when the U.S. sends in more troops." The high-level briefings, the grueling trips to the outer provinces, and the fear felt while serving in a combat zone do not compare to the grief of having a comrade killed in action. During my tour, I watched more than fifty coalition troops flown out in caskets.

In late June 2009, a West Point 2002 graduate and three soldiers from Crazy Horse Company died from an IED attack. A week later, a British combat engineer and friend, Ben Babbington-Browne, was lost in a helicopter crash outside Kandahar City. By the end of the month, July 2009, the surge of Marines who deployed lost their first soldier in Helmand province.

The funeral ceremonies, or what we called ramp ceremonies, tore at my heart. Whenever one was held, no matter what time of day, the entire base would shut down to pay last respects to the fallen. In the early part of my tour, I attended several midnight formations in subfreezing temperatures. In July, ceremonies continued even though it was a blistering 115 degrees on the tarmac. The eulogies were read in the casualty victim's native language, and we all saluted the heroes as they made their final taxi out of Afghanistan.

I vividly recall the Dutch sergeant major barking with a thick accent, "Haand . . . Sal-oote." Immediately, twelve hundred soldiers snapped upward with sharp salutes in honor of their fallen colleague. We sweat together as we held the salute. On my left was Jason Lewis-Berry, a Portland native who had left the moviemaking industry to be a State Department stabilization officer. On my right was Vicki Ferg, a Canadian reservist on a four-month rotation. Behind me stood Brian Madden, a USNA 2002 graduate, EOD supply officer, and the former star quarterback of the Navy football team. The composition of the group was surreal. How did we all end up here?

It didn't matter. We were reminded of our common purpose as we held a bicep parallel to the deck and a forearm canted at a forty-five-degree angle. As we listened to another nation's national anthem, we were all swelling with sadness for a fallen comrade and pride in our service. The sacrifice would be respected and remembered.

"Ready, Toooo. Troops—Fall out." Time to get back to work, the mission must go on.

PART V

★ ★ ★

INTEGRITY, TEAMWORK, AND SACRIFICE

It's not what we eat but what we digest that makes us strong; not what we gain but what we save that makes us rich; not what we read but what we remember that makes us learned; and not what we profess but what we practice that gives us integrity.

FRANCIS BACON

"Integrity" is a technical term sailors use to describe a ship's ability to right itself under the pressure of wind and sea. Certainly, the integrity of a ship can be threatened by enemy attack from the air, but the ship can also sink due to neglecting issues below the waterline. As with all things in life, it is often the unseen threat that is the most insidious. The unseen threat below the waterline—dust, rust, and unattended alarms—is the perfect analogy for the personal leadership challenges faced when no one is looking. As servicemen and servicewomen have all discovered, leadership, in the end, relies on personal integrity.

Teamwork is a value needed in complicated situations. The best teams are formed through the training, hard work, and dedication of its members. The concept of "team" in the U.S. military is at the core of its success as an organization. Not only do all the branches of service work together—referred to in military parlance as "joint"—but individual members often deploy in support of another service. Many from the Naval Academy Class of 2002 experienced this, serving as supporting members in Army units.

Sacrifice is sometimes essential when integrity is tested. Nothing good is ever achieved without a little bit of pain, some sweat, and often some tears. The trials experienced leading up to triumph are often what make a big win so satisfying. A leader who has integrity will never sacrifice life or treasure unless there is the potential for much greater gain. A good military leader must also be willing to sacrifice his or her personal rewards in the interest of the country.

The sailor or soldier deployed for six to nine months three times in four years is but one example. These young men and women truly give their lives for country, even if not through death. They spend weeks and months away from spouses and children, setting aside the comforts a normal life in service to their country and the Constitution. The dark sides of these sacrifices are broken marriages, posttraumatic stress disorder, depression, and estrangement. All are part of the sacrifices sailors and soldiers make while serving and the burdens they continue to carry after service.

The greatest sacrifice is for those who, as Lincoln described it, give their "last full measure of devotion" to the United States. It is impossible to understand fully how a mother or father feels when a military chaplain arrives at the door to announce that a son or daughter has perished on the battlefield, how a young widow copes with the news of the loss of her partner, or how a toddler grows up never knowing the guiding touch of his mother's or father's hand. The men and women in the armed forces know the risks when they sign up to serve. They also know that if they don't do it, there might not be anyone else ready and willing to fight so their families can continue to experience the American way of life.

Sacrifices for Country

Alex Katauskas

It was early afternoon, but it was already getting dark. I looked down and inspected my Class A green uniform one last time. I had spent the preceding hour obsessing over every insignia, ribbon, and rogue thread. Infantry insignia: centered five-eighths of an inch below the notch on my collar; U.S. insignia, captain insignia, unit crest, all meticulously placed within an eighth of an inch; ribbons pinned exactly an eighth of an inch above my left breast pocket. I'd used a Bic lighter to burn off the fraying threads that Navy folk call Irish pennants or IPs. I finished by using a roll of packing tape wrapped around my hand to remove every fleck of lint.

Never before, for an inspection or ceremony, had I cared so much about the minute details of this, my uniform, and never before had I felt so clearly the honor that it conveyed. Had the moment not been so heavy, I would have smiled at a job well done. I knew, however, that in this uniform on this day I would conduct the most difficult mission of my young military career.

★ ★ ★

In the fall of 2004, I transferred from the Navy to the Army and went from being a lieutenant junior grade to being a first lieutenant. After completing Infantry Officer Basic Course, I moved to Fort Richardson, Alaska, near Anchorage. In Alaska, I served as a rifle platoon leader in the 3rd Battalion, 509th Airborne Infantry. A few months before my unit deployed to Iraq in the fall of 2006, I was selected to be the battalion rear detachment commander for the first half of the battalion's yearlong deployment. This was not a duty that I had requested, and I felt guilty and a bit disappointed that I would not be accompanying my unit into combat (at least not initially). As rear detachment commander, I would serve as the commander of all those soldiers who were to remain behind, whether for medical, disciplinary, or administrative reasons. I was also supposed to train replacement soldiers who reported to the unit throughout the deployment. In addition, I would serve as the liaison between the deployed unit and the Family

Readiness Group (FRG), consisting of spouses and family members. This meant sending out information on the unit when available and trying to help any FRG members with problems they were having. Lastly, I had to serve as casualty notification officer, which would prove to be my most challenging duty.

As a casualty notification officer, I would be notifying the families when their soldiers had been wounded or killed in action. In the case of a wounded soldier, I would make a telephone call. When a soldier from our battalion was killed in action, I had to notify the family face to face, dressed in formal Army attire, with an Army chaplain present. I dearly hoped that I would not have to perform this duty, but in my gut I knew it was pretty much inevitable. The Army gave me some training on casualty notification, but there is only so much that you can learn on paper. Performing the duty itself turned out to be a whole different challenge, one for which nothing in my previous military experience had prepared me.

My first killed in action (KIA) notification came a few months into my unit's deployment, in the winter of 2006. It was a Sunday afternoon when I received the call from the U.S. Army Alaska Casualty Assistance Center that Sgt. Brennan C. Gibson had just been killed by an improvised explosive device (IED) while on patrol in Baghdad.

Senior officers had been telling me that a KIA was inevitable and to be prepared for it, but how does one do that? It felt as if I had a hole in my stomach; at the same time, a slight feeling of nausea came over me as I considered what I would have to do next. I checked and double-checked my Class A green uniform to make sure that it was in immaculate condition. Pride in the uniform, whether Navy, Army, Air Force, or Marines, takes on a lot more meaning after those you serve with die while wearing it. It represents the ideals and values that they died to protect. Even if no one had noticed a flaw in my uniform, I would have known, and that was unacceptable to me.

I drove to the Casualty Assistance Center at Fort Richardson to receive my briefing. There I met the chaplain who would accompany me for the notification. He was a lieutenant colonel who had done this quite a few times. In the briefing, we learned the specific circumstances of Sergeant Gibson's death and received the script that we would read to his wife. I had memorized it already and knew the procedure, but since this was the real thing, it was good to hear it one more time. We also learned that Gibson had a child who had been born shortly before he deployed. We then drove the white government SUV to Mrs. Gibson's home. She lived in post housing on Fort Richardson, so the entire ride lasted only a few minutes. I would have appreciated a longer drive during which to collect my thoughts, although I doubt any amount of time would have been enough.

The evening was young, but in the Alaskan winter it was already dark outside. When we arrived at the house, we could see that Mrs. Gibson had friends over for

Sunday dinner, most likely other wives from our battalion. I thought this was a good thing, since at least she wouldn't have to be alone after the notification. We parked the SUV in front of the house and walked up the steps to the front door. I saw through the window that one of the other wives saw us coming. The look on her face told me she knew why we were there. We rang the doorbell, and the sergeant's wife opened the door. We had met briefly at one of the FRG meetings, so she knew who I was. It took her a moment to realize what was going on. I asked if we could come in.

She did not cry at first, but stood, expressionless, in a state of shock. I asked her if she wanted to sit down. She said yes and had a seat at the kitchen table. The two other wives who were there gathered around her for support. One woman, whose husband was in the same squad as Sergeant Gibson, asked if anything had happened to her husband. I knew that he had been injured but did not know the details. When conducting a notification, the families of those killed in an attack must be notified before the families of the injured are notified. I told her that I believed he was injured and that she would be receiving a notification over the phone with the details. She was visibly shaken by this news, but she did her best to comfort her friend. I then took a deep breath and recited from memory the notification script:

> The Secretary of the Army has asked me to express his deepest regret that your husband, Sgt. Brennan C. Gibson, was killed in action in Baghdad, Iraq, on 10 December 2006. While conducting a combat patrol, his Humvee was struck by an improvised explosive device. The secretary extends his deepest sympathy to you and your family in your tragic loss.

I barely got through the notification without my voice cracking; my stomach was in knots. She had started to cry as I read the script—not sobbing, but tears flowed down her face. The truth was setting in, but she was trying to be strong. The chaplain then sat at the table and talked with her for a bit. He offered to stay as long as she wanted, but she declined the offer, saying that she had her friends there and that she wanted to call her family. I think she wanted us out of the house as quickly as possible, which was understandable. We departed and drove back to the Casualty Assistance Center to deliver our report. My first KIA notification had been completed, and I hoped I would never have to do another one. It had been worse than I had imagined, and I don't think there was anything that could have prepared me for it.

About a month later, in January 2007, I received a call that another of our soldiers had been killed in action. This time it was Spc. Jeffrey D. Bisson of Vista, California. He was killed when his vehicle struck an IED in Karma, Iraq, on January 20, 2007. He was twenty-two years old. Specialist Bisson had been a soldier in my platoon, one of the thirty-seven soldiers for whom I was responsible, when I was a platoon leader in A Company, 3rd Battalion, 509th Infantry (ABN). He was a really quiet guy, a good soldier. I also knew his wife, an outspoken woman not yet twenty years old who would often come to the battalion rear detachment office to visit. The day before I received the call about her husband, she had brought brownies to my rear detachment office for the soldiers working there.

Once again I prepared my uniform, making sure it was in perfect condition, and went to meet the duty chaplain. This time it was a major, a soft-spoken man who gave the impression that he would be good at providing comfort to a grieving family. We began the drive to Anchorage, where Mrs. Bisson lived, and I considered how, as difficult as the first notification was, this would be even harder. The chaplain had experience with casualty notifications, and his easy manner relieved some of the tension I'm sure we both felt. We talked on the way over about his life and experiences, though we both grew quiet as I turned the SUV into the apartment complex.

We parked and knocked on the door. It was a little before noon on a Saturday. Mrs. Bisson opened the door and for a brief moment thought that I had just stopped by to check on her. She gave us a small smile and was about to ask us inside, then a puzzled look came over her face. She noticed the uniform, and the chaplain next to me, and it began to register. I took a deep breath, knowing that if I didn't proceed immediately, I might not be able to proceed at all:

> The secretary of the Army has asked me to express his deepest regret that your husband, Spc. Jeffrey D. Bisson, was killed in action in Karma, Iraq, on 20 January 2007. While conducting a combat patrol his Humvee was struck by an improvised explosive device. The secretary extends his deepest sympathy to you and your family in your tragic loss.

She stood in shock and did not cry immediately. She then sat down on the couch, saying that she knew something had happened, that she had felt it. She had talked with him a couple of days before, and she said he had sounded good, but over the last few days she had felt a growing sense of unease.

Mrs. Bisson was from Anchorage, and her family lived nearby, so she called her parents, and they came over immediately. She then called the rest of her relatives to tell them the news. At the same time, in California, another set of casualty notification officers was paying a visit to Specialist Bisson's parents. The chaplain and I stayed longer this time; she wanted us there. I think it was because she knew me, and the chaplain had a calming way about him. She reminisced with us about Jeffrey, and I shared some of the memories I had of him from when I was his platoon leader. She would laugh for a bit when she remembered something funny he had done, but then she would become very quiet. We had been there a while, and she was becoming exhausted, emotionally and physically, so we left. Her parents stayed to comfort her.

Thankfully, that was the last KIA notification I had to do before I handed over command of the rear detachment and deployed to Iraq. As difficult and emotionally challenging as it was to serve as a casualty notification officer, I was honored to do it. It is the least amount of respect that soldiers, spouses, and parents deserve. It is a duty I hope to never do again, but I feel it is something that every officer should have to do at least once. That way they can experience the cost of war in a different way. We in the military usually feel the pain from the loss of a comrade in arms or a shipmate under our command. While that fills us with a deep sadness, it is quite a different thing to witness the loss felt by a wife, husband, mother, or father. Our loss of a shipmate pales in comparison, a fact all combat leaders would do well to remember.

Sometimes Dreams Do Come True

Carol A. Andersen

R ichard was a G.I. Joe and Microforce kid. He and his friends would play for hours, and I would occasionally find Sgt. Slaughter or a comrade safely tucked away between two cushions—or rock formations, depending on your point of view. He enjoyed building model airplanes and helicopters and of one day flying the real thing, and dreamed of attending the United States Naval Academy.

As always, hard work and focus was the order of the day, but this was never a difficult task for Richard. Part of his enjoyment of life was applying hard work and focus to every task he endeavored or had thrust upon him, and he did it all with a smile and a warm heart. As an NJROTC officer in high school, he earned the respect of all in the unit for his intelligence and nonjudgmental attitude, and his ability to make one want to strive a little harder. A few years later, we were reminded of all this, and were so proud.

Apply, accepted, depart—looking back it all seems to have happened so quickly. The Naval Academy beckoned, and Richard, like so many eager others, went forth into the jaws of plebe summer. The degradation of no hair, a silly hat, and a too big uniform, marching, drilling, push-ups, more, more and more push-ups, humiliation, square your shoulders, square your step, square your arm to eat—he loved it. Well, maybe not at the time, but at Parent's Weekend, the smile that greeted his father, his sisters, and me said it all. "We have endured, and will continue on," and they were all so bright and beautiful to behold.

Four grueling and demanding years don't go by so quickly, but one day (sometimes, I think, only yesterday), we watched them once again in their final march on Graduation Day. He had grown in so many ways over these years—physically, mentally. And yet, that inner strength and sense of honor he possessed all his life, his smile, his sense of humor, his humility had not changed, and I saw before me not only a naval officer who had become part of the glorious history of the Naval Academy, but my little boy.

Orders arrive; duty calls. Ensign Andersen spent the next two years in training at Pensacola, Corpus Christi, and Milton. He and his instructor flew from Pensacola to Norfolk one day, and his dad and I got to see him. You know—pictures with him and us, pictures with him and the jet, pictures of them taking off for their return flight. I wonder how it's possible that so much love and pride can be attached to such an insignificant moment in life. Anyway, Richard eventually chose helicopters and was off to Milton.

After he was winged and that childhood dream had become a reality, Lt. (jg) Andersen completed NATOPS and SERE at North Island and Naval Justice School in San Diego before receiving orders to HS-7, the Dusty Dogs, in Jacksonville. He enjoyed being in the squadron. He found it challenging and liked the guys he worked with, and when he called or could come home, we thoroughly enjoyed hearing about his life that we were no longer a part of. I could tell from that wonderful and sometimes mischievous smile that he was where he belonged.

When Katrina hit the Gulf of Mexico, HS-7 was one of many squadrons called in to support the hurricane relief efforts. Richard found this gratifying, but wished that there was more they could do. He wrote an article, "Behind the Heroes," in which he said that "a hero is not just one who goes in harm's way" but "anyone who takes a strain to get a job done, . . . whose actions are worthy of the respect of others." He was speaking of the maintenance crews who kept the pilots and aircrew on the job. He spoke of how the Dusty maintainers worked arduous hours, taking on roles in addition to their regular maintenance duties, and "rose to the occasion," and how maintainers from several squadrons put aside rivalries and worked together to get the job done. He did, temporarily, lose his computer at this time, and for Richard, this could be a "damn the torpedoes" kind of moment. Before they embarked on rescue missions, they dropped off their gear on the USS *Truman,* which was also hosting news crews. Apparently, when the news crews departed, someone accidentally picked up Richard's computer bag, which was the equivalent of his firstborn. When it was finally located several days later with the help of several people on each ship, to say that Richard was ecstatically happy would be an understatement. A couple of years later, guys from the squadron would confirm that this was all true.

Yosemite National Park has always been a favorite vacation spot for our family, but none of us had ever trekked to the top of Half Dome. The summer of '06, Richard and his father decided to change all that and set out on their "guy thing." They had a wonderful time, and although his dad didn't quite make it, Richard made it to the summit to take in the beauty around him. Two years later, his father would make the trip once again to finish a journey he started with his son, to stand where Richard once stood and see through Richard's eyes.

Richard's older sister had gotten engaged to be married that spring, and since HS-7 was scheduled to deploy sometime in the coming year, her wedding was planned for that same summer of '06. We could not take the chance that Richard wouldn't be able to attend because he was involved in training cruises or deployed, and looking back, we were all so grateful for that decision. The following March, his cousin also got married in Jacksonville, and Richard got to attend yet another very special family event, the kind of thing he always loved.

One evening in the middle of April '07, his father and I impatiently waited for him to call. The USS *Truman* was scheduled to return from a training cruise and with it HS-7. We would pick him up at the ship and take him for some dinner before they returned to JAX, which would be the last time we'd see him before the squadron left for Fallon, Nevada, in a couple of weeks. He finally called, and as always, I could not wait to put my arms around this young man—our boy.

One might wonder how such a little thing as entering an Applebee's restaurant can become worthy of a full measure of pride. Sometimes the little things are a great deal of what a mother might reason, and when I heard so many young enlisted people greeting my son with "Hello, Mr. Andersen," "Good evening, Sir," or "Hi, Lieutenant," I heard in their voices a great respect and a strong liking for our son, and once again felt the pangs of loving pride. When we dropped him off back at the ship, I asked my husband to wait a moment so I could watch him until he was through the gate. My mind reasoned that we might not see him for a very long time, and that I would miss him so much.

The squadron left Jacksonville for Fallon a week or so later. The last we and his sisters spoke to him was Saturday, 28 April—his birthday. He and some of the guys were just arriving in Las Vegas where they had decided to spend a day before work began at Fallon. He sounded happy. Why not; twenty-seven years old, setting off on a new adventure, work that he loved, people he liked, life ahead of him. He wrote in an email a couple of weeks earlier about being in the desert and "doing a lot of cool low level flying. It'll be busy, but it'll be worth it," he said. They would be practicing search and rescue in preparation for the upcoming cruise to the Persian Gulf.

Sometime during Monday night, or rather the wee morning hours of Tuesday, 8 May, I had a dream. I dreamed that I heard a commotion outside Richard's bedroom window and went to look. I saw two people in silhouette in our backyard, one with very dark hair, one with light. They spoke, and the one with light hair turned and walked away, and the one with dark hair became very angry. I won't go into the rest of the dream because it became quite frightening, and before I finally fell back to sleep, I couldn't help but wonder what the hell that was all about.

Maybe something, maybe nothing, but I thought of that dream when I opened our front door at about 9:30 a.m. and saw five uniforms standing there.

Someone asked if they could come in, and I said no. Maybe if I didn't let them in, it didn't happen. Richard's younger sister had just come home for a couple of days. She loves him so much, and this would devastate her. I yelled for my husband; I don't remember why he was home that day, a Tuesday, but he was. I yelled again for him; where was he, make this stop. When I finally saw him behind me and heard his sharp intake of breath, I let them in.

Richard, his CO, and three crewmembers had died in the desert the previous evening in a naval "mishap." We would learn so much more about this later, but frankly, at the time, how didn't seem to matter. Richard was gone, and life would never be the same. It's so true that children should never die before their parents, but it happens all the time, doesn't it. Young, bright, beautiful lives—snuffed out; gone from our yearning arms in a moment. That pure and wonderful mind and heart, that contagious smile, that patience and unlimited supply of love and caring—all gone, except in memory.

I didn't mention it earlier, but I had another dream about a year and a half before. I dreamed that Richard was going to die, and I'm pretty sure part of it took place at the Naval Academy. "Bunk" you might say, or "Oh yeah, sure," but I did. I tried to put it out of my mind because, after all, it was just a dream, wasn't it? I told myself God would never let anything happen to Richard even though it sometimes nagged at the back of my mind and tugged at my heart. I guess all kinds of dreams can come true.

Richard was buried the following Monday after Dover released his body. The previous day was Mother's Day, and thankfully, I didn't even know it. Much of the week is a blur, but the things I remember most are all the wonderful things that were said about him. Funerals are a time for saying nice things about the departed, aren't they, but the one thing that stays in my mind is the consistency of those precious comments about his good heart and kind ways, his desire to help, his ability to be nonjudgmental.

A young lieutenant from his squadron asked to speak on Richard's behalf at a memorial service out in Fallon, and later sent us an email and a copy of his comments. He said that he and his wife cared a great deal about Richard, and that "he was a truly good man." "What I saw was a quiet man, a humble man," he said, "without bitterness or ill will toward anyone." He called him kind, giving, forgiving, selfless, and said that his was a life worth emulating, and that he would always strive to be the man Richard was. I was so proud to know that others saw in him what I had always seen, and that Richard's life had, in some small way, touched so many we spoke with.

So—even though "Why?" never gets answered, faith is shaken, and a world gets turned upside down, it's true that life goes on. Richard lives in our memories now, and oh, what wonderful memories they are. I miss him more than anyone could ever imagine, and hope with every breath in me that I'll see him again someday. Do I wish I had encouraged him to choose another path? For myself—selfishly, yes; for him—no; he was doing what he dreamed of, and I think he was happy.

Strangely, when he was still at the Academy, he called me one day about his class ring order. I had requested to have his ring engraved with his name and "May God grant you strength, wisdom and long life." He said that the engraver could not accommodate all of that, and so it would only have his name and "May God grant strength and wisdom." He did. I don't pray a whole lot anymore; not yet, not ready, but I do wish fair winds and following seas to all of his mates and to Richard, our beloved son, wherever he may be.

Richard Andersen walks the streets of New Orleans. He was one of the pilots who flew in after Hurricane Katrina to support the thousands of people stranded and in need of assistance. (Courtesy Andersen family)

Forward Deployed to . . . Louisiana?

Kevin Stepp

I t was the Friday before Labor Day weekend in 2005, and swarms of people filled Raleigh-Durham International Airport, all anxious to visit their friends and family for the holiday. I too was fighting the crowds because I had been granted a well-deserved three-day leave to attend a friend's wedding in Colorado.

For the past three months, my unit—1st Battalion, 8th Marines (1/8, pronounced "One Eight")—had been stagnant because we assumed the duties as Alert Contingency Marine (ACM) Air Ground Task Force, the continental version of the forward-deployed Marine Expeditionary Units. While serving as the ACM battalion, all of our equipment (personal gear included) remained at the battalion headquarters, serialized and packed out, ready for any emergency in the Western Hemisphere. We maintained a constant state of readiness, deployable in six hours. It was only because of my commanding officer's compassion that I was untethered for this personal event.

From the terminal window, I watched my bag ascend the conveyor belt into the plane's belly. My row was called for boarding, so I joined the queue, boarding pass in hand. All the while, the televisions in the terminal blared with a constant stream of news about a deadly hurricane in New Orleans. Hurricane Katrina had flattened cities and townships all along the Gulf Coast; the levees on Lake Pontchartrain were breached, releasing floodwaters to cover New Orleans; families from Alabama to Louisiana waited and hoped for emergency crews to rescue their loved ones and restore essential services. Just as I approached the steward taking boarding passes, my cell phone rang.

"Hello?"

"Sir, it's Corporal Glover. We've been recalled. You have to come back. We're deploying to Louisiana."

★ ★ ★

A year prior, the battalion had returned from a seven-month deployment in support of Operation Iraqi Freedom. The Marines of 1/8 had fought with the 1st

Marine Division, primarily in the contested areas of Fallujah. These Marines were among the most combat-tested on the East Coast. In October 2005, the battalion was supposed to begin training for missions with the 24th Marine Expeditionary Unit. But what now?

We were on a new type of mission. As I sat listening to the drone of the engines in the darkness of the C-130 inbound for Louisiana, I looked around at the men of the battalion dressed in body armor, combat loaded, and sitting silently. I contemplated the gravity and scope of the mission we were about to conduct. Our task was unknown, intangible, and unfamiliar. Who was the enemy? Was there an enemy? We were in "condition one"—magazine inserted, round chambered, and weapon safe. We had heard reports of looting and murders. Could these stories be true? Was it up to *us* to enforce martial law in a U.S. city? In Iraq, the mission had been clear: Destroy the enemy to save the city. Normal rules of engagement (ROE) could not be applied in the French Quarter.

The New Orleans mission was planned in the same methodical manner that Marines use when going into battle. Even the medical officer took it extremely seriously: "Each Marine will receive a hepatitis shot prior to entry and following egress from the city of New Orleans," he said. "We will establish a medical and decontamination facility at the entry control point." This military control was to take place on the same streets where tipsy sorority girls used to flash enthusiastic Mardi Gras party-goers for prized beads.

We landed in Slidell, Louisiana, on an airstrip lit with chem lights because the nearby power plant was flooded. We immediately started to unpack the gear and stage equipment for convoys into New Orleans. As the sun began to rise over Slidell, the tremendous devastation came into full view. Anything not bolted to the ground had been tossed by the heavy winds. Boats and refrigerators hung like Christmas ornaments in the trees lining the streets and filled the backyards of the neighborhoods. Cars were not parked on curbs or driveways; they were in yards, behind houses, or "parked" halfway in living rooms. Fallen trees had ripped homes in two. Plate glass windows were destroyed. Oil, water, and a menagerie of chemicals had been mixed into soups that filled the gutters and walkways and were waist-deep in the streets. The heaviest hit area, the township of Irish Bayou, on the northeast coast of Lake Pontchartrain, had been gutted and laid flat. Nothing but the skeletons of the homes remained.

It quickly became clear that our mission was not what we had originally thought. Louisiana didn't need martial law; it needed divine intervention. We put down our weapons, picked up shovels, and began looking for anyone who needed assistance. We dug up rubble to release people in duress and helped others get their cars out of ditches so they could try to move on to help others.

The work in and around New Orleans involved a variety of efforts. Almost everything was being coordinated by local police, mayors, and civic leaders. Areas not flooded by water were flooded with Marines wielding sanitation and medical supplies and chainsaws. Local leaders led us to areas where trees and debris had to be cleared to provide residents access to their homes. Marines cut trees free from roofs, cleared roads, and helped distinguish trash from treasure for those unwilling to leave the hazardous zone.

The first few nights, we slept on the tile floor of a semi-flooded warehouse now emptied of any merchandise worth salvaging. Later we moved to the grassy expanse of the NASA assembly facility in Michoud, Louisiana. We would spend two to three days in one area and then move to a different area to assess damage, establish communications, and provide initial relief until local authorities could set up support services.

The flooding in New Orleans was subsiding slower than expected, but we were making progress. Then, as if conditions weren't bad enough, the water became a stagnant soup-like mixture of oil, mud, tree branches, and debris broken free from and within homes. The damage to structures and civilians was monumental. Houses and other buildings in the city were flooded to the rooftops, and people were trapped for days. People's possessions floated down roads, which now acted as canals. The putrid, fetid water grew worse each day, sickening hundreds of people. Our priorities shifted from disaster cleanup to rescue 9-1-1. Our commanding officer ordered the Marines to load up amphibious assault vehicles to rescue trapped citizens and to survey homes and facilities. We had to gear up to push through harsh terrain to save lives.

★ ★ ★

As the rescue effort progressed, another important mission was on the minds of many Marines. Nine months prior to Katrina, a member of 1/8 had lost his life on the streets of Fallujah while defending the city. LCpl. Bradley J. Faircloth was revered as a strong, courageous, and fun-loving Marine. The morning that we arrived in Louisiana, we learned that Faircloth's mother, Kathleen, in Mobile, Alabama, had suffered significant damage to her home as Katrina swept the Gulf Coast. We couldn't divert resources to our fallen brother's family in the first seventy-two hours, but when there was sufficient stability, we sent a team to find the Faircloth family and provide special support. The members of Bradley's platoon, using a private plane out of Slidell donated for the task, flew more than 115 miles to Mobile for a thirty-six-hour mission to clean up and fix Kathleen Faircloth's home. It was an unconventional mission, but one that upheld the Marine Corps' sense of brotherhood. We look out for our own—especially those who have paid the ultimate sacrifice.

During the thirty-six hours, the Marines had the opportunity to share with Kathleen their memories of Bradley and stories from the battle of Fallujah. Though it is painful to hear the facts of combat, most widowed mothers want to know some of the details. They want to know how their sons died. These stories often sustain families. They are honored to know that their sons died bravely.

The battalion's mission in New Orleans started with a declaration of martial law and ended with Marines extending hands of service to the neediest citizens. Nearly every aspect of the mission was challenging in new and unexpected ways. The Marines of 1/8 take pride in answering the call to serve, wherever, whenever.

Working Where the Land Meets the Sky

Katherine Kranz

hough fighter aircraft are a crucial part of naval aviation, most winged aviators do not end up strapped into the cockpit of a sexy fighter jet. Most are tasked with other unique missions within the naval aviation community that focus on supporting the war fighter. Some of the officers who graduated with the USNA Class of 2002 would enter the fray in the Middle East almost immediately as division officers on ships or submarines in the Persian Gulf or as leaders of Marines on the ground. For others, it would take longer to arrive at the "tip of the spear." For me, between syllabus training time and a weak stomach, it would take almost three years before I could earn sea duty pay.

When I packed up my car in 2005 and headed west to Point Mugu, California, to join the Black Eagles of VAW-113, I was headed into the unknown. During naval flight officer training, I had realized that I was "physiologically challenged" in an aircraft. The flight surgeon called it spatial disorientation, but most people just call it airsickness or puking your guts out. Prescription medications failed me, so I pounded saltines and ginger ale, wore acupressure wristbands, and held on for dear life every time I strapped into the T-34 Turbomentor. At the end of each day, I felt the way Dan Aykroyd and Chevy Chase looked at the end of the flight-training scene in the 1980s classic *Spies Like Us*, only worse. Twice I suffered through the dreaded airsickness adaptation program known as the "Spin and Puke," but I never really got over my problem. I would have done anything to get my wings, including feeling sick every time I went airborne, which is what I did.

My options for playing shotgun in the skies were diminishing fast. Both in heart and mind, I knew the indelible truth: I would never survive a career in the back seat of a tactical jet. With my health, sanity, and performance suffering, I asked to be selected into the E-2C Hawkeye community. I did not know much about the aircraft or the mission, but I knew the aircraft could not go upside-down, which was a good thing for me and for my stomach. As an officer in the Hawkeye, I would not be dropping ordnance in defense of troops in contact; I would not be head to head with a wave of hostile bandits threatening a carrier strike group, and I would not be hovering over a military mishap saving lives during a search and rescue mission. What *would* I be doing?

The Hawkeye is called the "quarterback of the skies" because it plays a role in so many missions. Built to augment the carrier air wing, the original platform design of the Hawkeye was to help combat the Russian bomber threat. Because American fighters did not have optimal radar-range capabilities, the Hawkeye became the eye over the horizon for the air patrol. Its aviators are trained to provide tactical assistance wherever and whenever needed. There are times when the environment is dynamic, when all five crew members are working frantically to identify forces in the battle space and disseminate this information to nearby assets. A Hawkeye crew can also lead, giving orders to air-wing assets to receive fuel, deploy ordnance, or run an air-to-air intercept. Other times, the mission is to simply be airborne, listening, observing, and assimilating data.

I was doing my part in the Fleet, but I often felt that my role was inadequate. So many others were enduring more. Even when operationally deployed, my nights were spent on USS *Ronald Reagan* (CVN 76), a floating city where they served four meals a day and the showers always had hot water. I vividly recall lying awake at night wondering how I was actually contributing to this historic war. In 2006, things began to change.

During *Reagan*'s maiden deployment, VAW-113's commanding officer, John Ring, drafted a concept of operations for the Hawkeye to expand its mission beyond its maritime interdiction mission and operate over land. Commander Ring had identified a gap in radar and radio coverage by the Air Force airborne warning and control system (AWACS) that he believed the Hawkeye could fill. The AWACS was overtasked and could be relieved if the Hawkeye was granted authorization to support ground assets. Our strike group admiral approved the operation, so the first OnStar mission was a go.

The new mission was a boost to our squadron. Each night, two Hawkeyes launched at ninety-minute intervals from *Reagan* to enter Iraq's airspace and provide a communication bridge for convoys traveling between checkpoints. Most of the time, our crew listened, received information, and monitored their operations in theater. We broadcast information about road closures and threats from improvised explosive devices and reported troops in contact. Every night, we landed safely back on board *Reagan*, feeling confident that we were contributing to the fight.

The first time we flew over land, or went "feet dry," it was like trying to communicate in a new language. Through coded frequencies battling environmental interference, these initial reports often came across as static until our ears attenuated.

Katherine Kranz stands in front of her E-2C Hawkeye on USS Ronald Reagan *while in support of the first OnStar support mission in Iraq.*

"Hawkeye (*tschhhh*), Hawkeye." That's us! I thought to myself. This must be important!

"(*tschhhh*) Alpha, checking in, checkpoint Kilo, heading from Ramadi to (*tschhhh*) Fallujah on Route X-ray. 20 Vicks, 30 Pax." What does that mean? What do I say? Who do I tell? Does he need something from me?

"Alpha, this is Hawkeye. Roger. Copy."

When the message was broken or completely incomprehensible, we would all do our best to decipher and write down what we had heard, and I would end up replying with a confident "Copy all," to leave no doubt in the minds of those in danger that we were there to support them. Between shuffling maps, notating the relayed information of garbled static, and attempting to write legibly in a vibrating aircraft, our mission had become more challenging. In a way, I welcomed the challenge, and we all soon became more comfortable with the new mission procedures.

One night midway through our Gulf deployment and halfway through a flight over Iraq, we were confronted with something new. Convoys had checked in with us, and we had passed on important information, but aside from chatter between convoy commanders, the net was silent. Suddenly the quiet ended: "Hawkeye, HAWKEYE, this is CONVOY Tango . . . (*tschtsch*) . . . hit us, we're under fire!" The panicked voice pierced the upper decibels of the frequency net. The man was gasping for breath between sentences. Somewhere far below us, his convoy was under attack, and we were the only asset they could reach to ask for help. The screams became incoherent, garbled words and babbling. If I knew where he was, I could provide immediate assistance, but it was impossible to discern his location.

Another of our crew members radioed to get two helicopters on standby to provide close air support and medical evacuations. At that point, I could only offer reassurance that help was on the way, but I still desperately needed the location of the convoy, and the soldier on the radio was still screaming. "Take a deep breath," I said in a calm voice. "I know you are scared, but everything is going to be fine." My mission commander solidified communications with a combat air support Blackhawk attack helicopter. I told the troops on the ground that help was on the way, and all we needed was good GPS coordinates. The soldier yelled, "Convoy located: 33, 15, 55 north 44, 36, 00 east." Finally, we had it. We relayed this to the inbound support aircraft.

The pilots came over the internal communications system, "Guys, we're on ladder. We gotta start heading back or we're going to run out of gas." This meant it was a matter of minutes until we were out of range of the convoy's radio. Had we done everything we could for them? We could only trust that we had provided what we could and turned the necessary information over to the AWACS. We headed back with confidence that help was on the way for them.

The Hawkeye only has a supporting role, but that support brings strength to the aviation community and the Navy. Someone flies the fuel tanker so the fighter jet has enough gas to drop ordnance, and someone turns the wrench on that fuel tanker so that it too can fly. Each piece of the military machine is linked to the rest and supports one common goal. There is no greater honor than supporting those who truly lay down their lives to protect this country, knowing that they would do the same for you if the roles were reversed.

On Building Submarines and Building Character

Lucas Adin

People sometimes ask me what it was like being in the Navy. As anyone who has served in the military likely knows, there is no single easy answer to that question. For me, it was a mix of frustration, hard work, and personal empowerment, which began with my freshman year at the Naval Academy. As we adjusted to our new lives in the military, we were reminded frequently about the commitment we had made to our country and to the people we would lead. Whether we would be directing ships at sea or leading Marines into combat, we all would one day have a vital role in defending our nation, even if it seemed relatively small, and the training we undertook at the Academy was preparing us for those roles. Yet, even late in my time at the Academy, despite all the training I had done and the weeks spent among ships, aircraft, and Marines, I still had trouble imagining what form my role would take. Being the kind who usually blended into the crowd, even at the Naval Academy, I never imagined myself in one that could be considered unique.

When I received news that my first duty out of the Academy was on USS *Virginia* (SSN 774), it nearly sent me into shock. *Virginia* was a brand-new, state-of-the-art attack submarine—the lead vessel of its class—scheduled to launch in late 2003. We had begun to learn about this new "boat" during my freshman year at the Academy, but the details were limited. Construction on *Virginia* was initiated in 1998 in response to the increasing cost of the *Seawolf* class of submarines. This new design was a less expensive alternative, and the new vessels would be more capable of operating in littoral areas, close to the shore.

When I arrived at the sub in the building yards of Groton, Connecticut, I was given a tour by a pair of junior officers who had arrived a few months before I had. I tried to make sense of my surroundings as we climbed through the boat's innards, but they were so jammed with workers, test gear, and construction equipment that it was hard to move, much less identify the various parts. Other than the obvious ones, like torpedo tubes or the crew's bunks, I recognized almost nothing. Over the next couple of years, I would learn the function of every pipe, valve, and electrical panel I saw that day. The boat was impressive, but it was hard to imagine it being ready for a mission at sea, and almost as hard to believe I'd ever know enough to help drive it.

The nuclear-powered attack submarine USS Virginia *under construction at Groton Shipyard, Connecticut, April 15, 2003.* (U.S. Navy)

Virginia was put to sea in the summer of 2004, and as is often the case, it got under way without the most junior crew members, who were not sufficiently qualified to help drive the boat, including me. We had been left behind so there would be sleeping capacity for engineers, testing personnel, and of course, the VIPs in a very crowded boat. While I knew I was perhaps two months from finishing my first major qualification, which would allow me to begin contributing on the watch rotation, it still seemed a lifetime away. Even as I watched the boat pull away from the pier on its historic voyage, I still felt like little more than a spectator. This was my first of many lessons on the importance of qualifications, but I had not fully embraced its significance. I was still more a midshipman than an officer.

In November 2005, when I pinned on my gold-plated dolphins, signifying the completion of officer qualification, I had been in the boat for nearly eighteen months. This was long past the normal completion time, and my enthusiasm for my assignment had faded significantly. Although we had spent a good amount of time at sea during the preceding year and had even conducted a brief tactical mission, the first for a *Virginia*-class submarine, my qualification for the most rewarding watch position at sea was immediately followed by another long year in the shipyard. I had trouble staying focused on my work and even had to redo one of my final qualification boards with the captain. I was bitter, discouraged, and at that point in my submarine career, I wanted little else than for it to be over.

To some people, my frustrations seemed unwarranted, and for good reason. After all, I was a member of the first crew of this first-of-class submarine. My name would be listed with all the other "plankowners" on a plaque that would remain on board the ship until it was decommissioned. I had seen and participated in testing exercises most submariners never experience in their entire careers, including unusual and dramatic tests of the propulsion plant as well as firing the ship's first torpedoes at sea. Yet it was impossible not to think of other junior officers in the submarine force like my own roommate, who was helping lead his boat on a long and technically challenging deployment that would take them under the polar ice and around the world. Meanwhile, I was stuck in a shipyard in New England, trying to pass qualification boards I knew I was smart enough to pass. Beyond my personal development, I was also having trouble identifying the contribution I was making to this ship and its crew and to the Navy in a meaningful way. I wanted to serve, to have some impact on national security; that was why I had joined.

Some of the setbacks for me and my peers in *Virginia* had to do with the practical difficulties of being on a new-construction ship. Training the crew required some creative adaptation. To put this in perspective, it is hard to learn how to navigate a boat out of port when it is still bolted to the pier and covered in scaffolding, and it is nearly impossible to qualify to operate a piece of equipment when it hasn't yet been installed. Most of the time, we used computer simulations and props to create scenarios we might encounter, which reminded me of some of the absurd things that we were told at the Academy as part of our military training. A classic example was the repeated notion that returning late to Bancroft Hall, the Academy's dormitory, was akin to missing a ship's underway movement, as if an eight-wing building would break from its moorings and set sail without us. The training lesson was to get us to appreciate the importance of timeliness, and more important, the consequences of being tardy in the Fleet. To the midshipmen, it was a joke. While I knew that the implications here were much more serious than they had been back at the Academy, it was still difficult to keep my focus day to day when my training scenarios were so far from reality.

Another year passed, but by then things had changed considerably, for me and for the boat. *Virginia* had completed all of its initial testing at sea and was eight months or so into a follow-on effort to inspect, repair, and upgrade its thousands of major components. The shipyard, in its furious effort to finish projects on time, was constantly scheduling one work activity on top of another, many of which were in direct conflict. While one system was being reassembled, another was being torn apart; one worker was asking to weld in a given space, while another was asking to do work with explosive gas only a few feet away. Through all of this, the ship's reactor plant was shifted from one unusual lineup to another to support work on its multitude of propulsion and electrical components. There were pumps running on power supplied by temporary cables, cooling systems running on temporary refrigeration units outside the boat, and many other strange setups.

One day, I was assigned to be the acting engineer on the boat while the captain was away. The shipyard planned its usual symphony of chaos, which included atypical alignments of the reactor coolant system for maintenance and tests. We proceeded to carry out the plan we had been handed, but as things tend to happen during shipyard testing evolutions, I was faced with making a choice about how to realign the plant's systems. I thought about the risks of two paths we could take and made a call to the captain. He reiterated an option we had considered earlier but because of the unique conditions I had thought might conflict with an obscure part of Navy engineering procedures. He was silent for a moment, but then said, "You're right, Lucas, we can't do that. Let's go with your proposal." It was a simple exchange of words, but it signified that I had independently reached a conclusion about a complex problem that the captain hadn't thought of first. Suddenly my contribution seemed clearer. Even more important, this man, who less than a year earlier hadn't seemed to trust me to do much of anything without supervision, was entrusting me with the safety of the entire crew. It had been a meeting of minds, and I was finally one of the minds, rather than just a follower or spectator, and there would be more moments like this during the remainder of my time on *Virginia*. They were moments of empowerment and personal reward and the feeling that I could still do something valuable. More important, I learned to focus less on my individual tasks and goals and more on the collective goals of the boat. This attitude served me well in the shipyard but would be even more important at sea.

By the time the boat was approaching the completion of its overhaul period in early 2007 and a third round of sea trials, the crew had not been to sea in over a year. Because of this hiatus, we once again had to undergo a thorough test of our ship driving and operational skills. This time around, I was no longer an unqualified observer but an active participant. At this point, we had only three qualified officers of the deck who had enough experience to stand watch during sea trials: a department head, another experienced junior officer, and me. This meant that I would finally have an opportunity to act in one of the most vital roles an officer can provide on board a ship at sea, in a dynamic and rapidly changing environment that is far removed from the relatively static conditions of the shipyard. All I had to do to secure my spot was to take an exam on my knowledge of ship driving and to demonstrate my abilities in an observed drill.

On the morning of my drill—which would simulate our initial departure from the Groton shipyard and our surface transit out to open ocean—I was the first to arrive on the boat's bridge. It was early, still dark, and the January wind whipping off the Thames River stung my face as I awaited our captain and the senior officer who would observe my performance. I did not know whether my hands were shaking because of the cold or because of nerves. In most cases I could depend on the expertise of the watch team to make up for any mistakes I might make, but in this case I was on my own. Once the others arrived, I initiated our computer-based transit, and things began to go downhill quickly. I had a hard time determining what was supposed to be simulated and what I was actually supposed to perform, such as a real blowing of the ship's whistle to indicate our getting under way from the pier. The observers kept interjecting into the simulated scenario, and by the time our imaginary crew member went overboard signaling the start of a drill, my head was spinning.

Even after a year of developing a newfound sense of confidence and establishing my merits as a competent leader, I still could not wrap my head around the task of demonstrating my abilities at sea while standing on a ship that was tied to the pier. After the drill, the captain called me into his stateroom and explained that he couldn't put me on the bridge for our outbound transit after such a harried performance. While this did not come as a surprise to me, I was deeply disappointed. Fueled by an unremitting determination to rebuild my image and earn back the trust of my superiors, I was considerably more focused from then on out.

We then ran a fire drill, which I had done many times before. As is usually the case, it isn't the repetition of something previously rehearsed that impresses the judges the most, it's how things are handled when they go wrong. As we were reaching periscope depth during the drill, the video system for the periscope froze, essentially rendering us blind. Almost instinctively, I unhooked the air hose for my breathing mask and rushed to the back of the control room to start the alternate periscope imaging device, all the while screaming orders through my mask. It probably looked ridiculous, but it was Oscar-worthy compared to my bumbling performance on the bridge. It sufficiently impressed my observers to get me back on the watch bill.

A few weeks later when *Virginia* was put back to sea, I was in control as officer of the deck, getting ready to direct its first submergence, a milestone following such a long shipyard overhaul. After a few initial tests in the depths, we conducted a surfacing, and I prepared to take over the watch from the bridge. When I reached the bridge in the early hours of the morning, it was snowing heavily, something I had never experienced at sea. The water was strangely calm for winter in the North Atlantic, and the wind gently swirled the snow around the sail and the bridge cockpit, some of it brightly lit by the masthead light above my head and intermittently in bright orange pulses by the submarine's ID beacon. I could hear nothing but the wind, and except for the lookout behind me, I was alone. Beneath me, 130 sailors were operating the Navy's newest national asset, a vastly complex machine that would eventually take its crew around the world in the silent depths of the sea. I had never felt such a powerful sense of responsibility in my life.

★ ★ ★

By the time I left *Virginia* to attend graduate school at Georgetown University, we had been to sea twice more. On our final return to home port, my father was on board as part of a three-day family cruise, a rare and unique event for a submarine. Seeing me issue orders and manage the watch team in a way that showed confidence, and the evidence of what I had accomplished in the nearly nine years since he saw me off on my first day at the Naval Academy, made him appear to truly appreciate how far I had come. It was a great capstone to my service in the Navy to show him this unique trade, submariners at sea, especially on this first-of-a-kind ship. The road to qualifying as a submarine officer was among the hardest I had ever traveled, but I am grateful for every moment. I had the chance to work with some of the most dedicated and professional individuals I've known, both officers and enlisted personnel, while contributing to jobs that, even if they seemed small on their own, added up to a lot.

Of most importance, I learned to set aside the doubts about my own abilities, get past my hindering anxiety, and do the job for which I was trained. My task was made challenging by technical complexities rather than the visceral dangers that many of my classmates from the Academy would face in other branches of the service, especially those in active combat. I'm certain that the way that we developed as leaders in these jobs, no matter where or how, has prepared us to make truly meaningful contributions to the country. We'll do it in different ways, both as civilians and as military officers, but we all have the potential to do great things that can improve our society and honor the sacrifices made by many over the past decade, including some of our own classmates. It all started with learning how to salute and how to put on a uniform on Induction Day at the Naval Academy. The valuable lessons that followed will stay with us for a lifetime.

Lost at Sea

Glyndell Houston

T he adventure of a lifetime was about to begin. None of us knew to what extent it would forever change our lives. In July 1998, our son, Joe Houston, left our home and sheltered life in Houston, Texas, to join the midshipmen at the United States Naval Academy. He was eighteen years old and so confident in his calling that he convinced us not to accompany him to Annapolis to send him off. He wanted his independence. He wanted to be a man. He wanted to embrace the challenge head on and say all his goodbyes in Houston. He was pumped. He was ready for anything and everything they could dish out. The apron strings were cut. It was his chance to make his dream come true: He wanted to fly. At the time, the Lord comforted me with the song "His Eye Is on the Sparrow." I was able to let go and launch our fledgling from our nest into his care.

We later learned that on the very first day, while the medics were taking blood, Joe passed out in line and had to have his blood drawn laying on a cot. Needless to say, this was not the first impression he wanted to make. I laugh now and wonder if the blood in his veins had been replaced by pure adrenaline. He was eager to absorb every aspect of USNA. His attitude was "bring it on." He would wax philosophical with each phone call home, analyzing what was expected, what he had achieved, how he could improve, how best to serve, as well as observations about relationships, loyalty, competitiveness, and camaraderie. Joe loved structure. The regimen, discipline, and daily grind of the Academy suited him well. He quickly became "Houston from Houston" and as a proud Texan enjoyed the attention. He laughed when he had to explain to his classmates that he didn't drive a pickup with a rack full of guns. He was miffed at being called John instead of Joe. His full name is John Joseph Houston, so all his official records refer to him as John.

Another of Joe's initial challenges was the need to study—perhaps for the first time in his life. He realized he was an "average Joe in the middle of the class" and "there are many people here a lot smarter than I am." He intentionally pushed himself to his maximum capacity and beyond. He became fiercely loyal to the brotherhood. There was a transformation occurring in Joe. He learned the wisdom of keeping his weapon secured after "losing" his rifle. (When a squad mate misplaces a weapon or ammunition the entire team suffers.) He learned to add green hot sauce to everything on his plate and that the mess hall cooked four hundred turkeys for Thanksgiving. He learned to turn to Scripture each night before bed for encouragement and strength for the next day. We noticed he began to refer to "Mother B" as home.

Four years at the Academy served as an anvil in Joe's life that helped sharpen and hone his character, honor, integrity, and mental, physical, and spiritual strength and endurance. We watched him expand his horizons and gain leadership and organizational skills. He learned to become efficient and to appreciate humility, sacrifice, and service to God and mankind. He learned to scuba dive, skydive, coach soccer, pay attention to world news, fold his T-shirts into tiny squares so they could neatly fit on his closet shelves, and appreciate his family more than ever. He developed perseverance and gained self-confidence.

By being blessed with admission to the first class offered corrective surgery for nearsightedness, Joe was able to qualify and be selected for aviation. Commissioned in 2002, he was winged two years later as a helicopter pilot at Whiting Field, in Milton, Florida. Following graduation, Joe faced many difficult personal and professional challenges. During periods of retrospection, he would comment on how lessons learned at the Academy had prepared him for later real-life situations. With God's help, he was able to achieve success while overcoming significant trials in flight school, a difficult marriage, the premature birth of his son, and three deployments to the Persian Gulf.

During survival training in advanced helicopter school in San Diego, Joe reported a humorous event. He was alone, evading the "enemy," taking shelter in a ditch to hide. Suddenly, the earth trembled and shook, scaring the wits out of him. For a moment he thought they were using live artillery in the training. It was impressively realistic and turned out to be his first experience with an earthquake.

Joe flew the Navy's latest helicopter, the SH-60 Sea Hawk, doing search and rescue and cargo/supply missions. He absolutely loved it. During Hurricane Katrina in New Orleans, Joe was assigned a humanitarian mission. He assisted people standing on roofs of houses waiting to be rescued. He witnessed the mass devastation of communities and infrastructure. He was frustrated with civilian air traffic and the media's erroneous reporting. He remembered the stench over the entire area. He embraced the opportunity to render aid.

During a workup training mission in San Diego, Joe was assigned to be first pilot in the Sea Hawk. At the eleventh hour, however, there was a decision to change pilots. One of his squadronmates flew instead. The helicopter went down in an instant, with no reported problems and in good weather. The entire crew perished. Joe struggled with survivor's guilt but realized that the Lord had spared his life for a purpose. Within days, he volunteered to fly again. His heart always wanted to fly. It's what he was trained and blessed to be able to do. He was a man of courage and commitment to the mission.

Joe served on USS *Peleliu*, USS *Bonhomme Richard*, and USS *Rainier*, flying search and rescue and supply missions. He was also involved in a counterpiracy expedition. He continued to excel. We were extremely proud of his service. During his deployment, we would send Joe care packages. He told us he would take all his goodies to the wardroom and spread them out on the table to share with those who had none. He was very appreciative of his blessings and privileges, empathizing with buddies who had few letters from home.

In Dubai, Joe rode a camel and reported crash landings when he ventured to snow ski on an indoor mountain. He relished trying all the exotic foods and loved the stuffed dates. On port calls to Guam, Australia, and Hawaii, he took advantage of the clear waters and beautiful reefs to go scuba diving. Once in Singapore he was walking down the street with a Navy buddy and decided he needed a drink of water. He saw a faucet on the side of a building and took a drink. He later realized it was a temple.

Joe had a great sense of humor and enjoyed making his squadronmates laugh. He would dress up in outlandish costumes, wigs and all, relishing their reactions and comments. His most renowned disguise was the Joker nurse in Batman. He developed an interest in flowers, taking beautiful photographs of blossoms from all over the world. After learning to macramé, he made lovely necklaces incorporating unusual shells collected on his dives.

In an effort to save his failing marriage, Joe requested and received a change in position and location. He believed that transferring to Corpus Christi, Texas, would strengthen his family bonds, stabilize his marriage, and allow him to be home three years without deployment. He became a T-34C Turbomentor flight instructor. Shortly before reassignment, however, his marriage ultimately failed. He came to Texas alone, leaving his wife and son in San Diego. He was in the middle of a divorce, wounded, broken, starting over again.

Joe applied himself fully to the Navy task at hand and enrolled in Embry University, pursuing a master's degree in aviation safety. He became an excellent flight instructor, with nerves of steel, great patience, and a heart full of compassion. He earned personal and professional respect at Corpus Christi Naval Air Station. Students would request his instruction and look forward to flying with him. He made sound decisions and quickly formed deep relationships with Christian friends in the area. Joe also received emotional healing and began moving forward again in his personal life. He soon reacquainted with a wonderful high school friend and became engaged to be married. Life was good; his hope

John Joseph Houston, beloved classmate, son, father, and friend.
(Courtesy Houston family)

was renewed and joy evident. He continued to be an incredible dad to his son, Asher, despite the physical distance.

On October 28, 2009, Joe unexpectedly completed his earthly assignment. He called his son, Asher, that morning and then flew a routine training mission with a senior instructor, Lt. Bret Miller (USNA Class of 2001). During the flight, their plane went off radar, plunging into the Gulf of Mexico. Two days later, Bret's body was found, raising questions about whether the canopy had been opened and whether Joe had been able to eject. A massive land and sea search ensued involving the Navy, Marine Corps, Coast Guard, and civilians. It lasted twenty-one days. Matt Kavanaugh, a classmate of Joe's from USNA 2nd Company, came from New Jersey to organize and facilitate the civilian search. On November 18, one day before Joe's thirtieth birthday, his plane was finally located. Joe's body was strapped in the cockpit.

Our precious son, Lt. John Joseph Houston, was buried on January 31, 2010, in Arlington National Cemetery with full military honors. Many family members, friends, and USNA shipmates attended the ceremony that clear frosty morning. A memorial trust was established by 2nd Company in Joe's name for educational resources for Asher. We learned that we truly have an extended Navy family. They continue to come forward in many ways, professionally and personally, to bless our family in providing support.

Joe loved life and lived it to the fullest. We miss him terribly, and our hearts are broken. It is comforting to know he was prepared to meet the Lord and lived a life worthy of his calling. Joe is eternally safe and secure in God's presence. Joe would want us to share his life verse: "Delight yourself in the Lord and He will give you the desires of your heart" (Psalm 37:4). His high school football team motto, his flight school banner, and the banner over his life continue to be "To God Be the Glory!"

Dual Military Couples: Twice the Challenge

Brooke Waller

JANUARY 2002

We thought we had it all figured out. As two seniors at the Naval Academy, my fiancé, Doug, and I had studied deployment schedules, talked with officers with Fleet experience, and paid close attention to our summer training opportunities. We were determined to put our heads together, figure out the right ships with the ideal underway schedules, continue on with our careers, and get married shortly after graduation. We were two midshipmen, ready to be officers and serve our country, but also wanting to start a life together. It had to be possible, right?

It soon became clear that we were being too naïve. We were going to need more than careful planning. The hard lessons started on the night of service selection at the Academy; it would be a milestone in our relationship. That evening, each of the one thousand members of the senior class was given a sealed envelope with a piece of paper inside, and on that piece of paper was a number ranking us according to our military and academic performance over the previous three years. Based on that number, students were given preference in choosing their assignments. As the night progressed, numbers were called out, and midshipmen were summoned to Memorial Hall, a huge room where admirals, generals, and loved ones all gathered. The walls were covered with charts of assignments. Doug and I knew our plan. He was to be called first, as his order of merit was higher than mine. (I still think his course load was easier!) He would pick the same ship on the West Coast as his good friend Chris Whyte. Eventually the voice over the loudspeaker called Doug's number. My heart raced as I thought of him in his Dress Blues walking down to the hall—he has a way of naturally marching wherever he goes—to make the first of many choices that would guide our careers.

My number was called a short while later, and I joined the other anxious seniors in a long line that made its way out of the hall and into the courtyard. My goal was to be an ensign on USS *Coronado*, the only West Coast command ship. As a bride to be, I wanted to try to balance our careers from the beginning and wasn't looking for the "toughest job in the Navy." I wanted to know I could share a holiday or two with my husband and family. Command ships, we were told, were usually in port a bit more often than other ships, and almost always for Christmas. As I waited in line, I wondered if it was foolish not to have a backup plan. I followed my classmates into the noisy, humid, and congested room. I had always thought this would be a serene and solemn night, but no, it was true Navy—boisterous, crowded, and flowing with alcohol. (There was access to an open bar after you had made your selection.) I stepped up to the red cloth railing, smiled at Doug, who was standing off to the side, and then looked up at the board.

That's when my heart sank, triggering a meltdown. My ship was gone! I later found out that a classmate ahead of me by three spaces had taken the last slot. Devastated, I walked up to the chart and asked the admiral what he recommended. He suggested a ship in his fleet, on the West Coast. I took the first ship he offered, grasping at the small hope that at least Doug and I would be in the same homeport, signed my name next to the ship's, and desperately looked around for the nearest exit. I didn't even wait for Doug because I knew he was right behind me. I could barely breathe and needed fresh air. How could this have happened to us? It was all wrong. We had planned and prepared for a life with some stability, being surface warfare officers in San Diego. Instead, I had an assignment to a destroyer about which I knew nothing, and to top it off, it had an active schedule that was quite the opposite of the amphibious schedule of my future husband's ship. This was just the first of many times that attempts to control our Navy careers would fail. I was comforted to know that despite the seeming failure of our plans, God was still in charge, and he had a plan for our lives. I prayed and tried to be encouraged that we would both be in San Diego.

FEBRUARY 2003

Fast forward thirteen months, and the challenge of service selection seems like a mere annoyance compared to what we were facing. Doug had been deployed in support of Operation Iraqi Freedom and was cruising in the Persian Gulf, protecting oil platforms. His ship did figure eights and resupplied (via small boats filled with fresh water, food, and ammunition) the sailors who stood watch on the platforms around the clock, without running water, no shade, and armed with automatic weapons. His ship was plagued by a faulty chem-bio alarm, which meant that whenever the wind blew unexpectedly, an alarm would sound, as if they had come under chemical or biological attack. He carried a gas mask with him at all times, even to the bathroom.

We wrote emails back and forth, his sometimes ending with "chem-bio is going off, gotta go." It was not reassuring to read, and honestly, I never got used to it. At the time that Doug was dealing with sandstorms so violent he could barely see his hand in front of his face, I was back at the Academy in Annapolis. I never joined the ship I'd chosen on service selection night and instead accepted a phenomenal opportunity to teach at the Academy after getting a master's degree in American history.

As pressure grew to invade Iraq, I sat in the faculty lounge at lunch, dining on Lean Cuisine and watching CNN's "Headline News" with my colleagues. There was constant banter between the liberals and conservatives, and we discussed the politics of the situation as only history instructors can—with plenty of references to antiquity. The only time I remember the lounge being silent was when we watched the fall of Baghdad unfold before us. We were riveted to the TV and glued to our chairs; everyone had questions but nothing to say. What would happen? Was Doug safe? Would he come home? I felt utterly helpless. I knew then and there that there wasn't a right way to rig a dual military marriage. This life was going to be tough, and there was no way around that.

2007

Four years later, we considered ourselves a seasoned military couple. We had three deployments between the two of us—I'd deployed as an intelligence officer with a helicopter squadron, HS-4, onboard an aircraft carrier, USS *Stennis*—we had missed four of five anniversaries, had never celebrated a Valentine's Day together, and had begun to receive friends' wedding invitations addressed to just one of us "and guest." We were finally due for a break, and we expected our shore tours to be just that. Almost all naval officers begin their careers with two tours at sea followed by one on shore. We had high hopes for ours—we would find cushy day jobs where we would wear "civvies" into work, and at night we would sleep in our own bed, not having to be on the ship every third night—but we were in for another surprise: I was transferred to a shore tour four months ahead of Doug. We needed a house, but I had not planned on finding one on my own. Why did our schedules never align?

Not ones to be discouraged, we made the most of the time we did have and quickly closed on a new home in ten days. While I waited for Doug to join me on shore duty, I made it my mission to create a home for us in our new place. Although I wanted him there to help me make decisions about paint colors or the arrangement of our furniture, I knew he was working hard and would have been with me if he could.

I reported for work at the National Geospatial Intelligence Agency well rested and bronzed from my time in the Southern California sun. I was scheduled to work four ten-and-a-half-hour shifts a week and had visions of spending my free time gardening or taking an art class. What was supposed to be an easy shore tour, however, was turning out to be harder than deployment. I barely had time to call Doug, let alone paint our new home or tend to a garden. I worked in the office that directly supported the director of the agency, and as a lieutenant I was expected to assume a leadership role immediately. Despite the intriguing sound of "national intelligence," the job was equal parts fascinating and mind numbingly dull. It was a heady experience to read the President's Daily Brief, or PDB as we called it, and to answer the red phone that connected to the White House Situation Room.

At first I was mesmerized by the seven phones on the watch desk, all of which had a different greeting because U.S. undercover agents might call one of the lines. Much to my dismay, the phone number for our undercover personnel was quite similar to the phone number for a local Domino's pizza. When answering the phone at 2 o'clock in the morning, I was less than amused by the caller who wanted a "large with onions and olives—fast." After telling him repeatedly that the number he had called was a national intelligence agency, not Domino's, I finally replied, "Sure, it'll be there in ten minutes." Happily, there were times when my mind and leadership were put to good use, which in the end made the job worthwhile.

2010

Now that Doug and I are out of uniform, we look back on our dual military careers as an adventure, with surprises and challenges around every corner, but totally and completely worth the sacrifice. I had never been so proud as to stand in uniform next to my husband and salute the colors as they passed. Never was I so honored than to greet him after he returned from an eight-month deployment. We understand what it means to sacrifice, for our country and for each other, and that our marriage is worth any hardship. The challenges of our dual military marriage are worth any hardship. They made us stronger.

When No One's Watching

*Lisa Freeman**

Some people have no direction, no purpose, and no idea where their lives will take them. Opportunities pass them by. The kids get raised, the mortgage gets paid, and the status stays quo. They're just along for the ride. Other people have a laser-like focus on where they need to be and a clear, but maybe less precise, idea of how to get there. They set goals and navigate a course undeterred by detours to the finish line. They are the world's drivers.

I always knew where I needed to be, I just wasn't sure how to do it. I wanted to be a pilot, like my dad, and I wanted to be a leader; everything else was just chaff. When I read President Theodore Roosevelt's "Man in the Arena" speech my first week at the Naval Academy, it reinforced my passion to be on the front lines. There I was, even during plebe summer, in the arena, my face marred with "sweat and dust and blood" from bear crawls on Hospital Point. I was doing what it took to achieve my goals, leaving behind the "timid souls" who know neither victory nor defeat.

In my early years, things were pretty much the same for me as they were for other military brats. I come from a Navy family. My dad, both my grandfathers, aunt, and an uncle were naval officers. During my first six years of education, I attended a different school every year. When my family moved to Richmond Hill, Georgia, however, I started the sixth grade and finally had educational stability because we never moved after that. It was there that I began the serious effort of earning an appointment to the Naval Academy. The Annapolis brochures said I should strive for good grades, have lots of extracurricular activities, and try to get leadership experience. Of course, I also needed a requisite dose of luck. In pursuit of the nomination, I received some much-needed character-building lessons.

Much of my interest centered on student government. I served on the student council every year in high school. As a freshman, I was the treasurer, and as a junior I ran for student council president but lost. This was a major blow to a young man focused on attending a college where leadership was a prerequisite.

*Written in Matthew's voice by Lisa Freeman, in honor of her son.

Pursuing school-wide office was uncommon for a junior, but I had the respect of so many different cliques that I gave it a shot, believing I could tally enough votes to win.

While living on different military bases, I never had the luxury of picking and choosing my buddies. I accepted anyone who accepted me. I lost the council president race because a malicious student council adviser, Mrs. Stenson, had shown favoritism toward another candidate. I was disappointed: How could I possibly get into Annapolis if I can't even land a high school leadership role? I accepted the loss, but I didn't give up. The next year I ran again and was elected council president. I learned something all successful military officers must learn—perseverance. Outside the Naval Academy leadership center is an Epictetus quote under the statue of Adm. James Stockdale that reads, "Lameness is an impediment to the body but not to the will." It really isn't important how many times you fail, fall, or get knocked down, or even how hard the blow. To truly win, you have to get back up and move forward.

My parents helped me fulfill my dream of attending the Naval Academy. Throughout my life, my mother has been my biggest cheerleader. She told me I could be anything I wanted to be. She told me I was blessed with brains, looks, and family, that I should use these strengths to help others, and that with the right choices and "checking the right boxes" my dreams would be realized. When things went wrong, she taught me to turn to God and learn from my mistakes.

The Marine Corps Mameluke sword, inscribed and presented to Matt Freeman at his graduation from the Naval Academy in 2002.

On Induction Day at the Naval Academy, I felt ready. My dad, Class of 1976, made sure I was prepared to be a plebe. Plebes are like freshmen at other, traditional colleges but without civil rights. They are broken down mentally and then built back up, reshaped as officers in the naval service. Last-minute instructions on how to fold T-shirts, polish boots, and memorize age-old sayings from Reef Points—a timeless bible that explains the Naval Academy and the Navy—were an advantage I had as a "legacy" student.

My dad told me if some sadistic upperclassman asked, "How's the cow?" I should be ready to respond by saying, "Sir, she walks, she talks, she's full of chalk, the lacteal fluid extracted from the female of the bovine species is highly prolific to the Nth degree, Sir." My dad also provided some intangible advice: To put my shipmates first, put 100 percent of my energy into every day, and never compromise my integrity. While other midshipmen were still developing their moral compasses, my self-awareness of right and wrong had already been calibrated.

My years at Annapolis were some of my fondest. I did my best as an aerospace engineer and developed close friendships. I wasn't Brigade commander, but I focused on being a good leader in company and taking care of my squad mates. Flying was in my DNA, but I was going to be different from the other aviators in my family: I was going to be a Marine as well. At graduation, my parents gave me an officer's sword. Marine Corps officers carry a Mameluke sword, in recognition of the one presented to 1st Lt. Presley O'Bannon by the Ottoman viceroy Prince Hamet during the First Barbary War in 1805. All Marine officers have since had it.

My parents engraved my sword "Matthew C. Freeman, USMC, USNA 2002. When No One's Watching." My dad wanted the phrase on the sword to remind me that character is one of the most important and essential parts of being an officer and leader, and the most telling method of measuring character is noting how someone acts and conducts his affairs when no one is watching.

After six months of officer training at the the Marine Corps Basic School at Quantico, Virginia, I went to flight school. Becoming a pilot required twenty-four months of additional education, and with a war going on, I was particularly impatient. Because of the needs of the Corps, I was assigned orders to a C-130 squadron based in Okinawa, Japan. Our mission was to take bullets, boots, and Band-Aids in and out of the area of combat operations, always in a support role.

Though my desire to be more involved in combat operations remained unfulfilled, personal things were on track living overseas. I was blessed to have my childhood friend and now fiancée, Theresa Hess, living with me in Japan. Theresa was an Air Force flight surgeon and had wrangled a job in Okinawa as well. We were able to enjoy the Japanese culture together and nurture our relationship. We took walks on the beach and bought eclectic Japanese delights. Our favorite was Norimake-Zushi, a delicious fresh fish wrapped in seaweed. We explored the island and snorkeled and scuba dived right in front of our apartment. I traveled to Australia and dove off the cliffs there. I played with monkeys in the Philippines and took pictures on Wake Island and Guam. Life was good, but something was missing. I felt disconnected from the history ongoing in Iraq and Afghanistan.

On a typical morning around the squadron hangar, my executive officer called a meeting for all the junior officers. He read an email explaining that the wars in Iraq and Afghanistan were continuing much longer than expected, and there was a shortage of troops on the ground due to extended Army deployments. There were not enough troops in the active, reserve, and guard components to maintain mission requirements. Positions were opening up for individual volunteers, or volun-"told," officers to augment Army forces on the ground. It was explained that an Army infantry unit responsible for mentoring the Afghan national army needed more personnel. Assignments to the unit were supposed to be for an entire year in Afghanistan.

Operations were slow in the Pacific region, and I felt the need to be closer to the fight. Aside from leaving Theresa, I was excited about the opportunistic deployment. My executive officer slated me to deploy individually to Afghanistan.

My pre-deployment checklist was in order: buy the right books, pack the seabag to the brim, and email friends an address for care package deliveries. I purchased and began reading Ahmed Rashid's *Taliban* and *Descent into Chaos*. I also bought and read the *Army and Marine Corps Counterinsurgency Field Manual* by David Petraeus, John Nagl, and James Amos. The Military Exchange had ample supplies needed to complete my rucksack: 1,000-mile-per-hour cord, lighter, knife, cold weather gear, canteens, harness, and survival gear. I had one other item on my to-do list: marry the love of my life.

Theresa and I secretly married on July 7, 2009, in a civil ceremony in Richmond Hill days before my departure. No one from our families was allowed to attend because we didn't want to detract from our "real" ceremony, scheduled for May 2010, upon my return. During my pre-deployment R&R (rest and relaxation), my USNA roommates Omar Garcia and Liam Hughes came to spend a few days with my family. We argued about politics, knocked back a few beers at the bar, and went shooting at the local range, having fun but also sharpening my rifle skills for operations downrange.

Arriving in Afghanistan was exhilarating: hundreds of helicopters, cargo planes, and combat aircraft were dancing around the airfield. Getting past Bagram Airfield, the dustiest place on earth, was the first hurdle, before arriving at my forward operating base in Kapisa province. I was working with the Georgia Army National Guard's 108th BCT, 48th Brigade. It was so ironic. A Georgia boy, stationed in Japan, sent to assist a random unit in Afghanistan. Of course, it had to be from Georgia.

We talked about the Georgia Bulldogs being the best team in the Southeast Conference and about the superior hunting and fishing in Georgia. We channeled that competitive spirit into plans for how the unit was going to better train and mentor the Afghan volunteers. We knew we needed the Afghans to take control of their own country and to be able to work as an organized army to do that. Otherwise, we would never go home.

I forged a bond quickly with the guys of the 108th. They respected my Marine Corps insignia, but I also did everything possible to put the soldiers first. I remember Gen. Charles Krulak telling us as midshipmen, "Officers eat last." We relearned that philosophy at Quantico, and I embraced that attitude every day.

During my early missions, I fell in love with the scenery and the people of Afghanistan. We would patrol villages, and once it felt secure, the locals would swarm our humvees with smiling faces, little children asking for candy and school supplies. In an email after my third patrol, I wrote my mother, a middle school teacher: "Mom, the kids would rather have pens and paper more than anything, even food or water. Would you please start a collection at your school and send them to me? I want to take the pens and paper to the kids so they can improve their education."

On August 7, 2009, our team planned to execute Operation Brest. We were supposed to approach a key area within our combat zone and perform "presence operations." Essentially, our task was to let the Taliban insurgents know that we had the confidence and ability to patrol in this particular area. As an officer adviser to the infantry company, I did not have to go on every mission. I had quickly become close with my team, however, and felt like I was responsible for the younger soldiers. Spc. Christopher "Kit" Lowe, from Easily, Georgia, was a particular favorite. He was young and earnest. He loved weapons and had a wonderful humor about him.

We went out of base camp and up toward an area where we knew there would be danger. Recent intel had reported that some eighty Taliban could be in the vicinity. Not more than ten minutes into our patrol, shots rang out. My team dismounted and cleared an enemy position in a mud house. I climbed atop the roof with Kit behind me and killed a man with an RPG during my ascent. I was visually acquiring layout of the area to call in air support when I was hit. Everything went black.

EXCERPT FROM MATT FREEMAN'S POSTHUMOUSLY AWARDED BRONZE STAR CITATION

Acting to conduct a reconnaissance of force in the valley, Captain Freeman's element received enemy fire almost immediately upon leaving the combat outpost. Pinned down as a result of this fire, Captain Freeman decided to clear a kulat in order to gain access to the top deck and achieve better observation of the enemy's firing position. Receiving a heavy volume of enemy fire, Captain Freeman led the way in clearing the house and was the first to reach the rooftop. Once on the rooftop, he spotted an enemy Rocket-Propelled Grenade gunman and immediately killed him. He and one of his team members spotted several other insurgents and began to engage while under fire. It was at this time that Captain Freeman fell mortally wounded. He fought with bravery and determination while demonstrating unwavering courage in the face of the enemy.

Matt Freeman, a brave Marine, loving husband, brother, and son, and a classmate never forgotten. (Courtesy Freeman family)

When his parents heard accounts of Matt's final minutes, they appreciated knowing the facts of that day. The soldier who retrieved his body after the battle said, "He was found with his finger on the trigger, his magazine almost empty, and he was facing the enemy. A proud death for a Marine." Everyone else made it home that day.

Matt had a warrior's homecoming. His brother-in-law, Mike Macias, a veteran of five ground tours in the Middle East, made a pact that if either of them needed an escort home, the other would do it. Matt's body arrived at the airport in Savannah, and for the entire seventeen miles home to Richmond Hill, people lined the roads in tribute. The police and the Patriot Guard provided an outstanding escort home. There was a five-hour wait for mourners to pay their respects at the funeral. It was as if the entire community of Richmond Hill had lost a son.

Two weeks later, at the chapel in Annapolis, there was another ceremony led by Lt. Gen. John Allen, USMC, who had been a classmate of Matt's father. Hundreds were in attendance, including family and friends and members of the Classes of 1976 and 2002 and the Naval Academy community. Specialist Lowe, still suffering from wounds and in a wheelchair, was also in the audience. After the ceremony in the chapel, we walked to the columbarium on Hospital Point, led by the 8th and I Marine Corps band. Matt was laid to rest on August 26, 2009.

Matt's last conversation with his mother had been about the school supplies for the Afghan children. Six months later, his family founded the Freeman Project (www.freemanproject.org), a non-profit whose mission is to procure, ship, and distribute school supplies to children in Afghanistan. Matt was hoping the pens and pencils would replace guns and grenades in these impoverished regions. To date, U.S. soldiers and Marines have distributed more than three tons of school supplies.

PART VI

— ★ ★ ★ —

THE NEXT GREAT GENERATION

After a decade of war, the nation we now need to build is our own . . . and just as our greatest generation left a country recovering from depression and returned home to build the largest middle class in history, so now will the 9/11 generation play a pivotal role in rebuilding America's opportunity and prosperity in the 21st century.

PRESIDENT BARACK OBAMA, Veteran's Day 2011

M ost Naval Academy graduates make a pivotal decision at the seven-to-ten-year mark of service: Do I stay in the military or move on to civilian life? Each decision is unique. A desire to start a family, the temptation of a higher salary, an eagerness to pick out one's own wardrobe, new interests and abilities, and so on, may deter some from staying in the military. Some go to graduate school, are hired by Fortune 500 companies, or start entrepreneurial endeavors. Whether in Silicon Valley, New York City, or Washington, D.C., the 9/11 generation is transitioning to positions of leadership out of uniform. We're using the lessons from the battlefield in the boardroom and break room to help America be great again.

One Wild and Precious Life

Joshua Awad

O n the twenty-second floor of the Deutsche Bank building in Sydney, Australia, I sat back in my desk chair and stared out over the iconic harbor; it was January 2012. I was employed at one of the world's top-tier management consulting firms, Bain & Company. My charcoal suit and silver cufflinks certainly made me look the part of a successful businessman. However, as I watched the sailboats gliding below, I thought back to the time I had worn my Navy summer whites and ribbons. One of my best friends had just been selected for early command at sea and had called to tell me. This was my third close friend from Annapolis to earn that distinction within a few months. Each would soon be in charge of a warship, lead their own crew, and deploy independently, conducting operations in the Persian Gulf. I was thrilled for each of them. They were all brilliant naval officers and highly deserving of the job, but I was conflicted over the career decisions I had made. Commanding a ship had always been one of my greatest aspirations. Now my friends were living my old dream, and I was rethinking decisions that had brought me to Australia. Why had I left the Navy? Where was I headed?

★ ★ ★

I have always been an adventurer at heart. I was drawn to a career in the Navy because it offered a chance to leave my hometown of Glenwood Springs, Colorado, and have an impact beyond America's borders. I wanted to join the Navy to see the world and to be a part of a "global force for good" as the slogan goes. By my senior year in Annapolis, I had been to six countries and was assured the opportunity to explore even more. For the first four years following graduation, I sailed throughout the Middle East, Asia-Pacific, and Europe.

At the end of my sea tours, I was selected to be the Navy Region Europe anti-terrorism officer, stationed in Naples, Italy. Bombings in England and Spain in the post-9/11 world demanded rigorous protection of U.S. bases abroad, and it was my job to ensure that they were equipped to combat the evolving threat from extremists. In my new role, I was exposed to the inner workings of a large Navy staff and observed how the Navy operates on a global level. The breadth of the operational duties meant a number of admirals were involved; this was the first time in my career that I had access to this level of seniority. The strategic perspectives the flag officers brought to the most pressing challenges was impressive to observe. They issued important orders with ease, moving ships and aircraft carriers around the coast of Africa and throughout the Mediterranean Sea.

Life in Naples had many rewards as well. The food was exceptional, and the people welcoming. My neighbor, Salvatore, and his two daughters regularly invited me over for Napolitano pizza or fresh pasta and his special homemade vino. The views of the bay of Naples from our shared villa were breathtaking. Some of the world's most beautiful islands—Capri, Ischia, and Procida—were on the doorstep and served as frequent destinations for weekend sailing or hiking. Furthermore, most of Europe's popular vacation destinations were just a short flight away. In fact, one of the biggest perks of my antiterrorism duties was the opportunity to travel for both work and pleasure. I skied in the Alps, celebrated Oktoberfest in Munich, and visited the Greek isles in summertime. It was during one of these trips, to Heidelberg, Germany, that I met my future wife, Nele.

Nele and I quickly fell for each other and took every possible moment to be together. During one holiday rendezvous in Athens, we began to talk about a looming decision: My tour in Naples was nearing its completion, and I needed to decide whether to continue my career as a naval officer. I had been selected for one of the Navy's graduate school scholarships. The program gave the best surface warfare officers time to complete a master's in business administration while on active duty. Things appeared to be on track. The scholarship was a wonderful enticement to stay in uniform, and I had been accepted at Stanford and Harvard. The Navy, however, then demanded that I pursue a shorter MBA program at a second-tier business school to avoid delaying other career milestones. Turning down the top graduate schools in the world because of career timing was a hard pill to swallow, but leaving the Navy I had come to know and love would be equally difficult. I sat with Nele on the rooftop deck of our hotel in Athens with a bottle of wine to discuss all the options.

She listened as I reminisced about my amazing journey to date. Steeped in tradition and history, Annapolis had been an incredible education in leadership and academics and the source of enduring friendships I would be hard pressed to replicate. I reported apprehensively to my first ship in San Diego, but after seven months deployed at sea, I became a confident mariner and qualified surface warfare officer. The mission was critical, disembarking the Marines who had invaded Iraq in 2003 and eventually escorting them home to California. I later became an engineering officer on the Navy's finest cruiser, USS *Hue City*, and led a division of sixteen damage-control personnel, protecting the ship against flooding, fire, and chemical, biological, radiological attack.

Staying in the military would provide me with a life and career of adventure, but a journey of service to which I was already quite accustomed; the private sector was completely unknown to me and exciting. Two admirals in Naples discovered that I was considering separation, and each tried to convince me of the rewards of a long naval career. They said the lifetime of stories, the robust retirement pay, and the intrinsic reward of service were immeasurable. I knew the Navy had a lot to offer, but I also believed I wanted more. I had an unquenchable desire to do more for a broader range of people in the civilian world. I followed my heart and my entrepreneurial spirit and accepted the offer from Harvard Business School for its upcoming semester. I have never again worn my summer whites.

★ ★ ★

When I left the Navy for civilian life, I felt as though I were reporting to that first ship in San Diego. It was a new unknown. I had no idea how I would be able to afford business school. I had no idea what industry I would enter. I was clueless about my career options in the short and long term. I had been in uniform since my eighteenth birthday; the preceding ten years had been filled with navigation, seamanship, naval history, and lots of regulations. I felt like the world was once more wide open to me. I just wasn't quite sure of my place in it.

Harvard provided an entirely new set of resources for navigating life. Roughly nine hundred brilliant and diverse students are admitted every year, a third of them from outside the United States, all with different backgrounds and aspirations. Beyond learning the mechanics of finance, operations, and marketing from the finest instructors, Harvard provided two years of conversation with hundreds of other students, all reflecting on their own career choices and future ambitions. There were military officers pondering their next steps, investment bankers who wanted to become entrepreneurs, teachers who wanted to reform the education sector, and consultants who wanted to train their problem-solving skills on fixing such complex issues as poverty, hunger, and the environment. I was surrounded by like-minded adventurers trying to navigate toward a career where they would have a positive impact on the world.

Attending Harvard Business School during the peak of the financial crisis meant that the school became an epicenter of debate about the roles and responsibilities of business and government in creating the crisis and responding to it. The debate hit close to home since many graduates were heavily involved in various aspects of the crisis. Some worked at the troubled investment banks whose demise had marked the start of the "great recession," while others, like President George W. Bush and Secretary of the Treasury Henry Paulson, played critical roles in determining how the government would respond to the Wall Street meltdown. At times, the classroom debate turned to the cost-benefit of funding two wars in Iraq and Afghanistan that appeared to be having limited success. My classmates would often ask for my perspective on the appropriate level of spending on national defense in the midst of soaring unemployment and national debt. I felt obligated to point out how critical defense is for America's security and economic growth but also acknowledged that defense could not come at the expense of good public schools, infrastructure investment, and needed technology at home.

I learned countless lessons in those Cambridge classrooms, from the faculty and my fellow students. Discrete events—like trekking through Patagonia with classmates, the one-on-one conversation I had with Jack Welch, and participating in the business plan competition—are not only unforgettable experiences but also provided me with confidence and a network of meaningful friendships that I hope to always carry with me. In the end, going to business school provided me with the foundation for a successful transition, bridging the divide between the military and civilian worlds.

After Harvard, Nele and I married and decided to move to Sydney, Australia. We were attracted by the breathtaking scenery, the abundance of outdoor activities available, the friendly people, and the booming economy. I joined Bain & Company as a consultant and have since worked with razor-sharp people in a number of industries on vastly different types of projects. While I think it is unlikely I will make a lifelong career of consulting, the boardroom access has helped refine my analytical and communication skills, continues to build my international IQ, and allows me to work hand-in-hand with Australian chief executive officers on some of the biggest challenges their businesses are facing. Like the Navy admirals I worked with in Naples, good CEOs have an uncanny ability to pinpoint the crux of critical issues with laser-like focus.

★ ★ ★

Mary Oliver's poem "The Summer Day" ends with the line

Tell me, what is it you plan to do
with your one wild and precious life?

One year removed from Harvard Square, looking out over Sydney Harbor, my answer to that question was less defined than it had been when I was in the Navy. I knew I want to live a life of purpose that makes a difference to others while finding the time to relish the small joys of life. I'm still not sure what shape that life will take, much less what it will be ten years from now. Will I start a non-governmental organization? Will I become an entrepreneur? Will I invest in ventures that have a social mission?

Although my postmilitary navigational chart is not yet plotted, my passions are as clear as when I was a naval officer. No matter the attire, I will lead a life of service. Having a positive effect in today's society requires perseverance, acumen, and a global perspective. My new life with Nele, my global network of hard-working friends, and the foundation of service derived from Annapolis bring confidence to my next chapter. I'm proud of the route my friends in uniform have chosen, but that path is no longer my life's aspiration. I will earn early command in my own way. I value having the freedom to set my own course. Our nation needs leaders in and out of uniform who are willing to serve with integrity and dedication. I'm still finding my path, but I wake up every day energized by the endless possibilities for this "one wild and precious life."

Serving Beyond the Uniform

Elizabeth Kreft

I never dreamed I'd find a line of work that could humble me more than military service. Then again, I also never expected to find myself snowshoeing through thirty-foot drifts on an Alaskan mountainside with a hundred military widows. While searching for a way to serve my country beyond my full-time uniformed years, I stumbled upon an amazing community of survivors who taught me that it's ok to cry and laugh at the same time.

When I first began military training, I assumed "real" service in the armed forces required an all-or-nothing approach. At least that seemed to be the mindset of most of my classmates, who already had the next forty years of their lives charted. They either intended to stay in the military for the minimum number of years and then move on to a civilian career—the "five and dive" plan—or to retire as an admiral. My problem was that neither plan appealed to me. I was sure I wanted to serve my country and be part of a team that accomplished great things, but signing on for a lifetime of military rules and regulations seemed daunting. I felt torn and longed to find a way to serve in a way that felt right for me.

Fast-forward ten years. I'm on the flight line at Nellis Air Force Base for my first Thunderbird air show, and I see Buzz Aldrin whip his head around and ask, "Well, how the hell did you end up in the Air Force young lady?" He overheard I was a Naval Academy alum turned Air Force officer. I fought a lump in my throat as I realized this man—who had been to the moon and back—was curious about *my* military service. I started talking. "Honestly Sir, I didn't know what I wanted to do in the military; I just knew I wanted to serve." I feared that might've come across as ungrateful or uneducated, but thankfully my sentiments seemed to resonate with the living legend. He nodded his head several times in approval. "Yeah kid, sometimes it's better not to have a plan and just go with it," he said.

I shared with Buzz my teenage dream of attending a military service academy and explained that Annapolis had accepted me into the Class of 2002. Although I didn't have a specific career mapped out, I knew I wanted to wear a uniform and serve my country in some way. I was a blank page, a clean slate, a service member without a predetermined path.

Buzz's face lit up as I told him about my first duty assignment: working side-by-side with NASA experts, shuttle operators, and rocket scientists at Kennedy Space Center and Cape Canaveral Air Force Station. I was humbled by his focused attention on my meager military experiences.

"Well, I think that's great," he said with a wide smile. "Maybe you can tell me more about it over a drink."

That's when I realized that Buzz Aldrin, the sharp-yet-goofy American icon, old enough to be my grandfather, was flirting with me. The day only got more interesting from there.

Elizabeth Kreft speaking with Buzz Aldrin. (Courtesy Elizabeth Kreft)

★ ★ ★

My conversation with Buzz wasn't the first or last time that I would explain to a friend, co-worker, or stranger why I cross-commissioned into the Air Force as a Naval Academy graduate. I have a passion for communication and enjoy sharing my stories of military service; in the Air Force, I could be that communicator immediately upon commissioning. The Navy, however, has greater restrictions on how an Academy graduate transitions from unrestricted to restricted warfare communities.

Cross-commissioning is a distinctive, unexpected path shared only by one or two other graduates annually from each service academy. Yes, it is a decision that still earns me a healthy dose of teasing, especially during college football season. (Of course I still root for the Mids every year.) However, this multiservice path gave me the broadened perspective on military life I would use to manage my toughest assignments. This is especially true of the tasks that came *after* I left active duty. By the time I finished my Thunderbird assignment, I had crossed the threshold of my military commitment and was on the hunt for a bigger challenge. I used the timing as a catapult to begin my part-time military career. This also meant that for the first time in ten years I had to find a civilian job.

At this crossroad, I wondered where the grass might be greener. I realized parting ways with the military community wasn't as easy as I had pictured it. By then, military service had blended with my soul. I loved working with warriors who chose to honor a higher calling and hold themselves to a distinct moral and ethical standard. I wanted to build on that bond of service beyond my years in uniform, but I was at a loss. In the summer of 2009, I began an internship at a local sports network covering the Washington Nationals to try something new.

Then, fate stepped in at a baseball game.

While the players took batting practice and the vendors filled the air with the smell of hot dogs and popcorn, I set up an interview for a visitor. Bonnie Carroll, the founder of Tragedy Assistance Program for Survivors (TAPS), was a special guest on the field to give an interview about supporting military survivors. "We offer emotional support and a place of healing for anyone who has suffered the loss of a military loved one," she said. Wow. Gut check. I had experienced the loss of military coworkers. I was immediately transported from the crowd-filled stadium back to Bancroft Hall.

Nick Juron had been a plebe squadmate of mine. From the first time I saw Nick, sitting next to me in alphabetical order on Induction Day, he came across as a big, intimidating athlete like so many guys at the Academy. Nick, however, had a funny, sly smile that would pop up right when you thought he might knock your lights out. I first saw that smile during our first platoon uniform inspection that plebe summer.

I spent hours that Sunday morning polishing our entire squads' shoes so we would pass our inspection. That afternoon, after our brooding upperclassmen gave us proper hell, they announced the inspection winner. Third Squad! My heart jumped. It was a small victory in an otherwise shitstorm of emotional and mental punishment. The upperclassmen then announced the individual winner:

Nick Juron! I still remember the smirk Nick had on his face after we ran back to our rooms. He simply gave me that sly smile and said, "Thanks, Kreft." It was worth it. Inadvertently, Nick and his newly shined shoes taught me one of my first and most enduring lessons of leadership: the team victory is more important than individual praise.

During our four years at the Academy, I saw that smile again and again, usually when Nick was teasing me about my non-engineering classes or giving me a hard time about the boys I chose to date. He was like the annoying big brother you love to hate but who, without question, had your back in a crunch. On Graduation Day, just as we had on Induction Day, Nick and I sat side-by-side as the Blue Angels screamed overhead and we tossed our hats in celebration.

In 2005, Nick's helicopter crashed at sea during a counternarcotics operation off the coast of Colombia. He passed away, along with two other sailors, that day, bravely serving his country.

★ ★ ★

"So, do you have a story like ours?"

Bonnie's question snapped me back to the present. From the moment she mentioned TAPS' mission, the pain of Nick's and other military friends' deaths rushed back into the pit of my stomach. I immediately felt connected to TAPS' cause.

"More than 20,000 spouses, children, parents, grandparents, and loved ones in the TAPS network offer a community of compassion and care so survivors can grieve together and find a place of understanding and hope," said Bonnie. I knew then and there that I wanted to be a part of the mission. Two days later I interviewed with Bonnie and her team, and two months later I joined them as the director of communications.

My most humbling experience at TAPS happened 3,500 miles from home. One of the healing tactics of our non-profit includes setting up opportunities for survivors of all types to gather and share their feelings, experiences, and issues. One concept is simple: No one can understand how a mother feels when she's lost her only son *except another mother* who has *also* lost her only son. The 2010 TAPS Widow's Retreat brought more than a hundred women to Alaska for the sole purpose of healing. We packed the schedule with opportunities to just live—skiing, snowboarding, dogsledding, and more—so they could bond over new experiences.

The contrast between the frigid environment and their warm hearts struck me the most. Here were these widows who understandably could have decided to be broken and defeated, giving in to the harsh reality of their loss. Instead, however, they were huddling together to beat the cold. Teeth chattering in between their big smiles, they laughed and hugged and stood together resiliently against the bitter Alaskan wind.

The huddle factor seems instinctive for survival. That is what these women and thousands of others did to endure the passing of their loved ones. Standing alone during a crisis—regardless of how strong or prepared someone feels—isn't natural behavior when adversity strikes. Yet it is the burden so many survivors feel when they've lost a loved one. They feel alienated or lost, so TAPS programs are created with the huddle factor in mind.

Our first outdoor adventure began in the early morning as the sun broke through the Alaskan clouds and highlighted the mountains all around us. We snowshoed past what seemed to be tiny, three-feet-tall Christmas trees, but then we realized the accumulated snow was packed so high, we were actually trekking past the tops of several thirty-feet tall (or taller) spruces! After an hour or so, we made it to a divide in the woods. One direction would take us back to the ski resort, the other up a steep incline. Our guide asked the group to decide which direction to go: "OK ladies, we can start heading back, or we can take this hill route, which will get us back in about forty-five minutes."

Their faces were blushed from the cold air and the cardiovascular workout, but they decided to press forward. "Oh, of course we are going UP the hill," shouted one widow with a laugh. The rest chimed in immediately. "Oh HECK yeah, we want the tough path!" Then I saw one of them take off, running up the hill in her snowshoes. I just kept thinking, damn, these women are gutsy. They were trying something new, challenging and pushing themselves to an unknown limit all in the name of healing.

The sleep I got that night was restless even though I was drained. My brain was in full gear. How could these women do it? I felt like an ass for complaining a single day in my life about such petty things as bad cell phone reception or bumper-to-bumper traffic.

I rolled over to see if my coworker Kyle was awake on the other side of the room. She had become a dear friend, and I identified with her story the most. She wasn't a widow, but a "wiance." Several dozen ladies created this term of endearment after they lost their military fiancés, putting them into a unique survivor category.

Kyle and her fiancé, Mike, had been deeply in love. Theirs was a storybook kind of love. They had met when she served him drinks and dinner at a bar just outside Fort Richardson; within hours they knew their futures were intertwined. Within months of meeting each other, Mike was deployed for a year in support of Operation Iraqi Freedom. When he returned for two weeks of leave, he sat Kyle down to tell her an important story. "It was the sweetest thing," she said. "I sat on the floor with him talking about his experiences in Iraq. He had been hit by an IED, and immediately after he didn't know if he was alright or hurt, but all he could think was that he *had* to be ok—because he had to get home to me and tell me he loved me one more time. And then he asked me to share the rest of his life with him." Less than two months later, Mike was killed while preparing a critically wounded patient for transport.

Fiancés aren't guaranteed support through official military or veteran's affairs channels. In fact, unless you are the military member's beneficiary or dependent, you aren't recognized in any of the official military survivor paperwork. By offering support to people like Kyle, TAPS was filling a void that needed to be filled. I rolled over and finally began to fall asleep as I thought about the widows and their family of survivors.

At times during that weekend, I felt like a stranger invited to a large, intimate family gathering. I carefully searched for common ground while trying not to overstate my own moments of suffering. It was uncanny the way each time, in my most uncomfortable moments, one of the widows would walk right up to me and bring me in.

"Do you think a non-widow could ever understand your feelings of loss?" I asked one of the women during a group chat session. She tenderly smiled saying, "We've all experienced some kind of loss. Relationships, pets, friends, loved ones. . . . Death happens, and if you understand even a small part of that, it helps." I blinked back tears as I thought about Nick. Yes, my classmates and I knew loss.

The next day we were out of the hotel before sunrise, making our way to the starting line of the Iditarod, the iconic race that takes mushers and their dog teams across roughly 1,000 miles of harsh yet breathtaking Alaskan landscape. The journey begins along crowd-lined streets in downtown Anchorage. That year, half a dozen veteran mushers wanted to honor the TAPS widows by carrying ribbons stitched with the names of their fallen husbands throughout the race.

I walked with one widow (who I'll refer to as Patty) through the crowds and down the snow-packed streets to find her musher. The air was bitter cold, and the smell of fish and dogs filled our noses.

"Do you think they really care?" Patty pondered aloud as we walked up to a group of dog teams.

"The dogs?" I asked. It was a lame attempt at humor on my part. Thankfully she laughed.

"No, I'm wondering if the mushers actually know how an act like this helps, or if it's just another nice PR stunt for them. Or maybe they care, but they have no idea why this sort of thing means so much to us."

Rather than attempt a complicated answer, I simply said, "Why not ask him?"

Patty looked back at me with a funny I-should-have-thought-of-that smile and walked up to her musher. He was intimidating, even for a brooding Alaskan male. Black scruff covered his face but didn't hide the wrinkles on his brow as he stared intensely at a map or chart. I imagined this guy being born with a pipe in his mouth and drinking whisky from a baby's bottle. He was clearly focusing on the race, which was scheduled to start in less than thirty minutes. Patty, within minutes, had brought this salty old man to the verge of tears.

Most of the widows I meet say the best way for an "outsider" or a "non-survivor" to support someone who has lost a military loved one is to simply ask about their story. They love to take the time to remember the amazing men they had in their lives, and they honor them by taking the time to remember their lives. That day in Anchorage, the mushers were helping the widows remember.

★ ★ ★

Remembering those who have gone before us is not always easy. Honoring their stories and their service is our calling, but not one that is free of pain. The process of healing is long, arduous, and unscripted. The emotional strength I cultivated as I served the TAPS survivors bolstered my abilities as a military leader. I believe the lessons I absorbed from these brave widows prepared me for my next tour of service in Operation Enduring Freedom.

During my time with TAPS, I continued my military service as a member of the District of Columbia Air National Guard. In the summer of 2010, I left my position with the non-profit to prepare for a six-month deployment to Kabul. There I was called upon to serve in another unique capacity—instructing President Hamid Karzai's team of spokesmen on public affairs and helping them establish a strategic plan to overcome the Taliban's sophisticated propaganda strategy.

I hid weapons under my sweaters. I wore a scarf on my head to blend in. I thought of my TAPS widows daily. People were dying in Afghanistan every other day. I was in harm's way but serving a purpose, breaking down barriers between radical Islamists and freedom-seeking Afghans. As I executed my mission, it gave me great peace knowing Kyle, Bonnie, and the rest of the TAPS team were conducting their mission as well.

As a veteran of the long wars, like so many of my classmates and military colleagues, I've experienced rare forms of professional and personal sacrifice. It was an odd juxtaposition of the desire to serve at the tip of the spear and longing for home. I felt an ache for family closeness, muted by the urge to execute my mission without weakness. It was a constant tension. These experiences sparked a new level of appreciation in me. I wanted to use my training to see those around me operate at their professional peak, and I now had more tools than ever in my war chest to achieve that goal.

Thus far, my service with TAPS and my service in Afghanistan have been the ultimate tests of my emotional strength. My favorite jobs have always offered the most challenging and rewarding tasks. As it turns out, maybe I was right during those early years at the Academy when I thought military service was an all-or-nothing attitude. I thought someday parting ways with military service would feel right—a time when I could comfortably trade in my camouflage uniforms for business casual. Without expecting it, however, through my experiences at TAPS and my Afghanistan deployment, I discovered national service can be continuous on both the civilian and military sides, wherever the greater need exists.

It's a lifestyle of service, in or out of the uniform, that I humbly and gladly accept. I'm all in.

Rings of Courage and Love:
Fighting for Gay Rights in the Military

Gary Ross

Naval Academy graduates are sometimes called "ring knockers" because of the large class rings they wear. The rings are sometimes knocked on a table to remind those around them that there is an Annapolis graduate in the room. In the Fleet, it is not necessarily a term of endearment, but at the Academy, especially for plebes, earning the name is an honor.

My class ring was gold with an antique finish, a beautiful blue stone in the middle, and a diamond set on either side. The diamonds were my mother's gift to me, which made me cherish the ring even more. On one side was the 2002 class crest, designed by Jason Chen, my friend in 28th Company, and on the other side were the Naval Academy seal and *Ex Scentia Tridens*, which translates as "Through knowledge, there is sea power."

A Naval Academy midshipman is first authorized to wear this ring at the end of junior year. The privilege is awarded at the Ring Dance, a century-old ceremony where midshipmen escort their significant others to a gala and dip their class ring into a grog of seawater collected from the seven seas.

I remember my classmates eagerly counting down the days to our Ring Dance, yet I did not share their enjoyment. Since 1993, the military had adhered to the "don't ask, don't tell" law. Under its mandate, commanders could not ask about sexual orientation, and gays in military service could not acknowledge (or *tell*) their sexual preference. Like most monumental events in my Navy career, my participation in our Ring Dance could have potentially revealed that I am gay. I had to make a decision: Do I pretend to be someone I am not, by bringing a "date," or do I find a plausible reason why I cannot go or why my "girlfriend" was unable to attend? I chose not to go.

The Ring Dance would be one of the countless events I would miss in the decade that followed. It would be ten years of making up stories and being dishonest with my colleagues. I was a naval officer, an Annapolis graduate, and I was gay. The laws of the land, however, denied me the freedom to be myself and to enjoy equal opportunities. At graduation, I was commissioned and sworn to defend the Constitution, to protect liberties that I could not enjoy myself.

★ ★ ★

I met Dan on a dating website during my sophomore year at the Academy. He was a flight attendant, and his schedule allowed us to spend most weekends together. He frequently planned his trips to meet me in various cities when I was on movement orders with the Yard Patrol Squadron, the training ships of the Academy. I also joined him on several of his trips during holiday breaks. He mailed me postcards every night he was away from home. By summer, we were hopelessly in love.

When I deployed on my first ship, USS *Valley Forge* (CG 50), Dan dropped me off at the pier, shook my hand, and watched as I walked up the gangway. As other couples exchanged their goodbyes, he went back to our car and started sobbing. We had been together for three years by that point, and Dan stood by my side even though my career kept us from freely expressing the love we had for each other.

While at sea, Dan wrote me daily emails and sent weekly care packages, but even these small gestures had to be "protected." Dan used a special email address just for our correspondence and signed everything as "Danielle" or simply with the letter "D." When I returned from weeks or months on patrol, Dan waited for me in off-base parking lots. I walked past my shipmates as they joyfully reunited with their loved ones. When I reached the parking lot, I threw my sea bag in the trunk, and we awkwardly saved our embrace until we got home, behind closed doors.

Those moments hurt. I deployed for months, enduring the trials of the seas, working ungodly hours on the bridge, and standing the watch. To return home from harm's way and not be allowed to show love for my boyfriend made me question everything. Who were my true friends? Who could I trust? Was military service worth this tremendous burden on my relationship?

I was not the only one asking questions. Whether they knew it or not, my shipmates often asked personal questions that put me in a difficult position of having to choose between being antisocial or telling a lie. They would often ask, "Are you married?" or "What are you doing this weekend?" Being antisocial would not have been good for unit camaraderie or morale since officers have a duty to espouse good order, positive attitudes, and motivation to accomplish the mission. On the other hand, lying would break the trust we shared as shipmates. I did not want to live a lie or be deceptive with my shipmates.

Unfortunately, I had to choose a combination of the two. For the good of my country and my passion to serve as an officer, I became somewhat abrasive toward intrusive questioning, while at the same time perfecting my ability to lie to those who had to trust me unconditionally in battle. I would not be rude to my department head or chiefs. I would instead tell "white lies." If I could get away with only changing a pronoun here or there, that's what I did: "Dan" was "Danielle"; "he" became "she." While this worked on USS *Valley Forge*, it was not effective for those who had known me since Annapolis. If you were not married by thirty in the U.S. military, someone would begin to inquire if you were gay. That's just the way it was. Everyone wanted to know why I hadn't married Danielle.

When I received new orders, Dan would fly to the area and search for a home. He specifically looked in communities that provided privacy and had few military residents. In some areas, this required a long commute. In others, it required two homes to minimize my commute a few nights per week. We rarely enjoyed dinner at restaurants or movies at theaters because we could not risk people seeing us together. Dan did most of the shopping by himself. There were a few times when we accidently encountered military people at the mall or grocery store. Dan would keep on walking while I stopped to talk to them.

★ ★ ★

On December 22, 2010, President Barack Obama, with the support of Adm. Mike Mullen, the father of one of my classmates and chairman of the Joint Chiefs of Staff, signed a bill into law that would repeal "don't ask, don't tell." Dan and I saw a glimmer of hope. In the months that followed, the realities of the policy shift began taking effect as the military implemented repeal training. On July 22, 2011, the president certified and notified Congress that the requirements for repeal had been met. In sixty days, a discriminatory law that had been in place for more than eighteen years would end, once and for all. Gays and lesbians serving in the military would finally be granted the freedom to be themselves. On September 20, 2011, the Department of Defense announced the implementation of the repeal of the policy:

> The Services will no longer separate Service members under DADT. Service members who had an approved separation date forecasted after repeal that was based solely on DADT will have that separation cancelled. The Services have ceased all pending investigations, discharges, and administrative proceedings commenced solely under DADT. Statements about sexual orientation are no longer a bar to military service.

When President Obama signed and certified the repeal, I was finally able to speak out against the law since previously even a simple gesture of protest might have jeopardized my career. When the laws finally changed, Dan and I wept

Gary and Dan Ross wed at the stroke of midnight on September 20, 2011.
(Courtesy Gary Ross)

with joy and could be married. We had wanted to get married for some time, so we quickly planned our wedding before the September implementation date.

We held our ceremony the first possible second we could—one minute after midnight on September 20, 2011, at the Moose Meadow Lodge in Burlington, Vermont. The location was perfect—a private and beautiful lodge on eighty-six secluded acres. When the day finally came, Dan and I arrived at the lodge full of hope. The fresh air and the smell of the woods were invigorating, and it gave me a feeling of newness for my upcoming life with Dan. We were saying goodbye to "Danielle" for good. It was wonderful; our marriage and unwavering love for one another were going to be recognized by the state of Vermont and, more broadly, would not have to be hidden from the military community.

Dan was asked if we would allow local media to attend our wedding, and he agreed. Our story was more than that, however; it became international news. On the morning of our ceremony, the Associated Press called Dan and me for an interview. Honestly, at the time, I only wanted to marry Dan, not to become the spokesman for gay and lesbian rights for the entire U.S. Navy. Dan and I talked about it and decided it was best to speak to the media instead of hiding. We changed into our tuxedos hours before the wedding and sat for several interviews. Dan looked sharp in his black tuxedo with white bow tie, and I was wearing my Formal Dress, with a white tie. Hundreds of media outlets, including major networks and cable stations, newspapers, and military publications, picked up our story. While we were apprehensive about the interest in our story, we were proud to be leaders in our country and to be the first same-sex military couple to marry legally.

The theme of our wedding was "Two people fall in love. Two people get married. Simple." We exchanged simple vows: "As I have promised before, I gladly promise again to give you my love, comfort, and support, and to be open and honest at all times. I renew this promise for the rest of my life as your husband." We also exchanged the same rings we had worn for more than ten years as we swore, "With this ring, I pledge my love to you."

At that point the wedding officiate, Greg Trulson, said, "As we all know, by law, I cannot pronounce you married until one minute after midnight." We anxiously watched a timer count down for thirty-nine seconds until he finally said, "I do hereby recognize, I certify, and I pronounce you legally married." At long last, we were finally free to share our lives openly and honestly. It was an indescribable moment.

★ ★ ★

Being married allowed us to live our lives openly and honestly. The first military event that Dan and I attended together was the annual command picnic, on October 14, 2011. From the moment we arrived, we felt accepted like everyone else at the command. From the commander to my coworkers, everyone seemed genuinely happy to meet my husband and exchange pleasantries.

After the picnic, Dan's involvement in the command grew. He helped with the annual chili cook-off and children's Halloween party. We even attended the Marine Corps Ball together. The media believed that an openly gay couple attending the ball was another historic event, and we granted several more media interviews. Following the ball, Dan and I enjoyed the post's Thanksgiving meal together. In every instance, Dan was accepted like any other spouse, and I was accepted like any other service member. No one seemed to care or mind that we were gay. Could it really be that easy? Could we finally have equal recognition, equal benefits, and equal pay for equal work and equal sacrifice?

Not long after we were married, Dan and I went to the ID office to report our marriage and get a dependent's card, just like other newly married military couples. We were treated like all the other applicants; for a moment, we thought that we finally really would be equal. Once we were called to the desk, however, the representative informed us that Dan could not be issued a dependent's ID card, since he is the same gender as I. While this was discriminatory and upsetting, it was expected. The so-called Defense of Marriage Act prevents the military from extending equal treatment to gay and lesbian service members. Without the ID card, Dan was unable to receive equal spousal benefits.

Sometimes we traveled to Davis-Monthan Air Force Base from my new duty station in Arizona. Since the military had not issued Dan a dependent's ID card, each time we went to the base, the government ran a background check on Dan. It was humiliating for him and frustrating for me to be told that my husband could not accompany me onto the base unless we submitted to another lengthy background check.

When I raised my right hand on Graduation Day in May 2002, I had sworn to defend the Constitution, against all enemies, foreign and domestic. Those who advocate the so-called Defense of Marriage Act are attacking my civil liberties, my freedom to marry and have a husband. They are also denying those same rights to thousands of gay and lesbian military members around the world. After Dan was denied equal military spousal benefits, I decided that it was my sworn obligation, as a leader, to bring this inequity to light.

With the partnership of the Servicemembers Legal Defense Network (SLDN) and the law firm of Chadbourne & Parke LLP, I filed a federal lawsuit against the Offices of the Secretary of Defense, the Attorney General, and the Secretary of Veteran's Affairs, as well as the United States of America, seeking equal recognition, benefits, and family support for equal sacrifice and service in the U.S. armed forces. Gay and lesbian military members deserve more than second-class citizenship. At a press conference in Washington, D.C., shortly after filing the complaint, I read the following from my note cards, with Dan standing at my side:

> Good morning. My name is Lieutenant Gary Ross and I'm a commissioned officer in the United States Navy. Today I am here with my husband, Dan.

We've been together for nearly twelve years, but we weren't allowed to be legally married in this country until just recently, right after the stroke of midnight, as the repeal of the Don't Ask, Don't Tell law took effect. For us to be married legally, and for our relationship to be publicly acknowledged for the first time has been an incredible experience for us. But allowing gays and lesbians to serve openly while at the same time treating their families unequally is simply not right! I've been in the Navy for more than 16 years, and I have spent my entire adult life serving this country. For the first time since service began, I am no longer required to stand by quietly and watch gay and lesbian service members be treated like second-class citizens. All service members deserve the same network of support! I would like to close with a quote that I recently read which I believe sums up our feelings quite well: "Inclusion without equality is incomplete. The job is not done."

I held my note cards with both hands as I read my prepared statement. On my right hand was my Naval Academy ring, a reminder of the pride I have in being a naval officer and my love for the institution that gave me a commission. On my left hand was my wedding ring, purchased when I was twenty-two years old and serving as a symbol of our marriage and lifetime commitment to one another. Together, we are ready to fight for our rights.

Command, Citizenship, and Government

Seth Lynn

T
o exit Camp al-Qa'im in Iraq, I remember we had to zigzag around a set of cement barriers staggered to prevent someone from driving into the camp at high speed. The names of famous battles were etched on the cement barriers so that whenever my Marines and I entered or exited the camp, we received a refresher in Marine Corps history and a reminder of the legacy of those who had gone before us.

We would steer our vehicles around the first barrier, marked "Tripoli, Chapultepec, and Barbary Pirates"; the next barrier, stenciled "Philippines, Boxer Rebellion, and Belleau Wood"; another one, lettered "Guadalcanal, Iwo Jima, and Tarawa"; the next one, marked "Pusan, Inchon, and Chosin Reservoir"; the following one, showing "Khe Sanh, Da Nang, and Hue City"; and next to last, one marked "Beirut, Kuwait, and Somalia." The final barrier carried the names of some of the Marine Corps' most recent battles: "Nasiriyah, Baghdad, and Fallujah." As we exited the wire, the battle names stopped abruptly, and we became part of history ourselves.

In November 2005, whenever I led a convoy out of Camp al-Qa'im and toward the Corps' current battle, upholding a legacy of honor was constantly on my mind and reinforced by the name of our destination—Camp Gannon. The position was named for the man most responsible for my becoming a Marine officer, and our mission was to take back the city where Capt. Richard Gannon had been killed.

★ ★ ★

Years earlier, as a midshipman, I had argued about my summer plans with Captain Gannon, then my company officer. I had wanted to be a Navy pilot since age seven, but Captain Gannon had piqued my interest in selecting Marine Corps ground, which would require me to complete Leatherneck, a one-month training program in Quantico, Virginia, that mirrors the six-month Basic Officer Course that Marine lieutenants complete after commissioning. I wanted to attend

Leatherneck to keep my options open and spend the second half of my summer with a naval aviation squadron. Captain Gannon predicted that I wouldn't enjoy Quantico and, therefore, insisted that I spend the second half of my summer with a Marine unit in the operating forces, where I would see how rewarding my job would be once I had completed the officer course.

Captain Gannon had been correct on both fronts. Leatherneck, because of its excessively restrictive nature, convinced me that I wanted to be a Navy pilot. The experience at Leatherneck was too much like plebe summer; it didn't make me feel like the leader I envisioned a Marine officer to be. I had completed the program, but I didn't put forth the effort I should have. Yet, spending the next half of my summer shadowing Marine officers convinced me that six more months in Quantico would be a small price to pay for the privilege of commanding a platoon of Marines.

The following month brought 9/11. America was under attack and interest in the Marine Corps skyrocketed. More than one hundred of my classmates were turned down, despite impressive records and terrific potential. I remain convinced that I only made the cut because Captain Gannon, who knew me well, convinced the other decision makers to overlook my middling Leatherneck performance at Quantico.

★ ★ ★

In April 2004, Captain Gannon was killed in a firefight in al-Qa'im, in the northwest of Iraq. The citation for his posthumously awarded Silver Star reads that while "maneuvering through the enemy fire, with complete disregard for his own safety, he entered the courtyard to search for [a] wounded Marine. Upon entering a house, he exchanged small arms fire and grenades with nine Mujahedeen fighters and fell mortally wounded."

By 2005, the situation in al-Qa'im had worsened significantly. The force of Iraqi insurgents known as Hamza was increasingly bolstered by arriving foreign fighters from just across the border with Syria. Eventually the Marines ceased operating inside the city, occupying only a few checkpoints and fortified positions on the outskirts. The Marines named one of the largest of these positions Camp Gannon following its namesake's death.

With the Marines no longer in the city, Hamza and foreign fighters began fighting each other for supremacy. The latter triumphed, effectively expelling Hamza from its own city. Now in control, the foreign fighters, known as al-Qaeda in Iraq (AQIZ), posted signs at the outskirts of the city proclaiming it the Islamic Republic of al-Qa'im. They barred girls from attending school, forced men to grow beards, and executed Iraqis in the streets.

As with most events in Iraq, the reasons for what happened next are unclear to me, but my understanding is that Hamza realized that the allied American and Iraqi government forces were not only the lesser of two evils, but also represented their best chance for returning home. When we retook the city, Hamza, now called the Desert Protectors, were on our side.

Operation Steel Curtain, to take back al-Qai'm, had begun on November 5, 2005. My AAV (amphibious assault vehicle) company had been attached to Regimental Combat Team 2, and one of my platoons would be conducting a feint attack on Ubaydi, the easternmost town in the region, with a light armored reconnaissance company. Meanwhile, another two of our platoons would support 3rd Battalion, 6th Marines, as they entered the town of Husaybah, joined to the south by 2nd Battalion, 1st Marines, who were responsible for the "440 District," a neighborhood that jutted westward from the southern end of Husaybah. To the north, soldiers from the 82nd Airborne patrolled the farmland between the town and the Euphrates.

As the AAV company's executive officer, I was responsible for ensuring that the Marines at the front were well-supplied. This meant that I spent the majority of my time running convoys from Camp al-Qaim, which had been built on a former rail depot several miles south of the city's populated area and about fifteen miles southeast of Camp Gannon.

The trip from Camp al-Qaim to Camp Gannon would have been easy but for the fact that the road between the two ran through Karabilah and Husaybah, where the AQIZ were still active, meaning that improvised explosive devices were everywhere. Convoys bypassed the area by driving through the desert toward the Syrian border, marked by just three strands of concertina wire, and then traveling north to Camp Gannon.

During one such convoy, we encountered a makeshift refugee camp. A large tent had been erected, and I saw sixty or so Iraqi children running around and playing, supervised by a handful of adults. I tried to speak to some of the adults, but I didn't have an interpreter with me. Our efforts to communicate were unsuccessful, until an elderly Bedouin woman appeared and spoke to me in broken English. I could see faded tattoos on her face although she held part of her headscarf over her mouth. It was clear that she had not spoken English in years, but I was able to discern that they needed food and water.

Upon our return to Camp al-Qaim, I went to find food for the Iraqis. We usually had supplies of "halal meals," which are similar to the Meals, Ready to Eat (MREs) that we ate, except they don't contain pork, and they are intended for civilians. On this occasion, however, all the supplies had been taken to a refugee camp that the Marines had set up inside Husaybah. Given the situation, we decided we would bring them some MREs and have an interpreter write a note in Arabic explaining which meals contained pork. We returned to the camp and dropped off the supplies. The children crowded around us and asked us to take photos with them while the adults shook our hands and thanked us profusely. It was undoubtedly the best day I spent in Iraq.

I sometimes felt guilty that I was running convoys through the desert while other Marines were fighting and dying nearby and wondered whether I was making a significant contribution to the mission. On the return to Camp al-Qaim that evening, a senior Marine put things in perspective for me. He said, "Twenty years from now, those kids will still remember the time they were hungry in the desert and the Marines brought them food."

★ ★ ★

Upon returning to the States, I was assigned to supervise a Marine Reserve training center in Tampa. The office of my commanding officer, Lt. Col. Kent Ralston, had been connected to mine. When he read the paper each morning, I was treated to a lengthy diatribe on the major issues. There was one point he made repeatedly, and it stuck with me: There were significantly fewer veterans serving in Congress than in the past. This, he felt, was a major component of many of the problems with government. Although I enjoyed my job, I couldn't shake the feeling that something was missing. I left active duty and enrolled in a graduate program at Princeton to study international relations and tried to figure out what I wanted to do next.

In graduate school, Lieutenant Colonel Ralston's words kept coming back to me, so I researched the changing proportion of veterans in Congress. I learned that the decline was even steeper than Ralston had realized. Whereas at the end of the Vietnam War, 75 percent of Congress had served in uniform, by 9/11 that proportion had dropped to just 33 percent. Even more startling was the continued drop since then: Today slightly more than 20 percent of Congress has military experience.

While at Princeton, I was invited to attend Ready to Run, a seminar on political campaigning for women. The goal was to teach women who were intensely involved in their communities how to run for office. The concept was inspiring. I immediately thought of another untapped resource of potential leaders—the men and women I had served with. I thought about the selflessness my Marines had shown through their service. We intimately understood the incredible capabilities, limits, and unintended consequences of U.S. foreign policy, and I thought about how so many of us, with different backgrounds and beliefs, had managed civil affairs situations far more delicate than anything one might experience in an American city. I concluded that there should be a program like Ready to Run for veterans and immediately decided to create one. Although I was in no way qualified to design such a program, I'd been similarly unqualified to command an AAV platoon; I'd simply been surrounded by Marines who were willing to share their knowledge with me. At Princeton, I was surrounded by classmates who had either worked on a campaign or had significant ties to campaign professionals.

Yet as one of only two veterans in my class, I wasn't sure how keen those who hadn't served would be about helping train veterans to run for office. I'd heard about the experiences of Vietnam veteran Pete Dawkins when he was a Princeton grad student. Dawkins, likely the most impressive cadet in the history of West Point, was a Heisman Trophy winner, Rhodes scholar, Brigade commander, captain of the football team, and president of his class. He deployed to Vietnam with the 82nd Airborne, earning two Bronze Stars. Later in life, he campaigned for the U.S. Senate, losing in a close race to Frank Lautenberg and a crack campaign team that included the not-yet-famous Jim Carville and Paul Begala.

As a graduate student at Princeton in 1970, Dawkins's Vietnam service and all-American pedigree had made him the target of student antiwar protestors. Students posted "Dump Dawkins" posters throughout campus, staged demonstrations, and demanded that he be removed from the university. Dawkins was saved by an unlikely guardian angel, a left-wing sociology professor named Marion Levy, who had served in the Navy in World War II. Levy challenged the students to a debate and ultimately shredded the students' arguments so thoroughly that they backed down.

We've come a long way since Pete Dawkins's time. Forty years later, with the proportion of veterans in Congress down by nearly two-thirds, my experience was starkly different. My fellow students, rather than demanding that I be removed from campus, helped lobby the administration to fund a workshop to train veterans to run for office. I spent the summer of 2009 in Washington, D.C., reaching out to people who could teach veterans the basics of campaigning. Lacking an office, I started the organization that would become Veterans Campaign out of the Army Navy Club's business center, which was now adorned with a memorial to Captain Gannon. A large, framed photo of him hung next to the doorway, inspiring me whenever I felt discouraged.

We held our first workshop in Princeton in September 2009. I felt confident that the program was solid, but it wasn't until the first evening that I realized that we had created something truly special. Chris LaCivita, a Marine who had served in the Persian Gulf War and had been the chief strategist for Swift Boat Veterans for Truth in 2004, gave a presentation called "Bulletproofing your Service Record." Simone Lightfoot, an Air Force veteran who was on the Ann Arbor School Board and served as director of the Michigan NAACP, spoke on a panel about preparing for a political campaign. Both needed to leave at dawn to travel home, yet at midnight, the two of them were still in a bar together, drinking

Seth Lynn standing in front of Camp Gannon in Iraq and later on stage as the founder of the Veterans Campaign, a national nonprofit organization. (Photos courtesy Seth Lynn)

beer and laughing about how they would never be caught dead with each other anywhere else. Shared military service is unquestionably the most effective antidote to partisanship.

Today, Veterans Campaign is housed at George Washington University. We've trained more than three hundred veterans and have begun to see some successes. Several of our attendees have become candidates, and a few won off-term elections. What really amazes me, however, is that nearly half of my graduate school classmates helped get Veterans Campaign off the ground, hosting workshop attendees in their apartments, assembling printed materials, and organizing a reception. Two of my classmates, Eric Melancon and Doug Palmer, neither one a veteran, wrote a comprehensive guidebook for veteran candidates in their spare time. Receiving that support gave me a feeling similar to what I felt when I got off the plane in Bangor, our first stop in the U.S. after departing Iraq.

For the esteem with which our country now holds its veterans, we have the Vietnam generation to thank. It's remarkable how much the Iraq and Afghanistan generation has received from those who have gone before us. They established a military tradition that set us up for success. They ensured that we would receive a better welcome home than they did, and they set an example of how to lead the country honorably upon returning.

I believe it's true that to whom much is given, much is expected. As the Iraq and Afghanistan generation returns home and begins taking the nation's reins of leadership, I'm reminded of exiting Camp al-Qa'im. Like the battle names on the stone barriers, we have the examples of patriots from George Washington to Teddy Roosevelt to Dwight Eisenhower to John F. Kennedy, who became some of our country's most esteemed leaders after returning from war. We can look to Senators Ted Stevens and Daniel Inouye, who both fought in World War II and despite representing opposing parties maintained a lifelong friendship. We can look to John McCain, Bob Kerrey, John Kerry, and Chuck Hagel, who, despite facing enormous challenges at war, upon returning took the lead in normalizing relations with Vietnam, helping to heal a wounded nation.

It's now our responsibility to uphold the legacy of those who have gone before us, as we, in keeping with the mission of the Naval Academy, "assume the highest responsibilities of command, citizenship, and government."

PART VII

★ ★ ★

CONCLUSION

From where have the United States' greatest leaders come? Was their success based on upbringing, education, opportunity, or a combination of the three? Decades from now, historians may cite the twentieth century as the period of America's most prominent rise. The Industrial Revolution and westward expansion unleashed a wealth of resources and opportunity, feeding the country's military and economic muscle. America's defense of democracy in two world wars and its extension of influence through economic progress were felt around the globe. Were it not for remarkable leadership, it is likely the United States would have taken a much different course.

Throughout U.S. history, some of the country's finest leaders have emerged from experiences defending its security abroad. In the late 1890s, Theodore Roosevelt's experience with the Rough Riders and his tenure as assistant secretary of the Navy laid the foundation for his passion toward maintaining military might. He devised the voyage of the Great White Fleet, which sailed around the world displaying American industrial strength and global reach. Later, after World War II, Gen. Dwight Eisenhower was elected president. He had led a million troops in Europe on the way to defeating Germany and its allies. These historical giants played important roles in leading the United States because they were veterans of war at historic moments.

The magnitude of World War II provided the opportunity and experiences that shaped twentieth-century American leaders. As men served abroad, women provided support at home. All overcame great odds and faced adversity that gave them confidence and shaped their outlook in the decades to come. This "greatest generation" returned from war, took advantage of the educational benefits offered through the GI Bill, and advanced the country's economy and transformed its society. World War II veterans, while fueling economic advancement, remained resolute in their value system: service, sacrifice, and community.

At Annapolis, the longstanding mission of the United States Naval Academy has been to develop midshipmen to assume the highest responsibilities of command, citizenship, and government. The discipline and rigor of training weave a common thread through the hearts of men and women from all walks of life, reinforcing honor, courage, and commitment as core values in their belief systems. This type of ethos forms the fabric of people's personality and drives them to a life of service, in and out of uniform.

In the Shadow of Greatness was envisioned to recognize and chronicle the service of brave men and women and through their stories establish connections with the broader, nonmilitary community. These first graduates of the Naval Academy after 9/11 entered a global war at sea, in the air, and on land. This war would last for more than a decade and define the United States in the early part of the millennium. The actions of the select few profiled here represent those of a much broader spectrum of patriots.

This book gives a megaphone to men and women who are normally reticent to tout their own actions. The entire Class of 2002 was canvassed, and the most inspiring stories were selected for the final manuscript. We cast a wide net and in doing so collected nearly one hundred stories, all brilliant and meaningful tales of heroism and devotion.

There are some heroes who chose not to write for this book but, regardless, should be recognized. Among them are Dan Cnossen, a member of the Class of 2002 and a Navy SEAL. Dan suffered injuries to both his legs in Helmand province in 2009. Two years after surgery to amputate his legs, he ran the New York Marathon in record time with prosthetics and is an inspiration to thousands. Dan and the fifteen other Navy SEALs from the Class of 2002 collectively chose not to write for the book out of respect for their silent, warrior community. Similar to the SEAL team members, Bale Dalton, a special operations helicopter assault pilot and terminal attack controller, could not disclose information about his covert duties out of deference to the special operations community he supported. Many members from our class earned Silver Stars, Bronze Stars, and Purple Hearts but did not contribute because of their painful memories from the front lines.

Some classmates voluntarily resigned from the military and went on to lead in their communities or to start companies. Ryan Long left the fighter aviation community to coach track and teach theology at Colorado Christian University. Justin Nasiri completed Stanford Business School and started a web company, VideoGenie. His business supports socially responsible initiatives connecting deployed soldiers to loved ones at home. The majority of the Class of 2002 is now out of uniform, but they continue to serve their communities.

This is not a book to simply celebrate Annapolis or Navy and Marine veterans. No matter the outcome of the counterinsurgency in Iraq, reconstruction efforts in Afghanistan, governance efforts in Africa, or counterterrorism missions in Southeast Asia, those who courageously volunteered to serve during this moment in American history have been forever changed. We would argue that these men and women are fit for greater leadership roles. They are stronger in mind and spirit, and they are some of America's finest citizens. Yes, some returned home with traumatic depression or severely disabled, but they do not quit. Their convictions are hardened. The optimism of this generation of veterans leads them to continue their service in uniform or to take their positive experiences of war and apply them in community and national leadership roles.

There are also many non-USNA veterans who are part of this "next great generation." Nathaniel Fick, a Marine Corps officer, was educated at Dartmouth and Harvard before turning to foreign policy and military affairs. He leads the Center for a New American Security, a think tank in Washington, D.C. Former Army officer Paul Rieckhoff founded the Iraq and Afghanistan Veterans Association to lobby and care for the wounded who return from war. Eric Greitens, Wes Moore, and Rye Barcott, three military veterans and academic scholars, took off their active duty uniforms but continued to serve. Eric founded the Mission Continues, a veterans rehabilitation and job placement organization. Wes is an entrepreneur and community leader in New York City, and Rye founded Carolina for Kibera, a non-governmental organization with the goal of advancing public health and grassroots government in a Kenyan urban community. These high-caliber individuals, and hundreds of other veterans, are out of uniform advancing ideals to improve America at home and abroad.

Other veterans are taking their ambition and heading to Congress, a venue that needs new ideas and collaborative leaders. In 2012, Tommy Sowers and Brandon Mullen will run for national office, committed to increasing job opportunities and curtailing unwise foreign policies. These men are a sample of the nearly two hundred veterans challenging for seats in government in the 2012 elections. Such men and women can offer new perspectives on problem solving without engaging in divisive partisanship. The successes of the 9/11 generation are everywhere and will continue to be in the years ahead.

The greatest generation of the twentieth century lived through the Great Depression and fought a two-front war. Our generation was called to defeat a faceless enemy and return to a country in economic turmoil. We aspire to be the next greatest generation, showing humility and respect for those who came before us. If we are to emerge from the shadows of our grandparents, we must persist in virtuous leadership on every battlefield and in every boardroom. From Baghdad to Washington and from Kabul to Silicon Valley, our commitment is resolute. Our nation's best days lie ahead, and we are committed to service and making our country great once again.

Epilogue

Adm. Mike Mullen, USN (Ret.)

On a trip to Iraq several years ago, I ran into a young naval officer on an individual augmentee assignment. He was working logistics in Baghdad; he seemed pretty good at it.

He could trace the best routes for ground movement on a map, could tell me how long it would take and how much it would cost to move a tanker of fuel to each forward base, and he could quote Army doctrine for keeping the lines of communication open and where reality conflicted with it. I asked where he came from and heard, to my surprise, that he was a Navy Reserve intelligence officer, with no experience in logistics, let alone logistics on land. He had volunteered to go to war. He did not care in what capacity. He did not care for how long. He did not care where they put him. He cared about contributing.

"Sir," he said, "I'm doing valuable work here, and I'm learning a lot. I'll be a better officer for all of this." I had no doubt that he was becoming a better officer. And I was confident then that he would take the lessons he had learned back to the fleet and to his command, making everyone around him better too.

Tens of thousands of other Navy and Marine officers have likewise deployed to fight in Iraq and Afghanistan these last ten years, including many graduates from the Naval Academy Class of 2002. Many deployed in classic roles: Marine ground combat, naval aviation missions, explosive ordnance disposal, and SEAL operations. Others served in more unconventional roles, like my logistician, or highly technical counter-IED work, economic development, rule of law, and good governance. All of them proved vital to the overall effort. Like that young man, they too had to learn new skills, often at the hands of extraordinary non-commissioned officers, adapt their own preconceived notions of what combat really means, what jointness means, and learn to lead America's sons and daughters in the chaos and fear—and unique challenges—of war.

You have heard it firsthand in these pages. You have read their stories, shared in their fears, celebrated their achievements. You have come to know about them what I have long understood: this is a new generation of great leaders, volunteers all, grateful for the chance to serve their country, stretched by the challenges they faced, and tempered by war. I believe they are positioned, because of their diverse experiences, to lead both in and out of uniform in the years to come.

It is through experience that one develops wisdom, and America will need their leadership through the challenges of tomorrow. Many have seen the worst of it, exposing themselves to danger and bringing back home with them memories and burdens they may find difficult to share with anyone. Some gave their limbs. Others gave their lives, leaving families behind to cope and mourn and move on as best they can. America is indebted to Matt Freeman, Rich Andersen, Joe Houston, and the other thousands who made the ultimate sacrifice. All of them—at sea and ashore—made an enormous difference.

Iraq is now a democracy, still struggling to come to grips with all that entails, but a democracy nonetheless. The Iraqi people have an opportunity now, one they never enjoyed under Saddam Hussein, to decide for themselves how to govern, how to prosper, how to defend themselves. These men and women helped bring about that opportunity. In Afghanistan, war still rages, but the hard and painstaking experience of counterinsurgency warfare wrought on the streets of Iraq are paying dividends in places like Helmand and Kandahar and Ghazni.

No one is underestimating the scope of the challenges that remain. Endemic and pervasive corruption still robs the Afghan people of their rights. Poor governance still denies them the rule of law. Safe havens in Pakistan still offer the enemy aid and comfort. All of this makes the task more difficult and dangerous, but no one can deny that—once again—this new generation of leaders has stepped up to provide a foreign government, this one in Kabul, the opportunity to be more responsive to its people.

They have done this by working with and through their civilian counterparts in the State Department and in other federal agencies, as well as with partners and allies from other nations. They have learned to be statesmen as well as soldiers, diplomats as well as warriors. Indeed, they have learned that in these new "savage wars of peace" the skills required of military leaders are often the same ones required of any good community leader: patience, understanding, decisiveness, and yes, to a degree, restraint. They have taken to heart the counsel given in the Army's new counterinsurgency manual that "U.S. military leaders require a strong cultural and political awareness of [host nation] and other multinational military partners." As Gen. Dave Petraeus put it, "Spend time, listen, consult, and drink lots of tea."

Yet these young men and women have never feared to fight. They helped kill Osama bin Laden and continue to decimate the ranks of al-Qaeda's senior leaders. They have defended vital sea lanes of ocean commerce, explored and discovered ways to protect the vast and as-yet-untamed wilderness of cyberspace, and they have kept sharp and sure the instruments by which U.S. national security is preserved.

In other words, this new generation of officers has had to do it all over the past ten years. The devastating attacks of 9/11 ushered in a new era of fighting, a new American way of war, without erasing the old. Even as the military continues to fight modern war, it must also contend with and plan to defeat traditional threats from regional powers who possess robust conventional and, in some cases, nuclear capabilities. The freedom to conduct naval operations in support of joint, allied, and coalition efforts—ensuring access and projecting persistent combat power—can only be preserved through enduring war fighting competencies.

Today's naval officers must therefore stay ready for wars big and small, for challenges global and local, for capabilities conventional and unconventional. Even a cursory glance through the pages of *In the Shadow of Greatness* should give any reader confidence that these leaders are battle hardened and ready and that they will remain ready for diverse challenges over the course of their careers.

When I graduated from the Naval Academy in 1968, the fighting in Vietnam loomed large in our minds. My first deployment was aboard the destroyer USS *Collett* (DD 730) to the waters off the coast of Vietnam, where we supported forces ashore with round-the-clock gunfire. In addition, the Cold War was very hot, indeed. We trained hard against the ever-present threat of the Soviets' navy, working doggedly to understand every tactic they employed, every weapon system they designed. One became good at being a naval officer in those days in large part by being successful in predicting the actions of the Soviets.

The young men and women coming out of Annapolis in 2002—my oldest son, John, among them—and succeeding classes did not have just a single foe, and neither will their juniors. Their world is a lot less predictable. In 2011 alone, economic and political dynamics were dramatically affected by natural disasters, energy competition, piracy, and the continuing development of weapons of mass destruction and their delivery systems. We have seen the power and speed with which actions, images, and ideas impact military operations, and we have seen the raw power that values-driven political protest can have in literally reshaping the map of the Middle East. This pace of change continually redefines the security environment in which we operate. It will also thus continue to redefine the type of officer we must field to lead it.

To the Class of 2002, I thank you for sharing your stories and opening America's eyes to the challenges faced by your generation, which in my view really is the next "greatest generation." For those in harm's way today, I commend you for the courage you are demonstrating and for the leadership you are developing.

My advice to you is simple: Continue to listen, learn, and lead in the decades ahead. Your families and your fellow citizens are counting on you. The nation looks to you, and the world needs you.

In Memory of

THE FALLEN NAVAL ACADEMY GRADUATES SINCE SEPTEMBER 11

*For their conspicuous gallantry and intrepidity above and
beyond the call of duty*

SEPTEMBER 11, 2001

Captain John D. Yamnicky, USN (Ret.), Class of 1952
Pentagon, American Airlines Flight 77, Passenger

Rear Admiral Wilson F. Flagg, USNR (Ret.), Class of 1961
Pentagon, American Airlines Flight 77, Passenger

Kevin P. Connors, Class of 1969
World Trade Center

Captain Charles F. Burlingame III, USNR, Class of 1971
Pentagon, American Airlines Flight 77, Pilot

Kenneth M. McBrayer, Class of 1974
World Trade Center

Kenneth E. Waldie, Class of 1978
World Trade Center, American Airlines Flight 11

Captain Gerald F. DeConto, USN, Class of 1979
Pentagon

Captain Robert E. Dolan, USN, Class of 1981
Pentagon

Commander Patrick Dunn, USN, Class of 1985
Pentagon

Commander William H. Donovan Jr., USN, Class of 1986
Pentagon

Lieutenant Commander Ronald J. Vauk, USNR, Class of 1987
Pentagon

Lieutenant Jonas M. Panik, USN, Class of 1997
Pentagon

Lieutenant Junior Grade Darin H. Pontell, USN, Class of 1998
Pentagon

POST–SEPTEMBER 11

Commander William C. McCool, USN, Class of 1983
Space Shuttle *Columbia*, accident, February 1, 2003

Commander Peter G. Oswald, USN, Class of 1984
Training mission, El Salvador, August 27, 2002

Lieutenant Kevin A. Bianchi, USN, Class of 1985
Training flight, helicopter crash, Italy, July 12, 2003

Lieutenant Colonel David S. Greene, USMCR, Class of 1986
Combat operations, al-Anbar province, Iraq, July 28, 2004

Lieutenant Commander William R. Muscha, USN, Class of 1987
Training flight, Gulf of Mexico, May 8, 2002

Lieutenant Colonel Brett M. Bekken, USMCR, Class of 1989
Training mission, jet crash, California, April 21, 2004

Major William R. Watkins III, USAF, Class of 1989
Combat operations, jet crash, Iraq, April 7, 2003

Lieutenant Colonel Mario D. Carazo, USMC, Class of 1991
Combat operations, Helmand province, Afghanistan, July 22, 2010

Lieutenant Commander Robert E. Clukey III, USN, Class of 1991
Fighter jet crash, Italy, November 3, 2002

Lieutenant Commander Anthony R. Domino, USNR, Class of 1991
Operational training, jet crash, Fallon, Nevada, April 18, 2003

Lieutenant Commander Christopher C. Tragna, USN, Class of 1991
Training flight, Naval Air Station Patuxent River, Maryland, April 2, 2002

Lieutenant Commander Scott A. Zellem, USN, Class of 1991
Operational mission, jet crash, Kita, Iwo Jima, August 10, 2004

Captain Matthew W. Bancroft, USMC, Class of 1994
Refueling mission, aircraft crash, Pakistan, January 9, 2002

Lieutenant Commander Scott T. Bracher, USN, Class of 1994
Operational flight, jet crash, Naval Air Station Jacksonville, Florida,
September 21, 2005

Lieutenant Kylan A. Jones-Huffman, USNR, Class of 1994
Combat operations, al-Hillah, Iraq, August 21, 2003

Lieutenant Joel A. Korkowski, USN, Class of 1994
Training mission, fighter jet crash, Monterey, California, October 18, 2002

Lieutenant Commander Frank C. Wittwer, USN, Class of 1994
Operational mission, fighter jet crash, El Centro, California, January 17, 2006

Lieutenant Commander Erik S. Kristensen, USN, Class of 1995
Combat operations, helicopter crash, Kunar province, Afghanistan, June 28, 2005

Major Megan M. L. McClung, USMC, Class of 1995
Combat operations, al-Anbar province, Iraq, December 6, 2006

Major Douglas A. Zembiec, USMC, Class of 1995
Combat operations, Baghdad, Iraq, May 11, 2007

Lieutenant Terri S. Fussner, USN, Class of 1996
Helicopter crash, Mediterranean Sea, March 12, 2002

Lieutenant Thomas M. Adams, USN, Class of 1997
Helicopter crash, on exchange with the British Royal Navy, March 22, 2003

Captain Franklin R. Hooks II, USMC, Class of 1997
Training mission, fighter jet went missing, Azores, June 26, 2004

Lieutenant Michael M. McGreevy Jr., USN, Class of 1997
Combat operations, helicopter crash, Kunar province, Afghanistan, June 28, 2005

Sergeant Steve Morin Jr., U.S. Air National Guard, Class of 1997
Combat operations, Umm Qasr, Iraq, September 28, 2005

Lieutenant Raul D. Jimenez, USN, Class of 1998
Operational flight maneuvers, injuries sustained near Corpus Christi, Texas,
January 27, 2006

Captain Seth R. Michaud, USMC, Class of 1998
Operational exercise, helicopter accident, East Africa, June 22, 2003

Lieutenant Matthew Shubzda, USN, Class of 1998
Fighter jet crash, Pacific Ocean, October 18, 2002

Captain Jennifer J. Harris, USMC, Class of 2000
Combat operations, helicopter crash, al-Anbar province, Iraq, February 7, 2007

Lieutenant Christopher H. Snyder, USN, Class of 2000
Anti-drug operations, helicopter crash, Pacific coast of Colombia,
December 20, 2005

Second Lieutenant John N. Wilt, USMC, Class of 2000
Training flight crash, T-39 Sabreliner, Gulf of Mexico, May 16, 2002

Lieutenant Bret Miller, USN, Class of 2001
Training mission, T-34C Turbomentor crash, Gulf of Mexico, October 28, 2009

First Lieutenant Ronald D. Winchester, USMC, Class of 2001
Combat operations, Iraq, September 3, 2004

Lieutenant Richard F. Andersen, USN, Class of 2002
Operational mission, helicopter crash, Fallon, Nevada, May 7, 2007

Captain Matthew C. Freeman, USMC, Class of 2002
Combat operations, Kapisa province, Afghanistan, August 7, 2009

Lieutenant John J. Houston, USN, Class of 2002
Training mission, T-34C Turbomentor crash, Gulf of Mexico, October 28, 2009

Lieutenant Nicolas J. Juron, USN, Class of 2002
Anti-drug operations, helicopter crash, Pacific coast of Colombia,
December 13, 2005

Second Lieutenant James P. Blecksmith, Class of 2003
Combat operations, Fallujah, Iraq, November 11, 2004

First Lieutenant Brian R. S. J. Deforge, USMCR, Class of 2003
Training exercise, fighter jet crash, Fort Hunter Liggett, California, June 26, 2006

First Lieutenant Michael Licalzi, USMC, Class of 2004
Combat operations, al-Anbar province, Iraq, May 11, 2006

Lieutenant Brendan A. Looney, USN, Class of 2004
Combat operations, helicopter crash, Zabul province, Afghanistan,
September 21, 2010

First Lieutenant Travis J. Manion, USMC, Class of 2004
Combat operations, al-Anbar province, Iraq, April 29, 2007

Captain Aaron D. Cox, USMC, Class of 2005
Training mission, Super Cobra crash, San Diego, California, May 5, 2009

Captain Brandon A. Barrett, USMC, Class of 2006
Combat operations, Helmand province, Afghanistan, May 5, 2010

Captain Daniel B. Bartle, USMC, Class of 2006
Helicopter crash, Helmand province, Afghanistan, January 19, 2012

ACKNOWLEDGMENTS

The whole is greater than the sum of its parts. This sentiment is exhibited throughout *In the Shadow of Greatness: Voices of Leadership, Sacrifice, and Service from America's Longest War*. Drawing on contributions from more than one hundred authors, advisers, friends, and family members, this book is a team endeavor.

The U.S. Naval Academy alumni and financial donors from the Class of 2002 involved in this project are too numerous to list, so to avoid leaving anyone out, we would simply like to express a collective and heartfelt thank you to all for their generosity and the time they spent on this group effort. We must, however, recognize a small number of folks by name.

Emmy Spencer Probasco, Logan Plaster, Bryce Holt, Barbara Welle, and Chip Crane sacrificed months to mentor untrained writers in the art of nonfiction. Some of our classmates submitted contributions that did not make it into the book. Their efforts are equally praiseworthy and can be found on the book's website. Special appreciation goes to T Alford, Caroline Murtagh, Nick Huber, and Julia Floraday Wells, leaders in our class who advocated the project when others were skeptical. Another thank you goes to our dear friend Meg, our most constructive critic and detailed observer and now an honorary member of our class.

Rodney Cocks, Fred Kacher, and Jon Kirby, leaders in military and political affairs, advocated for this book among senior officials in government and business. Without their support, we would have fallen short. Special appreciation goes to a behind-the-scenes group of believers: Maj. Guy Berry, Claude Berube, Chris Brownfield, Capt. James Campbell, Rajiv Chandrasekaran, Angela Mikolajewski, Bill Murphy Jr., Charles Nolan, Gordon Peterson, Cdr. Tom Robertson, and Michael Zuckerman. Each of them provided motivation when the project could have lost steam. We would also like to acknowledge the Center for a New American Security for supporting the book and providing a forum to share our stories with the Washington, D.C., community.

The Naval Institute Press is a publisher that cares about its authors, not just their sales numbers on Amazon.com. Tom Cutler, director of Professional Publishing, fearlessly worked to meet a tight deadline, and his team—which included Susan Corrado, managing editor, and freelance copyeditor Robin Surratt—made it happen. We also received support from the institute's talented marketing team. George Keating and Claire Noble provided incredible marketing guidance. Our publicist, Judy Heise, and Brian Walker, special sales manager, were passionate about the book's success. Vice Admiral Peter Daly, USN (Ret.) and chief executive officer of the U.S. Naval Institute, supported the book from day one. Special appreciation goes to the U.S. Naval Academy Alumni Association and all our supporters on and off the Yard. Our literary agent, Maryann Karinch, is a true patriot and savvy adviser who made us feel cared for and respected throughout this process.

At the front of the pack, we are honored to have earned a place on this book's cover. We are indebted to our parents, friends, and other loved ones. They were patient during countless conference calls, writing road trips, and whiteboard strategy meetings. It was on the second floor of the Nimitz Library, in December 2010, that we decided to make this book a reality. The stories were too good, the passion too rich, and the vision too important. John Ennis's creativity, Katherine Kranz's analysis, and Graham Plaster's poetic prose all brought the book to life. As for Joshua Welle, he was the navigator in chief, charting the book's course from idea to bookstore. We wrote, edited, and labored together, classmates and teammates.

Thank you readers, who by picking up this book have expressed faith in the United States of America. We hope it helps you to better understand its modern military and inspires you to learn more about its veterans. Whether civilian or military, Americans must always stand together in service, promoting freedom and protecting democracy against all enemies, foreign and domestic.

READ MORE
ONLINE

Nearly one hundred stories were collected for *In the Shadow of Greatness.* The submissions printed in this bound volume were chosen because each best fit the thesis and contributed to fulfilling the goal of offering a variety of perspectives. The stories that do not appear in the print volume can be found online. To read the electronic submissions of the members of the USNA Class of 2002 listed below, please visit www.shadowofgreatness.com.

Joseph Achenbach	Ryan Long
Theodore Achimasi	George Messner
Patrick Alfonzo	Stephanie Muskovac
Benjamin Drew	Heather Honnette Myers
John Ennis	M. Alexis Wright Piet
Susan Gormley	Benjamin Foster and Melissa Rains
Bradley Harrison	Jeffrey Raunig
Benjamin Heineike	Amy Jones Satrom
Zachery Henry	George Schmuke
Joseph Hooper	Brandon Smith
Derrick Hunt	Rebecca Smith
David Bintliff Johnson, Jr.	James Southerton
Casey Kirkpatrick	Timothy Steigelman
Casandra Koistinen	Marlon Terrell
Victor Lange	Shevonne Wells

About the Editors

Joshua Welle is an entrepreneur and commander in the Navy Reserve with experience serving around the world. He was a political science instructor at the United States Naval Academy and the chief of staff to the NATO Civilian-Military Cell in Kandahar, Afghanistan. Joshua was a military fellow at the Center for a New American Security and Council on Foreign Relations term member. He is president of the USNA Class of 2002 and holds graduate degrees from the University of Maryland and the Harvard Kennedy School.

John Ennis is a sales manager with CenturyLink and a 2002 USNA graduate. He previously managed Gartner's Marine Corps team, was an account manager with Microsoft and IBM, and served in Lockheed Martin's International Business Development Group. He advised the presidential campaigns of Mitt Romney and Marco Rubio. John last served in uniform as chief speechwriter to the Deputy Chief of Naval Operations.

Katherine Kranz Jordan is the director of Women's Programs for Veterans Campaign, a nonprofit organization committed to encouraging, mentoring, and preparing veterans for a second service in civic leadership. Kate served in the Navy until 2014, most recently as a special assistant to the Commander of Naval Forces Europe/Africa in Naples, Italy. She is a 2017 graduate of the Fletcher School of Law and Diplomacy at Tufts University and a member of the Truman National Security Project's Defense Council.

Graham Plaster is the CEO of TheIntelligenceCommunity.com, managing a social network of 100,000 national security and intelligence professionals worldwide. Previously he served as the assistant dean of students for the Naval War College and as U.S. military liaison for UN peacekeeping missions across the Middle East. He is currently advising on policy for the Office of the Secretary of Defense and is also the editor in chief of the *Foreign Area Office Association Journal of International Affairs*.

The Naval Institute Press is the book-publishing arm of the U.S. Naval Institute, a private, nonprofit, membership society for sea service professionals and others who share an interest in naval and maritime affairs. Established in 1873 at the U.S. Naval Academy in Annapolis, Maryland, where its offices remain today, the Naval Institute has members worldwide.

Members of the Naval Institute support the education programs of the society and receive the influential monthly magazine *Proceedings* or the colorful bimonthly magazine *Naval History* and discounts on fine nautical prints and on ship and aircraft photos. They also have access to the transcripts of the Institute's Oral History Program and get discounted admission to any of the Institute-sponsored seminars offered around the country.

The Naval Institute's book-publishing program, begun in 1898 with basic guides to naval practices, has broadened its scope to include books of more general interest. Now the Naval Institute Press publishes about seventy titles each year, ranging from how-to books on boating and navigation to battle histories, biographies, ship and aircraft guides, and novels. Institute members receive significant discounts on the Press's more than eight hundred books in print.

Full-time students are eligible for special half-price membership rates. Life memberships are also available.

For a free catalog describing Naval Institute Press books currently available, and for further information about joining the U.S. Naval Institute, please write to:

Member Services
U.S. Naval Institute
291 Wood Road
Annapolis, MD 21402-5034
Telephone: (800) 233-8764
Fax: (410) 571-1703
Web address: www.usni.org